# BEST of the BEST
# from
# MISSOURI

*Selected Recipes from Missouri's*
*FAVORITE COOKBOOKS*

# BEST
## of the BEST
## from
# MISSOURI

### Selected Recipes from Missouri's
## FAVORITE COOKBOOKS

EDITED BY

**Gwen McKee**

AND

**Barbara Moseley**

*Illustrated by Tupper England*

QUAIL RIDGE PRESS

*Preserving America's Food Heritage*

**Recipe Collection ©1992 Quail Ridge Press, Inc.**

Reprinted with permission and all rights reserved under the name of the cookbooks or organizations listed below.

**Library of Congress Cataloging-in-Publication Data**

Best of the best from Missouri : selected recipes from Missouri's favorite
cookbooks / edited by Gwen McKee and Barbara Moseley ; illustrated
by Tupper England.
  p. cm.
includes index.
ISBN-10: 0-937552-44-5
ISBN-13: 978-0-937552-44-5
  1. Cookery—Missouri. I. McKee, Gwen. II. Moseley, Barbara.
TX715.B4856413  1992
641.59778—dc20                                              92-25259
                                                                CIP

First printing, October 1992 • Second, October 1993 • Third, March 1995
Fourth, January 2000 • Fifth, March 2001 • Sixth, May 2004
Seventh, November 2005

Manufactured in the United States of America
Designed by Barney and Gwen McKee
Back cover photo by Greg Campbell
Front cover photo of Alley Spring Mill near Eminence and
chapter opening photos courtesy of Missouri Division of Tourism

**QUAIL RIDGE PRESS**
P. O. Box 123 • Brandon, MS  39043 • 1-800-343-1583
Email:  info@quailridge.com • www.quailridge.com

*The Lexington Courthouse. A misfired Civil War cannonball is still lodged in the top portion of the first column.*

# Contents

*Editors Gwen McKee and Barbara Moseley pack up the QRP van*
*several times a year to search for and promote cookbooks.*

# Preface

In the very heart of America . . . there is Missouri. It is not considered a northern state or a southern state. It's not east, and though the pioneers thought that by the time they got all the way to Missouri, they were in the West, it's really not west. Perhaps because the Pony Express starting point was St. Joseph, Missouri became known as the Gateway to the West. Today an awesome gateway arch reaches high into the sky in downtown St. Louis to welcome visitors from every direction to this fair state.

We felt very welcomed everywhere we went. "What do people in Missouri like to eat?" we asked. And they looked at us incredulously. "What every other red-blooded American likes to eat," most said . . . "meat and potatoes!" But then came the list, "and vegetables, of course. And casseroles . . . and desserts . . . certainly barbeque . . . lots of apples . . . we like walnuts . . . etc., etc., etc." We came to the conclusion that Missourians like a little bit of everything! So we said, "Show me," and indeed they did. Deliciously!

Missouri's cooking heritage is as Mid-American as its locale. It's a wonderful culinary mixture with a solid base of simple country, a touch of elegantly fancy, a generous helping of ethnic cuisine, a few dashes of flavorful barbeque, and lots of modern and healthy dishes mingled in. From "Shrimp Salad with Apricot Mayonnaise" to "Stir-in-the-Pan Cake"; from "Favorite Apple Betty" to "Dippity Stix"; from "Barbequed Pork Loin Baby Back Ribs" to "Frog Eye Salad" . . . the variety of Missouri cooking seems endless.

The sixty-five cookbooks that contributed recipes to this collection are all very deserving of their "Best" rating. Our correspondence with the authors, editors, committee chairpersons, and publishers enabled us to get acquainted with the people behind the books and recipes, and we hereby thank them all sincerely for their cooperation in making this book possible. We invite you to order their individual books directly from them (see the Catalog of Contributing Cookbooks section that begins on page 279). And please forgive us if we have inadvertently overlooked any book that should have been included.

We thank our "Best" artist, Tupper England, for her delightful drawings. We are indebted to the knowledgeable newspaper food editors and home economists all across the state who helped us with our research, and to the many book and gift store managers who made suggestions and offered comments, making our work so much easier. We also thank some mighty helpful folks at the Missouri Division of Tourism for their use of pictures and information.

When you travel through Missouri, there are so many wonderful discoveries that one often exclaims, "Really?" We have included a sampling of historical facts throughout the book to convey the unique nature of the state. If you take the time, Missouri will most definitely live up to its "Show Me" nickname, and then some. Our travels throughout the state were both enlightening and rewarding, made especially so by the delightful people we encountered all along the way. We hope that the recipes and information within the pages of this book will enable you to experience the taste and spirit of bountiful, beautiful Missouri.

*Gwen McKee and Barbara Moseley*

# CONTRIBUTING COOKBOOKS

*Above & Beyond Parsley*
*Adventures in Greek Cooking*
*á la Rose*
*Apples, Apples, Apples*
*The Art of Hellenic Cuisine*
*Baked With Love*
*Beyond Parsley*
*Blue Ridge Christian Church Cookbook*
*Bouquet Garni*
*Breakfasts Ozark Style*
*Chockful O' Chips*
*A Collection of Recipes from the Best Cooks*
*in the Midwest*
*Company's Coming*
*The Cook Book*
*Cooking for Applause*
*Cooking in Clover*
*Cooking in Clover II*
*Cooking on the Road*
*Covered Bridge Neighbors Cookbook*
*Delicious Reading*
*Eat Pie First...Life is Uncertain!*
*Finely Tuned Foods*
*From Generation to Generation*
*From Granny, With Love*
*From Seed to Serve*
*From the Apple Orchard*
*From the Ozark's Oven...*
*Gateways*
*Gourmet Garden*
*Grandma's Ozark Legacy*
*Heavenly Delights*
*Home Cookin'*

# CONTRIBUTING COOKBOOKS

*Hooked on Fish on the Grill*
*It's Christmas!*
*Kansas City BBQ*
*Kansas City Cuisine*
*Kitchen Prescriptions*
*Kohler Family Kookbook*
*Lavender and Lace*
*Luncheon Favorites*
*The Never Ending Season*
*The Passion of Barbeque*
*PAST & REPAST*
*Recipes & Stories of Early-Day Settlers*
*Recipes From Missouri...With Love*
*Recipes Old and New*
*Remembering the Past—Planning for the Future*
*Rush Hour Superchef!*
*Sassafras!*
*The Shaw House Cook Book*
*Silver Dollar City's Recipes*
*Sing for Your Supper*
*The Sportsman's Dish*
*St. Ambrose Parish "On the Hill" Cookbook*
*Steamboat Adventures*
*Talk About Good*
*The Tasty Palette Cook Book*
*Thyme for Kids*
*Treasured Recipes Book I*
*Treasured Recipes Book II*
*Turn of the Century Cookbook*
*USO's Salute to the Troops Cookbook*
*The Vegetarian Lunchbasket*
*Wanda's Favorite Recipes Book*
*With Hands & Heart Cookbook*

## Appetizers

*The bridge at Hannibal crosses the mighty Mississippi.*

# Piña Coolada

1 cup pineapple juice
½ teaspoon coconut extract

1 cup skim milk
1 cup crushed ice (optional)

Blend and serve cold. Makes 2½ cups.

*Breakfasts Ozark Style*

# Cranberry Tea

1 quart water
1 cup red hots

1 cup sugar
12-15 whole cloves

Boil together and set aside.

3 quarts water
1 small can frozen orange
    juice

2 quarts cranberry cocktail
1 small can frozen lemonade

Mix above ingredients together. Then mix with first mixture.
Serve hot or cold.

*Lavender and Lace*

# Apple Tangy Fizz

2 cups apple juice
2 cups ginger ale

1 pint orange sherbet

Drop scoop of orange sherbet in each of 4 glasses. Pour juice
and ginger ale over sherbet. Yield: 4-6 servings.

*From the Apple Orchard*

A really good apple squirts juice when you take the first bite.
The big three in Missouri apples are Jonathan, Red Delicious,
and Golden Delicious.

# Strawberry Lemonade Punch

½ cup instant tea (not
  lemon flavored)
1 (12-ounce) can lemonade
  concentrate
5 cups water

½ cup sugar
1 package frozen sliced
  strawberries
Vodka or champagne
  (optional)

Mix tea, lemonade, water, and sugar together, then add strawberries. Vodka or champagne may be added to taste. Easy.
Do ahead (except strawberries.) Serves 8-10.

**With Hands & Heart Cookbook**

# Cranberry Foam Punch

1 (6-ounce) can frozen
  cranberry juice (or
  cranberry cocktail)
1 (6-ounce) can frozen
  pineapple juice

1 container vanilla ice
  cream
1 (28-ounce) bottle seltzer
  water

Mix ingredients. Pour in seltzer just before serving.

**Delicious Reading**

# USO Jubilee Punch

1 (46-ounce) can red
  Hawaiian Punch
1 (6-ounce) can frozen
  lemonade concentrate
1 (6-ounce) can frozen
  orange juice concentrate

1 (6-ounce) can frozen
  pineapple juice concentrate
4-6 cups water
1 (28-ounce) bottle ginger ale

Chill punch and mix with other ingredients, except ginger
ale. Add ginger ale just before serving. Make frozen ice rings
or blocks out of club soda or Hawaiian Punch. This can be
served in a hollowed out watermelon shell.

**USO's Salute to the Troops Cookbook**

# Cappuccino

6 cups light cream
6 cups coffee
1 cup dark crème de cacao

½ cup rum
½ cup brandy

Mix cream, coffee, crème de cacao, rum, and brandy in saucepan. Heat over low heat. Serve hot. Serves 10-12.

*Cooking for Applause*

# Hot Cheese Crab Dip

3 large (8-ounce) packages cream cheese
2 (6-ounce) packages frozen crabmeat, thawed and drained
3 crushed garlic cloves
½ cup mayonnaise

2 teaspoons prepared mustard
¼ cup sherry or white wine (or more to taste)
2 - 2½ teaspoons powdered sugar
1 teaspoon onion juice
Seasoned salt to taste

Mix all ingredients together and heat. Serves: 8-10.

*Gourmet Garden*

# Vegetable Dip

1 cup mayonnaise
½ cup sour cream
¼ teaspoon salt
1 tablespoon onion
1 tablespoon parsley
2 tablespoons capers

½ teaspoon curry powder
1½ teaspoons lemon juice
1 tablespoon Worcestershire sauce
1 tablespoon salad seasonings

Mix in blender. Sometimes it is hard to find the capers, but it is good without them. I use Miracle Whip instead of mayonnaise. This is very good with raw cauliflower plus any other raw vegetables.

*A Collection of Recipes from the Best Cooks in the Midwest*

# Eggplant Caviar

1 medium eggplant, peeled
and cut into ½-inch cubes
⅓ cup chopped green pepper
1 medium onion, chopped
3 cloves garlic, crushed or
½ teaspoon garlic powder
⅓ cup olive oil
1 (4-ounce) can mushrooms,
drained
1 (6-ounce) can tomato paste

⅛ - ¼ cup water
2 tablespoons red wine
vinegar
½ cup stuffed sliced green
olives
½ teaspoon seasoned salt
1 teaspoon sugar
⅛ teaspoon pepper
½ teaspoon oregano

Mix the eggplant, green pepper, onion, garlic, and olive oil in a pan. Cover and cook slowly for 30 minutes. Then add the remaining ingredients. Cover and simmer another 30 minutes. Serve hot or cold with pita bread or crackers. Easy. Can do ahead. Serves 6-8.

*Cooking in Clover*

# Missouri Crab Grass

If only real crab grass disappeared so quickly!

½ cup butter
½ cup chopped onion
1 (10-ounce) package frozen
chopped spinach, cooked
and drained

1 (7-ounce) can crab meat,
drained
¾ cup grated Parmesan
cheese
Crackers

Sauté onion in butter. Stir in spinach, crab meat and cheese. Heat through. Serve in a chafing dish with crackers. Makes 3½ cups.

*Sassafras!*

Missouri is honeycombed with more than 5,000 known caves. They have been used not only for shelters, but to grow mushrooms, and for wine cellars during prohibition. These limestone caverns are still used for food and industrial storage.

# Dill Dip in Pumpernickel Loaf

1 (16-ounce) carton sour cream

1 pint mayonnaise or salad dressing

4 tablespoons dill weed

2 tablespoons chopped onion

4 teaspoons Lawry's seasoned salt

½ teaspoon garlic powder

1 round loaf pumpernickel bread

Mix all ingredients together except bread. Refrigerate for several hours before serving. To serve, cut top off of round loaf of pumpernickel bread. Scoop out inside of loaf and cut into small pieces for use as dippers. Place bread on large serving plate, put dippers around edge. Another loaf may need to be purchased to cup up into dippers. Pour dill dip into bread shell. Serve with toothpicks for dipping. Rye bread may be used instead of pumpernickel or a long loaf of French bread. Other seasoned salts may be used. Beau Monde is a good brand to use.

*Remembering the Past—Planning for the Future*

# Dippity Stix

1 (8-ounce) package cream cheese

1 (7-ounce) jar marshmallow creme

2 tablespoons orange juice

Mix and serve with fruit. (Can use fruit for table decorations and then dip it).

*Lavender and Lace*

# Homemade Boursin Cheese Dip

1 (8-ounce) package cream
  cheese
⅛ cup mayonnaise
1-3 teaspoons Dijon mustard
2 teaspoons horseradish
1 clove garlic, minced

1 teaspoon dill weed
1 teaspoon dry thyme
1-2 tablespoons freeze-dried
  chives or fresh cloves or
  green onions, finely
  chopped

Combine all ingredients and beat in electric mixer or food processor until smooth. Refrigerate to give added firmness. Decorate with paprika or parsley sprinkled around edge of bowl or down the middle.

Serve with assorted crackers. Mixture can also be used to stuff mushrooms or cocktail tomatoes. Keeps well, but do not freeze.

*Tasty Palette*

# Roast Garlic Spread

2 heads whole garlic
4 sprigs fresh thyme
½ teaspoon fresh rosemary
2 cups grated Monterey Jack
  cheese

2-4 tablespoons olive oil
Coarse ground black pepper
  to taste
Pink and green peppercorns
  for garnish

Preheat oven to 350°. Cut heads of garlic in half. Place 2 sprigs fresh thyme and ¼ teaspoon fresh rosemary between garlic halves. Wrap garlic in 2 thicknesses of aluminum foil and place in oven for 30 minutes. Remove from oven, unwrap, and let cool. Peel garlic.

Place grated cheese and herb-roasted garlic in a food processor and process briefly. Add ground pepper and 2 tablespoons of olive oil. Process until smooth and creamy, adding more olive oil if necessary. Garnish with pink and green peppercorns.

Serve in a crock or bowl alongside toasted French or sourdough bread or crackers. This spread is also excellent to brush on grilled lamb chops. Makes 2 cups.

*Kansas City Cuisine (Californos)*

# Zesty Italian Tuna Spread

1 (7-ounce) can white tuna
1 (3-ounce) can ripe olives
 (½ cup)

1 package Good Seasons
 Italian Salad Dressing Mix
1 cup sour cream

Drain off oil or water from tuna and rinse meat in cold water. Cut olives in fourths. Combine tuna, olives, salad dressing mix, and sour cream. Stir until well mixed. Place in serving dish, sprinkle with paprika, and serve with crackers (preferably a plain cracker). Preparation time: 6 minutes. Makes 2 cups.

*Note:* If no ripe olives on hand, omit.

*Rush Hour Superchef!*

# Crabmeat Spread

2 (8-ounce) packages cream
 cheese
1 small onion, finely
 chopped
½ cup mayonnaise
1 tablespoon lemon juice

1 teaspoon garlic salt
1 tablespoon Worcestershire
 sauce
1 bottle chili sauce
1 (10-12-ounce) container
 crabmeat (or crab sticks)

Soften cream cheese. Add all remaining ingredients except chili sauce and crab. Blend well. Shape on large flat serving platter and cover with Saran Wrap. Refrigerate overnight. Just before serving, cover spread with chili sauce, then put shredded crabmeat on top. Serve with biscuit-type cracker or Bremmer wafers.

*Kohler Family Kookbook*

---

Daniel Boone arrived in Missouri territory to open a whole new era in America's westward push. In the early 1800s, in the peaceful Femme Osage valley, this perpetual wanderer found the place he would always call home. The Daniel Boone Home is near Defiance.

---

# Decorated Cheese Wheel

Christmas entertaining is an expression of the generosity of the season, and a bounteous buffet is a beautiful way of giving. Extend your dining room table to its fullest point and include this festive gem in your holiday presentation.

6 (8-ounce) packages cream cheese, softened
½ cup chopped green onions, including tops
1 garlic clove, minced
8 ounces sharp cheddar cheese, grated
8 ounces Roquefort cheese, softened
2 tablespoons red caviar
2 tablespoons chopped black olives

2 tablespoons minced fresh parsley
2 tablespoons chopped pimiento
2 tablespoons crisply cooked diced bacon
2 tablespoons chopped pitted green olives
2 tablespoons black caviar
2 tablespoons chopped capers

Mix 2 packages of cream cheese with green onions and garlic; set aside. Mix 2 packages of cream cheese with cheddar cheese, set aside. Mix remaining 2 packages of cream cheese with Roquefort cheese; set aside.

Line bottom of a well-oiled 8- to 10-inch round springform pan with waxed paper; oil paper. Carefully layer cheeses in pan in order mixed; refrigerate. To serve, loosen cheese from side of pan with moistened thin-bladed knife; invert on serving dish. Remove waxed paper.

Thoroughly drain caviars, olives, pimiento and capers.

Using kitchen twine, mark top of cheese in 8 pie-shaped sections for toppings. Cover each section with 1 of the 8 toppings in order given. The more precise the division between the toppings, the more attractive the appetizer will be. Refrigerate until ready to serve, with Melba toast rounds or crackers. Serves 40.

*Note*: Bleu cheese may be substituted for Roquefort.

*PAST & REPAST*

# Mint Ball Appetizers

1 (8-ounce) package cream
  cheese, softened
1 tablespoon milk
¼ teaspoon salt
2 tablespoons walnuts,
  chopped fine

½ teaspoon sugar
¼ teaspoon cinnamon
¼ cup fresh mint leaves,
  chopped fine

Combine cream cheese, milk, salt, walnuts, sugar, and cinnamon. Form into small bite-size balls and roll in mint. Chill before serving.

*From Seed to Serve*

# Log Cabin Cheddar Sticks

An original recipe from the kitchens of Silver Dollar City; these are a favorite of the Log Hewers. To serve, arrange the sticks as if assembling a miniature log cabin and serve around your favorite party dip.

¼ cup butter, softened
1 cup grated Cheddar cheese
¼ cup milk
¼ teaspoon salt
Dash of Tabasco

Dash of paprika
Dash of cayenne
¾ cup sifted flour
1½ cups fine, soft bread
  crumbs

Soften butter to a creamy state and blend in cheese, milk, salt, Tabasco, paprika, and cayenne. Combine flour and bread crumbs and add to mixture. Divide mixture in half and refrigerate overnight.

After it's chilled, roll out half of the dough at a time between 2 pieces of wax paper until very thin. Work quickly. Take a knife or pastry wheel and cut into strips about 5 inches long and 1 inch wide. Place strips on cookie sheet and top with coarse salt or grated Parmesan cheese. Bake at 350° about 15 minutes or until golden brown. This will make about 40 sticks.

*Silver Dollar City's Recipes*

# Saganaki
### (Fried Greek Cheese)

1 pound any Greek cheese except Feta (Kasseri or Kefalotiri are best) cut into ¼-inch thick slices
1 egg, beaten
¼ cup milk or water
½ tablespoon oil

½ teaspoon salt
¾ cup flour
Oil for frying
Juice of 1 lemon
2 tablespoons brandy (optional)

Beat egg. Add milk or water, oil, and salt. Mix. Stir in flour and mix thoroughly. Let stand ½ hour. Dip cheese slices into batter and fry for about 2 minutes until browned. Sprinkle with lemon juice and serve immediately.

A nice royal touch, place 2 or 3 slices fried cheese on heat-proof plate. Pour 2 tablespoons brandy over cheese, light and serve a flaming Saganaki. As soon as flame dies out, sprinkle with lemon juice and serve immediately.

*The Art of Hellenic Cuisine*

# Stuffed Nasturtium Flowers

16 ounces cream cheese, softened
½ cup crushed pineapple, well-drained

¼ cup pecans, chopped
¼ teaspoon nutmeg
30-36 fresh nasturtium flowers

Combine first 4 ingredients, then stuff center of nasturtium flowers with a well-rounded teaspoonful of mixture. Arrange on a bed of lettuce or nasturtium leaves.

*Thyme for Kids*

James Hart Stark is credited with growing the first cultivated fruit west of the Mississippi. Stark Nursery, where the popular Red and Golden Delicious apples were first developed, is today one of the largest in the world and the oldest in America.

# Tortillitas

1 (8-ounce) package cream
  cheese, softened
1 cup sour cream
5 green onions, chopped
1 (4-ounce) can chopped
  green chiles

1-2 teaspoons garlic salt
6-7 (12-inch) flour
  tortillas
Picante sauce

Combine all ingredients except tortillas and picante sauce. Mix until smooth. Cover 1 tortilla with about 3-4 tablespoons of the mixture, spreading to the edges. Place another tortilla on top of this and spread with mixture. Continue layering until tortillas and mixture are used, ending with a tortilla on top. Chill thoroughly and cut into squares. Spear with a toothpick and serve with picante sauce. Can be made a day in advance. Makes 35-40 tortillitas.

*Gateways*

# Puerto Vallarta Wheels

¼ cup cooked black beans
2 jalapeño peppers, seeded
1 whole pimiento, seeded
1 teaspoon cumin
¼ bunch cilantro

¼ teaspoon salt
2 (8-ounce) packages cream
  cheese
2 (10-inch) flour tortillas
Salsa or picante sauce

Combine beans, peppers, pimiento, cumin, cilantro, and salt in a food processor with blade attachment and chop coarsely. Add cream cheese and blend until smooth. Spread mixture on tortillas, roll up, and chill. Remove from refrigerator and cut into ½-inch slices. Serve with your favorite salsa or picante. Serves 6.

*Kansas City Cuisine (Joe D's Wine Bar & Cafe)*

# Toasty Cheese Crackers

2 cups shredded cheddar
  cheese
½ cup grated Parmesan
  cheese
½ cup butter or margarine,
  softened

3 tablespoons water
1 cup flour
¼ teaspoon salt
1 cup uncooked oatmeal

Beat cheeses, butter, and water until smooth. Add flour and salt; mix well. Stir in oatmeal until blended.

Shape dough to form 2 (12-inch) rolls. Wrap securely and refrigerate 4 hours. Cut ⅛ - ¼-inch slices. Flatten slightly and bake at 400° on greased cookie sheet until edges are light brown. Easy. Do ahead.

*With Hands & Heart Cookbook*

# Sausage-Onion Snacks

As quick as can be.

1 pound bulk pork sausage
1 large onion, chopped
2 cups biscuit baking mix
¾ cup milk
2 eggs

1 tablespoon caraway or
  poppy seed
1½ cups dairy sour cream
¼ teaspoon salt
Paprika

Grease a 13x9x2-inch baking pan. Cook sausage and onion over medium heat until browned. Drain. Mix biscuit mix, milk, and 1 egg together. Spread in baking pan. Sprinkle with caraway seeds. Top with sausage mixture. Mix sour cream, salt, and remaining egg. Pour evenly over sausage. Sprinkle with paprika. Bake uncovered at 350° until set, 25-30 minutes. Cut into rectangles. Serve warm. Makes 32 rectangles.

*Finely Tuned Foods*

# Milanese Appetizer Cups

Use miniature muffin pans for intriguing, individual appetizers.

1 (10-ounce) package frozen chopped spinach
8 ounces ricotta cheese (1 cup)
½ cup grated Parmesan cheese (1½ ounces)
1 cup chopped mushrooms (about 3 ounces)
2 tablespoons minced onion

¼ teaspoon dried leaf oregano
¼ teaspoon salt
1 egg, lightly beaten
24 thin slices prosciutto, about 2 inches square
Dairy sour cream, if desired
2 green onions, if desired, thinly sliced

Cook spinach according to package directions. Pour cooked spinach into a sieve; drain thoroughly by gently pressing out excess juices with back of a spoon.

In a medium bowl, combine drained spinach, ricotta cheese, Parmesan cheese, mushrooms, minced onion, oregano, salt and egg. Preheat oven to 375° (190°C). Lightly butter 24 (1¾-inch) muffin cups. Place 1 slice prosciutto in each cup; press against bottom and side of cup. Spoon cheese mixture into prosciutto-lined cups. Bake in preheated oven 20-25 minutes. Complete now or make ahead.

To complete now, let stand 5 minutes. Gently run a knife around side of each cup to loosen appetizers; remove from cups. Serve hot or cold. If desired, garnish each appetizer with a dollop of sour cream and 2 or 3 green onion slices.

To make ahead, cool in pan at room temperature 10 minutes. Cover with foil or plastic wrap; refrigerate up to 24 hours. To serve hot, preheat oven to 350° (175°C). Remove cover; heat in muffin cups 6-10 minutes. Cool in pan 5 minutes, then gently loosen and remove from muffin cups. Garnish as directed above, if desired. Makes 24 appetizers.

*St. Ambrose "On the Hill" Cookbook*

# Caponata
### *(Eggplant Appetizer)*

2 eggplants (medium),
  unpeeled, cut into
  ½-inch cubes
Salt
Salad oil
2 medium onions, chopped
4 ribs celery, ½-inch slices
3 cups Italian plum tomatoes,
  chopped

1 teaspoon sweet basil
1 teaspoon salt
⅛ teaspoon pepper
¼ cup capers (optional)
1 cup green olives, chopped
1 tablespoon sugar
3 or 4 tablespoons red wine
  vinegar (to taste)

Place eggplant in colander, sprinkle salt over it and place inverted plate over eggplant. Place heavy object on plate to weight down, thus squeezing water out as it is secreted by eggplant. Let stand about 1 hour; rinse thoroughly. Drain and dry with paper towels.

Heat 2 tablespoons oil; add onions and celery, sauté 5 minutes. Add tomatoes, basil, salt, and pepper. Simmer 10 minutes. Add capers and olives and cook 5 minutes more.

Meanwhile, heat some oil and fry eggplant in small batches until browned; drain on paper towels. Combine eggplant with tomato mixture, add sugar and vinegar. Simmer 8 or 10 minutes more.

Store in jars in refrigerator, will keep 2 weeks. Recipe makes about 9 cups and contains about 60 calories for ¼ cup.

### *St. Ambrose "On the Hill" Cookbook*

# Spinach Balls

2 (10-ounce) boxes frozen,
  chopped spinach, cooked
  and drained well
1 box herbed stuffing mix
2 medium onions, minced

¾ cup melted butter
½ cup Parmesan cheese,
  grated
½ teaspoon garlic salt

Mix all of the preceding. Shape into balls (about 1 inch in diameter). Bake at 350° for 20 minutes, turning once. These may be frozen.

*Silver Dollar City's Recipes*

# Mushroom Squares

6 slices bread (trim crusts
  off and cut in quarters)
Butter
4 slices bacon, fried and
  crumbled
1 small can mushrooms,
  chopped and drained

2 tablespoons grated Swiss
  cheese
2 tablespoons mayonnaise
1 tablespoon parsley flakes
⅛ teaspoon rosemary leaves
Few grains of salt

Spread butter on bread and place, butter-side-down, on baking sheet. Top with small amount of other ingredients mixed together. Bake at 400° for 5 minutes.

*Delicious Reading*

# Missouri Pâté

A well-spiced pâté is a convenient dish for a country picnic or a festive buffet table. Cornichons add an elegant touch to this mildly flavored regional version of a classic.

4 tablespoons unsalted
  butter
½ pound fresh mushrooms,
  chopped
1 shallot, minced
2 tablespoons bourbon
1 tablespoon cognac
8 ounces liverwurst

2 (8-ounce) packages cream
  cheese, softened
1 teaspoon chopped fresh
  dill
1 teaspoon chopped parsley
2 teaspoons Dijon mustard
Salt and freshly ground
  pepper to taste

Melt butter in a skillet. Sauté mushrooms and shallot until soft. Stir in bourbon and cognac, cool.

Place mushroom mixture and remaining ingredients in a food processor or blender; process until very smooth. Transfer to a crock or serving bowl. Refrigerate for at least 24 hours before serving. Garnish with sprigs of fresh dill. Serve with party rye and cornichons. Serves 12.

*PAST & REPAST*

# Smoked Fish Pâté

1½ pounds smoked fish
  (sable, salmon, trout or
  whitefish, not lox)
⅓ cup minced scallions
  (white part only)

4 ounces cream cheese
⅓ cup mayonnaise
Garlic powder to taste
Liquid smoke to taste
  (optional)

Blend all ingredients together; chill and serve. Serves 6-8. Easy. Can do ahead.

*Cooking in Clover II*

# Egg Roll Borek

1 pound deer burger (or
  hamburger)
½ pound pork sausage
1 medium onion (chopped)
3 tablespoons chopped dried
  parsley (or ½ cup fresh)

½ teaspoon black pepper
½ teaspoon salt
1 pack egg roll sheets

In a skillet, cook meat, onion, and spices together over medium heat until meat is done; drain off all liquid. Put about 3 tablespoons meat on each sheet, roll and seal according to package instructions.

In a non-stick skillet, put a light coating of cooking oil. Over medium heat, cook rolls to a golden brown, turning and adding oil as necessary. Drain thoroughly on paper towels. Serve hot.

*The Sportsman's Dish*

# Polish Mistakes

1 pound hamburger
1 pound Italian sausage
1 pound Velveeta cheese
1 teaspoon garlic powder

½ teaspoon oregano
Salt and pepper to taste
Rye bread squares

Cook hamburger meat; do not overcook. Drain. Cook Italian sausage, drain. Mix with hamburger meat. Add cheese and cook until cheese is melted. Add other seasoning.

Put good serving on small square of rye bread. Place on cookie sheet, heat 10 minutes in 350° oven.

May be frozen; cover with plastic wrap or foil. Remove cover, heat 20 minutes in 350° oven.

*Wanda's Favorite Recipes Book*

# Glazed Barbequed Salami

1 pound log of salami
1 bottle of sweet and sour sauce

¼ cup barbeque sauce
1 tablespoon Dijon mustard

Peel and score the salami, making large X's. Combine the remaining ingredients to make a sauce. Bake in a 275° oven for 1½ hours, basting frequently with sauce. This can be made ahead.

Serve at room temperature and slice thinly. Surround with cocktail tomatoes, parsley, party rye and dollar rolls. Place bowl of sauce or mustard on the side. Serves 8.

*From Generation to Generation*

# Cranberry Meat Balls

An excellent blend of ingredients.

2 pounds ground beef
1 cup cornflake crumbs
⅓ cup dried parsley flakes
2 eggs
2 tablespoons soy sauce

¼ teaspoon pepper
½ teaspoon garlic powder
¼ cup catsup
2 tablespoons onion, chopped

In a large bowl mix ground beef, crumbs, parsley, eggs, soy sauce, pepper, garlic powder, catsup, and onion. Blend well and form into small balls. Brown in oven at 400° for 15 minutes. Pour off grease.

SAUCE:

1 (16-ounce) can jellied cranberry sauce
1 (12-ounce) bottle chili sauce

2 tablespoons brown sugar
1 tablespoon lemon juice

While meat balls are baking, combine cranberry sauce, chili sauce, brown sugar, and lemon juice. Cover drained meat balls with sauce and bake uncovered at 300° for 15 minutes. Serve in chafing dish. Makes 80-90 meat balls.

*Finely Tuned Foods*

# Chicken Cordon Blue Appetizers

Ham cubes (½ x ½ inches)
Swiss cheese cubes (½ x ½ inches)
Chicken strips (breasts, deboned, sliced in ½-inch strips and pounded thin)

Eggs (for dipping batter)
Italian bread crumbs
Butter, melted
Parmesan cheese

Spear 1 ham cube and 1 cheese cube with a toothpick. Wrap chicken strip around it. Dip in egg. Cover with Italian bread crumbs. Brush on butter. Sprinkle on Parmesan cheese. Bake for 15 minutes at 350°. Brown for 10 minutes.

*Kohler Family Kookbook*

# Smokey Frank "Bites"

When these are served, there will be an onslaught by the young set.

1 pound frankfurters
2 tablespoons butter
1½ teaspoons aromatic bitters

¼ teaspoon onion salt
¼ teaspoon celery salt

Cut frankfurters into 1-inch pieces. Heat butter in skillet. Stir in aromatic bitters, onion salt, and celery salt. Add frankfurters; stir to coat. Cook over medium heat, stirring occasionally, until pieces are dark brown and crusty. Spear on toothpicks and serve hot. Yield: 40 "Bites."

*Treasured Recipes Book II*

---

Would you answer an ad that read, " Wanted: Young, wiry fellows, not over 18. Must be expert riders willing to risk death daily. Orphans preferred. Wages: $25 per week."? One who did answer the ad in the 1860s was Buffalo Bill Cody, who once rode 300 miles without stopping...for The Pony Express.

---

# Meatball Appetizer
### (Microwave)

1½ pounds ground round
1 small size package
Pepperidge Farm Herb
Stuffing

⅔ cup evaporated milk
2 teaspoons curry powder

Mix ingredients together. Form into small balls. Cover with waxed paper to microwave. Microwave on HIGH power for 5 minutes. Makes about 65 small meatballs. Serve warm.

*Sing for Your Supper*

# Puppy Chow - Dog Food
### (Crispy Cereal Snack)

1 stick margarine
1 small bag chocolate chips
1 cup peanut butter

1 box Crispex cereal
1 box powdered sugar

Melt together the margarine, chocolate chips and peanut butter; add Crispex and stir. Pour warm mixture and powdered sugar into a brown paper bag, close tightly and shake to coat. Turn out on foil or waxed paper. Spread out and stir around a little to cool. Put in large plastic container with a lid and shake often. Keeps well. If you want to make a big hit—buy a large dog dish to serve it in.

*Lavender and Lace*

# Chocolate-Peanut Butter Cornucopias

1 package cone-shaped corn
snacks
¼ cup peanut butter

3 (1-ounce) squares
semi-sweet chocolate

Choose 60 nicely shaped corn snacks. Stuff each one with peanut butter. Set aside. Melt chocolate in top of double boiler; dip open end of each corn snack in chocolate. Place on waxed paper. Yield: 60 cones.

This is a great snack for kids to make as it takes a minimum of supervision. It is also an attractive addition to any tray of assorted cookies for a reception or party.

### *Remembering the Past—Planning for the Future*

In 1907 Harold Bell Wright wrote *The Shepherd of the Hills*, which has become one of the best selling books of all times. At the Shepherd of the Hills Farm, a reenactment of the story is performed from May to October.

# Bread and Breakfast

*Performers in Shepherd of the Hills drama at
Old Matt's Cabin in Branson.*

# Plum Bread

2 cups flour
1 teaspoon soda
1 teaspoon cinnamon
½ teaspoon salt
½ teaspoon nutmeg
1½ cups sugar

2 small jars Gerber baby
food puréed plums
1 cup salad oil
3 eggs, beaten
1 cup nuts

Sift all dry ingredients together. Add remaining ingredients. Bake at 275° for 1 hour. Test center. May need to bake longer.

**TOPPING:**
¼ cup oleo
¼ cup sugar

2 tablespoons milk
⅛ teaspoon soda

Put on stove to warm until the soda boils up. Drizzle over bread when cool.

*Blue Ridge Christian Church Cookbook*

# Oatmeal-Raisin Bread

This recipe will be a favorite with all the raisin bread lovers.

½ cup whole wheat flour
½ cup firmly packed dark brown sugar
1 teaspoon salt
½ cup butter or margarine, softened
1 cup quick-cooking oats, uncooked
¾ cup raisins

2 cups boiling water
1 package dry yeast
½ cup warm water (105°-115°)
5-6 cups all-purpose flour
½ cup sugar
1 tablespoon ground cinnamon
Melted butter or margarine

Combine first 6 ingredients in a large bowl; mix well. Add boiling water, stirring to melt butter; cool mixture to 105°-115°.

Dissolve yeast in warm water; let stand 5 minutes. Add to oats mixture, and mix well. Gradually stir in enough flour to make a soft dough.

Turn dough out on a floured surface, and knead 8-10 minutes until smooth and elastic. Place in a well-greased bowl, turning to grease top. Cover and let rise in warm place (85°), free from drafts, 1 hour or until doubled in bulk.

Punch dough down; turn out on a floured surface, and knead 2 minutes. Divide dough in half, and let rest for 10 minutes  Roll each half into an 18x9-inch rectangle.

Combine sugar and cinnamon. Sprinkle half the sugar mixture evenly over each rectangle. Roll up, jelly role fashioned, beginning at short end. Fold under ends, and place in two greased 9x5x3-inch loaf pans. Brush with melted butter. Cover and let rise in a warm place (85°), free from drafts, 40-50 minutes, or until doubled in bulk. Bake at 375° for 40-45 minutes or until loaves sound hollow when tapped. Remove loaves from pans, and cool on wire racks. Spread top with powdered sugar glaze, if desired. Yield: 2 loaves.

*From the Ozarks' Oven...*

# Christopsomo
### (Christmas Bread)

| | |
|---|---|
| 2 packages active dry yeast | 1 cup warm milk |
| 1 cup warm water | 3 large eggs, beaten lightly |
| ¾ cup, plus 2 teaspoons | ½ cup melted sweet butter |
|   granulated sugar | ¾ coarsely chopped |
| 7-7½ cups flour |   walnuts, or pecans |
| 1 teaspoon salt | ½ cup light colored raisins |
| 1-1½ teaspoons mastiha | |
|   (a spice) | |

Dissolve yeast with water and 1 teaspoon sugar; allow to stand, covered, until doubled in volume.

Meanwhile sift 7 cups flour with ¾ cup sugar and salt into large bowl. Pound mastiha with remaining teaspoon sugar until powdered. Then add to flour.

Make a well in the flour and add milk, eggs, butter, swollen yeast, walnuts, and raisins, and mix until smooth. If necessary, add more flour to form a soft but not sticky dough, and knead for 10-15 minutes.

Place in a lightly-oiled bowl in warm place to rise until doubled in bulk (about 2 hours). Uncover dough, punch down and divide into 2 parts. Knead each part for a few minutes. Then form into round loaves and place in greased 9-inch pans. Cover and set aside to rise in a warm, draft-free place until doubled in bulk (about 1½ hours).

Bake in a 375° oven for 20 minutes. Spread on the preferred glaze.

| GLAZES: | Or: |
|---|---|
| 2 tablespoons honey | 1 beaten egg white |
| 2 tablespoons orange juice | Fine granulated sugar |
| ¼ cup slivered almonds, | ¼ cup glacéed fruit |
|   mixed | |

The first glaze may be brushed on with a pastry brush. If the second glaze is used, brush on the egg white, then sprinkle with sugar, then the glacéed fruit.

Continue baking at 325° for 35-40 minutes more or until bread is a deep shiny light brown color. Cool on racks. May be baked in advance. Yields 2 round 9-inch loaves.

*Adventures in Greek Cooking*

# Apricot Coriander Pecan Bread

So moist and smells so good!

¼ cup butter, softened
1¼ cups sugar
1 egg, beaten
2 cups flour
½ teaspoon baking powder
½ teaspoon baking soda
½ teaspoon salt
1 tablespoon ground
  coriander

1 (16-ounce) can (1 cup)
  apricots drained
  and mashed
2 tablespoons sour cream
½ teaspoon almond extract
½ cup chopped pecans
½ cup halved maraschino
  cherries

Preheat oven to 350°. Beat butter. Add sugar and continue beating until fluffy. Stir in egg. Sift flour, baking powder, baking soda, salt, and coriander onto waxed paper. Stir into sugar mixture alternately with apricots, sour cream, and almond extract. Add pecans and cherries. Turn into greased 9x5x3-inch loaf pan or 2 smaller loaf pans. Bake at 350° for 50 minutes or until toothpick comes out clean. If using smaller pans, baking time may be between 30-40 minutes.

Cool in pan(s). Wrap in foil or plastic wrap. Refrigerate. Allow to ripen 24 hours. Easy. Do ahead. Freeze.

### *With Hands & Heart Cookbook*

# Little Boy Blueberry Orange Bread

2 tablespoons butter
¼ cup boiling water
½ cup plus 2 tablespoons
　orange juice, divided
4 teaspoons grated orange
　rind, divided
1 egg
1 cup sugar

2 cups sifted flour
1 teaspoon baking powder
¼ teaspoon soda
½ teaspoon salt
1 cup fresh or frozen
　blueberries
2 tablespoons honey

Melt butter in boiling water in small bowl. Add 1/2 cup juice, and 3 teaspoons rind. Beat egg with sugar until light and fluffy. Add dry ingredients alternately with orange liquid, beating until smooth. Fold in berries. Bake in greased 9x5x3-inch pan at 325° for 1 hour and 10 minutes. Turn out onto rack. Mix 2 tablespoons orange juice, 1 teaspoon rind and 2 tablespoons honey. Spoon over hot loaf. Let stand until cool. Or frost with:

**ORANGE GLAZE:**
1½ teaspoons butter
　flavoring
1½ teaspoons almond
　flavoring

1½ teaspoons vanilla
　flavoring
¼ cup orange juice
⅓ cup sugar

Mix ingredients and use as glaze on warm bread.

*Recipes From Missouri...With Love*

# Apple Bread

1 cup sugar
¾ cup vegetable oil
2 eggs
1½ cup flour
1 teaspoon cinnamon

1 teaspoon baking soda
¼ teaspoon salt
¼ cup nuts
1½ cups chopped apples
Sugar and cinnamon

Mix together sugar, oil, and eggs. Add flour, cinnamon, baking soda, and salt. Add nuts and apples. Pour into greased 9x5-inch loaf pan. Sprinkle top with sugar and cinnamon. Bake at 350° for 55 minutes. Makes 1 loaf.

*Cooking for Applause*

# Flower Pot Bread

A fun way to present the "staff of life."

| | |
|---|---|
| 1 package (1 tablespoon) active dry yeast | 1 teaspoon salt |
| ½ cup warm water (114°-120°) | 1 (13-ounce) can evaporated milk |
| ⅛ teaspoon ginger | 2 tablespoons vegetable oil |
| 3 tablespoons sugar | 4 - 4½ cups unsifted flour |
| | Butter, melted |

Season a 6-inch clay flower pot before first use by greasing well and baking 30 minutes at 350°. Cool and repeat seasoning procedure. Set pot aside to cool while preparing dough.

In a large mixing bowl, dissolve yeast in warm water. Blend in ginger and 1 tablespoon of the sugar. Let stand in a warm place until bubbly, about 15 minutes. Stir in the remaining 2 tablespoons sugar, salt, evaporated milk, and oil. Mix at low speed. Add flour, 1 cup at a time; beat well after each addition. The dough should be stiff, but too sticky to knead. Place dough in lightly oiled pot. Let rise in warm place until dough is 1½ inches over top of pot, about 60 minutes.

Preheat oven to 350°. Bake 60 minutes. (For smaller loaves, use two 4-inch pots and bake 40-45 minutes.) Crust will be very brown. Brush top with melted butter. Let cool 5-10 minutes and loosen crust around edge. Store in flower pot for freshness. Makes 1 loaf.

*Sassafras!*

# Armenian White Bread

This is a beautiful bread to make you proud.

2 packages dry yeast
½ cup warm water
1¾ cups warm water
3 tablespoons olive oil or
   salad oil

2 tablespoons sugar
1 teaspoon salt
2½ - 3 cups flour

Dissolve yeast in ½ cup warm water. Add milk, oil, sugar, and salt. Beat together (5-8 minutes). Then stir in enough flour to make a stiff dough. Turn out onto bread board; knead until smooth and elastic (5-8 minutes). Cover with plastic and let set 20 minutes. Knead and divide into half or fourths and make into 2 flat, round loaves. Place on greased sheet (pan). Brush with oil, cover and let set for 20 minutes.

Bake 25-30 minutes in 350° preheated oven. Cool and rack. For glazed top: Before placing into oven, brush with 1 egg yolk mixed with 2 tablespoons water and sprinkle with sesame seeds.

*Treasured Recipes Book I*

# Best-ever Jewish Challah
### (Egg Bread)

1 package active dry yeast
5 cups all-purpose flour
1 teaspoon salt
⅓ cup sugar
1¼ cups very warm water
(125°)
⅓ cup soft butter or salad
oil

2 eggs
Pinch of saffron or few
drops yellow food coloring
1 egg yolk, blended with 1
tablespoon milk
Poppy Seeds

Combine yeast, 1½ cups flour, salt, and sugar in a mixing bowl. Pour in water and beat until smooth. Mix in butter or oil, eggs, and saffron or food coloring. Gradually add enough remaining flour to make a soft dough. Turn out on floured board and knead until smooth and elastic or knead in a large food processor with dough hook. Place in greased bowl, butter top of dough lightly and cover with a clean towel. Let rise in warm place until doubled in size, about 1½ hours. Punch down, turn out onto floured board and knead lightly.

Divide into 4 equal parts. Roll each into strand 20 inches long. Place 4 strands on greased baking sheet. Pinch top ends together and braid as follows: Pick up the strand on the right, bring it over the next one, under the third and over the fourth. Repeat until braid is complete. Cut enough dough off ends to make ¾ cup. Tuck ends under and pinch to seal. Roll reserved dough into 3 strips and make a small braid. Lay on top of large braid. Cover and let rise until doubled. Brush with yolk mixture and sprinkle with poppy seeds. Bake at 350° for 35 minutes or until loaf sounds hollow when thumped. Makes 1 loaf.

*Gourmet Garden*

The Anderson House in Lexington served as a field hospital for both sides during the Civil War.

# Stuffed Bread

5-6 submarine or other hard
  crusted rolls
½ pound liverwurst
2 (8-ounce) packages cream
  cheese
¼ cup beer

1 tablespoon dry mustard
¼ cup watercress, chopped
  (or spinach)
¼ cup chopped onion
¼ cup chopped radish

Heat oven to 350°. Slice off ends of rolls and scoop out as much of the inside as possible. Crumble or cube this bread and toast lightly in oven. Cut liverwurst into small cubes. Beat cream cheese until smooth and soft. Mix beer, mustard, and cream cheese. Add watercress or spinach, onion, radish, and mix well. Add liverwurst and toss lightly.

Cool toasted crumbs to room temperature and stir into cheese mixture. Pack stuffing into bread shells. Wrap and chill at least 4 hours or overnight. Slice thin. Makes beautiful hors d'oeuvres to take on a boat or picnic.

*Kitchen Prescriptions*

# Vegetable Cheese French Bread

1 cup shredded mozzarella
  cheese
½ cup grated carrot
2-3 green onions, sliced

½ teaspoon dried Italian
  herb seasoning
¼ cup mayonnaise
8 slices French bread

Combine all ingredients except bread in a medium bowl. Cover and chill.

When ready to serve, place bread slices on an ungreased baking sheet. Broil 2-3 minutes until lightly browned. Turn and spread cheese mixture on untoasted side. Bake at 350° until cheese melts. Serve immediately. Serves 6-8.

*Gateways*

# Pimento Cheese Bread

Quick to prepare.

3¾ cups biscuit mix
1 egg, beaten
1½ cups milk

1 cup cheddar cheese, grated
1 (4-ounce) can pimentos,
   drained and diced

Combine all ingredients with an electric mixer. Do not over beat. Pour into well-greased 8½ x 4½-inch loaf pan. Bake at 350° for 50-60 minutes. Best if served warm. This delicious bread can be rewarmed. Serves 8.

*Finely Tuned Foods*

# Corn Cakes

1 can creamed corn
1 egg
4 tablespoons sugar

¾ cup flour
Salt and pepper to taste

Combine all ingredients. Mix well. Drop by heaping table-spoons into a lightly oiled skillet. Fry till crusty and golden on each side. Serve with syrup, and bacon or sausage for a hearty winter supper.

*From Granny, With Love*

# Corn Pone

This method was used in the late 1800s. Cornbread made with water instead of milk was often called Adam's Ale Bread. This is similar to the bread made by the Indians for the early settlers which was also shaped by hand.

Take 3 cups of corn meal and sprinkle over it 1 teaspoon salt. Pour over the meal 1½ cups of boiling water, or enough to make a real stiff dough. Have an 8x10-inch bread pan "simply swimming" in grease. Shape the dough into a flat loaf by using your hands and pressing fingers into the dough, leaving long ridges on the top. Bake in a hot oven until brown around the edges. Serve with lots of butter.

*Grandma's Ozark Legacy*

# Broccoli Cornbread

| | |
|---|---|
| 2 sticks butter | 4 eggs |
| 1 teaspoon dried or fresh | 1 cup cottage cheese |
| onion, (optional) | 1 (10-ounce) box frozen |
| 2 (8½-ounce) boxes corn | chopped broccoli |
| muffin mix | |

Melt butter in 9x13-inch pan. Mix all ingredients together. Spoon mixture into pan with melted butter.

Bake according to instructions on corn muffin box. (May need to bake longer.)

*The Never Ending Season*

# Float Trip Hush Puppies

Serve these around the campfire with the fish you caught.

| | |
|---|---|
| ¼ teaspoon baking soda | ½ teaspoon salt |
| ½ cup buttermilk | 1 egg, beaten |
| 1 cup cornmeal | ¼ cup finely chopped |
| ½ teaspoon baking | onion |
| powder | Vegetable oil for frying |

Dissolve soda in buttermilk, stir well. Combine cornmeal, baking powder and salt. Stir in buttermilk mixture, egg and onion, mixing well.

Drop batter by tablespoonfuls into deep hot oil (350°). Fry about 3 minutes per side or until golden brown, turning once. Drain on paper towels. Makes about 2 dozen hush puppies.

If you are on a float or camping trip, mix dry ingredients ahead in a plastic bag.

*Recipes From Missouri...With Love*

In Missouri's nearly one million acres of water, there are almost 200 species of fish, including bass, bluegill, catfish, striper, crappie, walleye, northern pike, and muskie.

# Chive Rolls

| | |
|---|---|
| 5-5½ cups flour | 2 cups milk |
| 2 tablespoons sugar | ¼ cup butter |
| 1 package dry yeast | ¾ cup chives, chopped |
| 2 teaspoons salt | Cornmeal |

Combine 2 cups flour, sugar, yeast, and salt in a large mixing bowl. Heat together milk and butter until very warm. Gradually add dry ingredients and beat 2 minutes at medium speed, scraping bowl occasionally. Add 1 cup flour; beat 2 cups chives and enough additional flour to make a stiff dough. Turn out on lightly floured surface; knead until smooth and elastic (5-10 minutes).

Punch dough down and divide into 20 pieces. Shape into balls and flatten slightly. Place about 3 inches apart on buttered baking sheets which have been lightly sprinkled with cornmeal. Cover and let rise in warm place until double in bulk again (30-45 minutes). Preheat oven to 400°. Brush tops with melted butter, sprinkle tops with remaining chives, and bake for 18-20 minutes. Cool on wire rack.

*From Seed to Serve*

# Caraway Crescent Rolls

A "quickie" for busy days!

| | |
|---|---|
| 1 cup Rice Krispies, crushed | 1 (8-ounce) package crescent |
| 1 teaspoon salt | refrigerator rolls |
| 2 tablespoons caraway seeds | ½ cup milk |

Mix crushed cereal with salt and caraway seeds. Remove rolls from container and cut each triangle in half to make 2 small triangles. Dip each piece of roll dough in milk, then in dry cereal mixture. Starting with narrow side, roll up dough and place on a cookie sheet. Bake rolls in preheated oven 450° for 10-12 minutes. Serve warm. Yields 16.

*The Cook Book*

Lambert's Cafe in Sikeston is home of the "throwed rolls." They literally throw you a roll when you ask for one!

# Quick Herb Crescent Rolls

1 package Pillsbury Crescent Rolls

¼ cup shredded cheese, (cheddar or Monterey Jack)

2 tablespoons chopped fresh herbs (your choice)

Preheat oven to 400°. Open package and unroll the dough. Sprinkle the center of the wide-end of each roll with a small amount of cheese and a pinch or two of herbs. Roll and bake in preheated oven according to the directions of the package. Makes 8 rolls.

*Thyme for Kids*

# Pumpkin Apple Streusel Muffins

2 cups sugar
2½ cups flour
2 teaspoons cinnamon
½ teaspoon ginger
2 eggs, slightly beaten
1 cup pumpkin
½ cup vegetable oil

2 cups apples, peeled and diced
1 teaspoon soda
¼ teaspoon salt
¼ teaspoon cloves
¼ teaspoon nutmeg

Mix dry ingredients in large bowl. Combine eggs, pumpkin, and oil; add to dry ingredients. Mix only until moistened. Stir in apples. Spoon into greased or paper-lined muffin tins, filling ¾ full. Sprinkle with Streusel Topping. Bake at 350° for 35-40 minutes or until toothpick comes out clean.

**STREUSEL TOPPING:**
2 tablespoons flour
¼ cup sugar

½ teaspoon cinnamon
4 teaspoons butter

Combine dry ingredients; cut in butter until mixture is crumbly.

*Apples, Apples, Apples*

# Southwest Missouri Blueberry Cream Cheese Muffins

| | |
|---|---|
| 1 cup Missouri blueberries | 2 teaspoons lemon juice |
| 2 cups flour | 2 teaspoons vanilla |
| ¾ cup sugar | ½ cup milk |
| 1½ teaspoons baking powder | ¼ cup butter, melted |
| 3 ounces cream cheese | 2 eggs |
| | Pinch of salt |

Toss blueberries with 2 tablespoons flour; set aside. Combine remaining dry ingredients; set aside. With blade in food processor, blend cheese, lemon juice, vanilla, milk, and butter. Add eggs, pulse 4-5 times. Add flour, pulse 6 times. Stir in blueberries by hand. Fill greased muffin cups ⅔ full. Bake at 400° 18-20 minutes.

*The Never Ending Season*

# Streusel Filled Apple Muffins

| | |
|---|---|
| 1½ cups flour | ½ cup milk |
| 2 teaspoons baking powder | 1 egg, beaten |
| ¼ cup sugar | 1 medium apple, peeled and grated |
| ½ teaspoon nutmeg | |
| ¼ cup vegetable oil | |

Sift together dry ingredients. Make a well and pour in oil, milk, beaten egg, and grated apples. Mix only until moistened. Spoon ¾ of batter into well-greased muffin tins. Sprinkle streusel filling over each, then top with 1 teaspoon batter. Bake at 350° for 20-25 minutes.

**STREUSEL FILLING:**

| | |
|---|---|
| ¼ cup brown sugar | 1 tablespoon butter or margarine, melted |
| 1 tablespoon flour | ¼ cup chopped nuts |
| ½ teaspoon cinnamon | |

Combine above ingredients. Yield: 1 dozen muffins.

*From the Apple Orchard*

# Pineapple Oatmeal Muffins

1 cup quick-cooking oats
1 (8-ounce) can crushed
   pineapple (juice pack,
   undrained)
½ cup milk
1 egg beaten
¼ cup butter-flavored
   Crisco, melted

1 cup all-purpose flour
½ cup sugar
⅓ cup chopped pecans
1 tablespoon baking powder
¼ teaspoon salt

**STREUSEL TOPPING:**
¼ cup brown sugar, firmly
   packed
¼ cup quick oats
¼ cup flake coconut

¼ cup finely chopped
   pecans
2 tablespoons melted
   margarine

Preheat oven to 400°. Grease 18 medium muffin pans or 6 jumbo muffin pans well. Set aside. In a small mixing bowl, mix oats, pineapple and juice, milk, and egg. Let stand for 3 minutes to soften oats. Stir in melted butter-flavored Crisco.

In a medium mixing bowl, combine flour, sugar, pecans, baking powder, and salt. Make well in mixture. Add oat mixture. Stir only until dry ingredients are moistened. Fill muffin cups about ⅔ full.

Mix Streusel Topping ingredients together and sprinkle 2 teaspoons mixture on top of each muffin. Bake 20-25 minutes or until deep golden brown.

*Remembering the Past—Planning for the Future*

# Morning Glorious Bread or Muffins

Served at Ramblewood in Camdenton.

2 cups flour
1¼ cups granulated sugar
½ teaspoon salt
2 teaspoons soda
2 teaspoons baking powder
2 teaspoons cinnamon
3 tablespoons Tang

¾ cup coconut
1½ cups grated carrots (4 medium)
3 eggs
1 cup oil
1 teaspoon vanilla
1½ cups chopped apples

Combine dry ingredients, add liquids. Bake at 350° in 2 greased loaf pans for 1 hour; 20 minutes for two-inch muffins; 15 minutes for mini-muffins.

*Breakfasts Ozark Style*

# Apple Biscuit Coffee Cake

2 tablespoons butter or margarine
2 cooking apples, peeled and sliced
¼ cup raisins
1 can refrigerated ready-to-bake biscuits

¼ cup brown sugar
½ teaspoon cinnamon
¼ cup light corn syrup
1 egg
¼ cup chopped walnuts
1 tablespoon butter or margarine

Melt 2 tablespoons butter in bottom of 9-inch round cake pan. Arrange sliced apples over butter. Sprinkle raisins over apples. Cut each of the biscuits into fourths and place over apples.

Mix together brown sugar, cinnamon, corn syrup, and egg until well blended and sugar is dissolved. Pour over biscuits. Sprinkle walnuts over top. Dot with 1 tablespoon butter.

Bake at 350° for 25-30 minutes. Invert onto serving plate, spooning juices over top. Yields 6-8 servings.

*From the Apple Orchard*

# Gooey Butter Coffee Cake

Don't count the calories in this St. Louis favorite.

1 (16-ounce) box pound cake
   mix
4 eggs, divided
½ cup butter, melted
1 (16-ounce) box
   confectioners' sugar

1 (8-ounce) package cream
   cheese, softened
1½ tablespoons vanilla
   extract

Preheat oven to 300°. Combine cake mix, 2 eggs, and the butter. Pour into a well-greased 8x12-inch baking pan. Reserve 2 tablespoons of sugar. Combine cream cheese, vanilla, remaining eggs and sugar; mix well. Spread over batter. Bake 15 minutes.

Remove from oven; sprinkle reserved sugar on top. Return to oven, continue to bake for 25 minutes. Serve warm, or cool on rack. Serves 10-12.

*PAST & REPAST*

# Karen's Cranberry Upside-Down Cake

Served at Benner House in historic Weston.

| | |
|---|---|
| 2 cups fresh cranberries | 1 cup granulated sugar |
| ½ cup granulated sugar | 1 cup flour |
| ½ cup chopped pecans | ½ cup melted butter |
| 2 eggs | ¼ cup melted shortening |

Clean, rinse, and drain fresh cranberries. Grease 10-inch pie plate or springform pan. Spread drained cranberries on bottom of pan. Sprinkle with ½ cup granulated sugar and pecans.

Beat eggs until foamy and gradually add 1 cup granulated sugar. Beat well; add flour, melted butter, and melted shortening. Pour over cranberries. Bake 325° for approximately 1 hour. A wonderful fall and winter breakfast treat!

*Breakfasts Ozark Style*

# Marge's Marshmallow Puffs

| | |
|---|---|
| ¼ cup sugar | ¼ cup margarine, melted |
| 1 teaspoon cinnamon | 2 cans crescent rolls, |
| 16 marshmallows |   separated |

LIGHT GLAZE:

| | |
|---|---|
| 2 cups powdered sugar | Milk to make glazing |
| 1 tablespoon melted |   consistency |
|   margarine | 1 cup nuts, chopped |

Combine sugar and cinnamon. Dip marshmallows, one at a time, into the melted margarine, then into the sugar mixture, and roll into one crescent roll. Seal all seams very securely. Dip each roll into the melted margarine, and put in muffin tin. Bake at 375° for 10-15 minutes. Remove from tins as soon as set enough and put on racks to cool. When cool, dip tops in Light Glaze and then in nuts. These freeze well.

*Breakfasts Ozark Style*

# Stuffed French Toast with Orange Sauce

**FILLING:**

1 (3-ounce) package cream cheese, softened to room temperature

3 tablespoons toasted, chopped pecans

2 tablespoons apricot preserves

Combine cream cheese, pecans, apricot preserves. Set aside.

1 (1-pound) rectangular loaf challah or egg bread, unsliced

8 tablespoons butter

3 large eggs

½ cup milk

2 tablespoons Grand Marnier

Powdered sugar, to garnish

With a bread knife, trim short ends from loaf. Cut bread into four 1½-inch thick slices. With a sharp knife, on 1 edge of each slice, make a horizontal cut to center of bread to create a pocket. Stuff each pocket with cream cheese filling, taking care not to poke a hole through top or bottom of slice.

In a large skillet, melt butter over medium heat. In a pie plate or wide shallow bowl, combine eggs, milk, and Grand Marnier. Dip each side of stuffed bread slices into egg mixture for several minutes until bread is saturated. Reduce heat and fry bread slices, turning once to brown both sides, about 7 minutes per side.

**SAUCE:**

½ cup (1 stick) butter

⅓ cup sugar

2 oranges, thinly sliced, peeled and pith removed

¼ cup fresh orange juice

¼ teaspoon cornstarch

In a large skillet, melt butter and then add sugar. Cook until mixture is bubbly. Add orange slices and cook, stirring occasionally for 5 minutes. In a small bowl, combine orange juice and cornstarch. Add orange juice mixture to butter mixture. Cook, stirring constantly until sauce thickens slightly, about 4 minutes. Remove sauce from heat and pour into a serving bowl. Keep warm.

Spoon sauce onto plates. Cut slices in half diagonally, top with powdered sugar and place on plates. Serves 4. A wonderful contrast of textures—crispy outside, creamy inside.

*Above & Beyond Parsley*

# Bake Ahead Butter Cheese Biscuits

2 cups flour
3 teaspoons baking powder
½ teaspoon salt
½ cup butter

½ cup grated cheddar
   cheese
¾ cup milk

Combine dry ingredients. Cut in butter to consistency of corn meal. Add cheese and mix lightly. Stir in milk. Turn onto floured board and roll to ½-inch thickness. Cut with a biscuit cutter and place on ungreased cookie sheet. Bake at 350° for 12-15 minutes. Brush with melted butter after baking.

Biscuits may be stored in plastic bag until time to serve. Slice, butter and toast lightly. Wonderful when piled high with chicken salad. Biscuits freeze beautifully.

*Silver Dollar City's Recipes*

# Microwave Apple Pancakes
## (Microwave)

3 tablespoons butter or
  margarine
2 medium cooking apples,
  peeled and sliced

⅓ cup sugar
¼ teaspoon cinnamon
¼ teaspoon allspice

PANCAKE BATTER:
1 cup pancake mix

¾ cup water

In glass 9-inch pie pan, melt butter in microwave. Mix in sliced apples, sugar, and spices. Cover. Microwave until apples are tender (3-4 minutes).

Mix together pancake batter and pour over apples in pie pan. Microwave until a toothpick inserted 2-inches from edge comes out clean (about 3-5 minutes). Let stand few minutes, then invert on serving plate. Cut into 6 pieces. Serve. Yield: 6 servings.

*From the Apple Orchard*

# Ham and Eggs 4th of July

8 frozen Pepperidge Farm
  Patty Shells
2 ounces mushrooms, sliced
2 tablespoons butter
2 tablespoons flour
⅛ teaspoon thyme
1 cup milk

⅓ can condensed cream of
  chicken soup
1 cup cubed ham
4 eggs, slightly beaten
¼ teaspoon salt
¼ cup milk
Parsley sprigs

Prepare the patty shells according to the directions on the package. Brown the mushrooms in the butter and stir in the flour and the thyme. Add the milk and cream of chicken soup. Stir until smooth. Add the ham. Heat, stirring occasionally.

Gently scramble the eggs with the salt and milk. Put the eggs into hot patty shells and top with the ham mixture. Garnish with sprigs of parsley. Serves 6.

*Bouquet Garni*

# Egg Casserole

1½ pounds Monterey Jack
  cheese
½ large onion, chopped and
  sautéed
¾ pound mushrooms,
  sautéed
¼ cup oleo, melted

1 cup cubed ham
7 eggs
1¾ cups milk
½ cup flour
1 tablespoon parsley
1 tablespoon seasoned salt

Use a 9x13-inch pan or dish. Put half of the cheese in bottom. Add onion and mushrooms sautéed in oleo. Add ham and rest of cheese. Beat rest of ingredients in blender and pour over top. Bake for 45 minutes at 350°. Serves 10.

This is a family favorite for Christmas morning.

***Kohler Family Kookbook***

# Oeufs en Bas

Young Mary Finney Barret mentions in her journal that this dish was prepared by Jenny Lind at a party given in his townhouse by Mr. Shaw.

4 tablespoons olive oil
1 clove garlic
1 onion, minced fine
2 cups tomato sauce
1 teaspoon minced parsley

Salt and pepper
1 teaspoon minced mixed
  herbs
8 eggs
Parmesan cheese

Heat the oil in the cooking pan; make sure that it has a cover that fits tightly. Split the garlic clove lengthwise and run a toothpick through each half, so you can find it when the cooking is finished—no lady of the '50s would risk eating a piece of garlic! Brown the garlic slowly in the oil. Add the onion, minced, and cook until golden. Then add the tomato sauce (canned does very well) and the seasonings and herbs. Cook about 10-15 minutes, stirring often, then take out the garlic.

Into this sauce break the eggs, carefully. Spoon the sauce over them, cover closely, and cook over the hot water pan until the eggs are done—about 15 minutes. When done, put each egg on a piece of dry thin toast, cover with sauce, and sprinkle with freshly grated Parmesan cheese. Serves 8.

***The Shaw House Cook Book***

# Blintze Casserole

**BATTER:**

1 cup butter, melted
3 eggs
¼ cup milk
1 teaspoon vanilla

1 cup flour
½ cup sugar
3 teaspoons baking powder
Dash salt

**FILLING:**

2 pounds small curd cottage cheese, blended until smooth

3 eggs
¼ cup sugar
Juice of 1 lemon

Mix all batter ingredients together. Mix all filling ingredients together. Can make and refrigerate each separately up to one day before assembly.

To assemble casserole: Preheat oven to 300°. Butter bottom of 2-quart baking dish. Place one-half of batter in baking dish. Then pour in all the filling. Top with remaining batter. Bake 1½ hours and serve with sour cream or blueberry sauce. Easy. Do part ahead. Serves 10.

*Cooking in Clover*

# Cheese and Eggs Olé

The green chilies add distinction to an easy and tasty brunch dish. Serve with bowls of salsa, guacamole and sour cream and a huge basket of crispy tortilla chips.

1 dozen eggs, beaten
½ cup flour
1 teaspoon baking powder
1 pound Monterey Jack cheese, shredded

½ cup butter, melted
2 (4-ounce) cans green chiles, diced
1 pint cottage cheese

Preheat oven to 350°. Combine all ingredients. Pour into a buttered 9x13-inch baking dish. Bake 35 minutes or until done. Serve immediately. Serves 8-10.

*PAST & REPAST*

# Yolkless Ranch-Style Eggs

1 medium onion, finely
  chopped
2 garlic cloves, finely
  chopped
⅛ teaspoon salt
⅛ teaspoon black pepper
¾ teaspoon dried oregano
1 teaspoon chili powder
¼ teaspoon ground cumin
1 green bell pepper, diced
¼ cup canned chopped green
  chilies

2 cups canned tomatoes,
  drained and chopped
  (reserve juice)
¼ cup tomato juice (from
  canned tomatoes)
4 egg whites
½ cup part-skim mozzarella
  cheese
4 corn tortillas, heated

Combine the onion, garlic, spices, green pepper, chilies, tomatoes, and tomato juice. Cook over low heat, uncovered, until vegetables are soft.

For each serving, pour ¾ cup of the sauce into a small skillet and put 1 egg white on top of the sauce. Cook, covered, for about 10 minutes or until the egg white is opaque. Sprinkle with 1½ tablespoons mozzarella. Place a hot tortilla on a heated plate. Carefully place the sauce with the egg and cheese on the tortilla. Spread extra sauce over the top of the cheese. Serves 4. The sauce is good to use on other egg and cheese dishes.

*Breakfasts Ozark Style*

# Turkish Eggs

Chop enough cold chicken to make one cupful, add half the quantity of breadcrumbs, season to taste; add a little gravy or hot water, and warm it in hot butter until it absorbs the butter. Spread it on small round dishes. Break an egg on top of each; sprinkle with salt, and set in the oven until the egg is firm.

*Turn of the Century Cookbook*

# Impossible Bacon Quiche

12 slices bacon, cooked and
    crumbled
1 cup shredded natural Swiss
    cheese, about 4 ounces
1/3 cup chopped onion

2 cups milk
1 cup Bisquick baking mix
4 eggs
1/4 teaspoon salt
1/8 teaspoon pepper

Preheat oven to 400°. Lightly grease a 10-inch pie plate. Sprinkle bacon, cheese, and onion in the pie plate. Beat milk, Bisquick, eggs, salt, and pepper in a medium-size bowl with electric mixer until smooth, about 1 minute. Pour into pie plate.

Bake in hot oven for 35 minutes or until top is golden brown and knife inserted halfway between center and edge comes out clean. Let stand 5 minutes before cutting. Garnish with tomato slices and bacon strips, if you wish. Refrigerate any leftovers.

*Covered Bridge Neighbors Cookbook*

Calamity Jane, born Martha Jane Canary in Princeton, Missouri, was a rough-riding, sharpshooting frontier woman of the early West. She received her nickname as a result of her statement that she would cause calamity for any man who tried to court her. Wild Bill Hickok, though, reputedly ignored that warning.

# Kangaroo Pouches
### (Sandwiches)

1½ cups chicken breast,
  cooked and diced
½ cup seedless grapes,
  halved
½ cup Jarlsburg cheese,
  cubed
¼ cup green bell pepper,
  or ½ cup apple, diced
¼ cup red onion, minced

2 tablespoons fresh basil,
  minced
1½ cups mayonnaise or
  Miracle Whip
1 tablespoon lemon juice
6-8 pita bread pockets
¼ cup sunflower seeds
½ cup fresh salad burnet
  leaves
1 cup alfalfa sprouts

In a large bowl, mix together chicken, grapes, cheese, green bell pepper or apple, onion, basil, mayonnaise, and lemon juice. Stuff pita pockets with mixture, leaving some space inside. In this space sprinkle with some sunflower seeds and burnet leaves and then finish stuffing with alfalfa sprouts.

*Thyme for Kids*

# Bun-Steads

¼ pound American cheese
  (1 cup cubed)
3 hard-cooked eggs, chopped
1 (7-ounce) can tuna, flaked
2 tablespoons chopped green
  pepper
2 tablespoons chopped green
  onions

2 tablespoons chopped
  stuffed olives
2 tablespoons chopped sweet
  pickles
½ cup mayonnaise or salad
  dressing
8 Coney buns (I fill 12 with
  this amount)

Combine ingredients (except buns). Mix lightly. Split buns and fill. Wrap in aluminum foil. Place in slow oven (250°) about 30 minutes until filling is heated and cheese melts. Serve hot.

*Talk About Good*

# Scrapple

This scrapple is a long-time favorite.

| | |
|---|---|
| 1½ pounds bulk pork sausage | ½ teaspoon sage |
| 4 cups water | 1 cup cornmeal |
| 1 teaspoon salt | 1 cup cold water |

Crumble pork sausage in a frying pan; add 4 cups water, and heat to boiling. Reduce heat, cook for 20 minutes. Then drain meat, reserving 3 cups stock. Add salt and sage to stock. Bring to boiling. Combine cornmeal and 1 cup cold water. Gradually add to stock, stirring constantly. Cover and cook over low heat for 10 minutes. Stir occasionally. Then add sausage, stir it all together and pour into loaf pan. Refrigerate overnight. Next morning slice and fry until set. Serve with syrup, if desired.

*Grandma's Ozark Legacy*

# Soups

*The Bollinger Mill and Covered Bridge. Near Burfordville.*

# Avgolemono

The most popular Greek soup is Avgolemono (chicken with egg/lemon sauce). Make the soup with a whole chicken as a main dish, or with broth only as a first course.

| | |
|---|---|
| **6 cups chicken broth** | **1 chicken bouillon cube** |
| **½ cup rice** | **3 eggs** |
| **1 teaspoon salt** | **Juice of 1½ lemons** |
| **Pepper to taste** | |

Combine chicken broth, rice, salt, pepper, and bouillon cube in a large saucepan. Bring to a boil. Reduce heat, cover, and simmer until rice is tender. (Long grain rice should cook in 15 minutes.)

In a bowl beat eggs until fluffy and pale yellow. Add lemon juice and mix in. While still running the mixer, slowly pour about 2 cups of the hot broth into the egg-lemon mixture so that the eggs do not curdle. Pour this mixture into the rest of the broth and stir. When ready to serve, garnish with a sprig of parsley or dill, if desired. Yield: 6-8 servings.

*The Art of Hellenic Cuisine*

# Wild Rice Soup

This is a must to try! It's our four star choice!

| | |
|---|---|
| **½ cup wild rice, uncooked** | **2 cans potato soup** |
| **9 slices thick bacon** | **(undiluted)** |
| **1 medium onion, chopped** | **2 cups shredded American** |
| **2 cups whole milk** | **cheese (8-ounces)** |
| **2 cups half-and-half** | **Parsley** |

Cook wild rice 20 minutes. Drain. Add fresh water and cook 20 minutes more. Drain. Add fresh water again and cook 20 minutes or until rice is fluffy (makes 3 cups).

Dice bacon. Cook until crisp. Drain on paper towels. Sauté onion in bacon grease. Drain. Combine all ingredients in a heavy saucepan and cook over low heat until cheese melts. Garnish with parsley if desired. Serves 6-8.

*Finely Tuned Foods*

# Dilled Potato Soup

1 (10³/₄-ounce) can cream
  of potato soup
1 soup can milk
Dash white pepper

⅛ teaspoon salt
1 teaspoon dried dill
⅔ cup sour cream

Mix soup, milk, pepper, salt, and dill in soup pan. Heat until hot, stirring constantly with wire whisk. Stir in sour cream. Pour into soup bowls and sprinkle with paprika for color. Preparation time: 10 minutes. Serves 2 heartily, 3 well, 4 in small bowls.

*Rush Hour Superchef!*

# Ham and Potato Chowder

¼ cup melted butter
1 medium onion, minced
¾ cup diced ham
½ cup chopped celery
1½ cups finely diced raw
  potatoes

¼ cup flour
1½ teaspoons salt
¼ teaspoon pepper
4 cups milk

In large saucepan, melt butter and sauté onion, ham, and celery. Add potatoes and cook 10 minutes longer. Remove from heat and add flour, salt, and pepper. Mix well. Add milk and return to heat. Warm slowly—do not let boil. If not served immediately and soup thickens, add warm water to thin to desired consistency. Serves 4-6.

*Silver Dollar City's Recipes*

Two of Missouri's most popular, yet controversial, historical figures, Jesse and Frank James, were never convicted of a crime. Factual accounts of the events surrounding his life are preserved in the Jesse James Bank Museum in Liberty, and the Jesse James Farm in nearby Kearney.

# Red Pepper Bisque

One of our favorite starters.

1 cup unsalted butter
2 tablespoons vegetable oil
4 cups chopped leeks
6 large red peppers, sliced
3 cups chicken broth

Salt
6 cups buttermilk
White pepper to taste
Chives or lemon slices and
  caviar

Melt butter and oil in a large saucepan. Add leeks and red peppers. Reduce heat and cook, covered, until vegetables are soft. Add chicken broth and salt to taste. Simmer, partially covered, over low heat for 30 minutes or until vegetables are very soft.

Blend mixture in a food processor until smooth. Strain into a large bowl. Stir in buttermilk and white pepper to taste. Chill. Garnish with chives or a thin slice of lemon with a small scoop of caviar in the middle. Serves 10-12. For single servings, dole the soup into green pepper shells.

*Gateways*

# Gazpacho Blanca

3 medium cucumbers, peeled,
  seeded, and coarsely
  chopped
3 cups chicken broth
3 cups sour cream or 2 cups
  sour cream and 1 cup
  yogurt
3 tablespoons white vinegar
2 teaspoons salt or to taste

2 cloves garlic, crushed
4 medium tomatoes, peeled,
  seeded, and chopped
¾ cup chopped almonds,
  toasted
½ cup sliced scallions
¼ cup chopped fresh
  parsley

Whirl cucumber chunks in a food processor a very short time with a little chicken broth. Pour into mixing bowl; add remaining broth, sour cream, vinegar, salt, and garlic. Stir just enough to mix. Chill thoroughly, at least 2-3 hours. Before serving, stir again. Pour into chilled bowls. Sprinkle with remaining ingredients on top. Makes 8 servings.

*Beyond Parsley*

# New Plantation Gumbo

½ pound raw ham
½ pound raw chicken
½ pound fresh okra
3 medium onions
1 large bell pepper
¼ cup fresh parsley
¼ cup bacon drippings
3 quarts boiling water
56 ounces tomatoes

1 clove garlic, minced
2 bay leaves
⅛ teaspoon thyme
¼ teaspoon salt
⅛ teaspoon pepper
1 pound raw shrimp
1 pound fresh crabmeat
2 tablespoons seafood
   seasoning

Cut ham, chicken, okra, onions, bell pepper, and parsley into small pieces and fry in the bacon drippings. When browned add the boiling water, tomatoes, garlic, bay leaves, thyme, salt, and pepper. Cook slowly for 1 hour.

Add the shrimp and crabmeat and cook for 30 minutes longer. Add the seafood seasoning and stir well. Remove from heat and refrigerate overnight.

Reheat and serve over steamed rice. Serves 16.

*Bouquet Garni*

---

 Six Ionic columns in the heart of the University of Missouri's Francis Quadrangle, are all that remains of the original Academic Hall destroyed by fire in 1892.

# Gail's Cheesy Broccoli Soup

¾ cup chopped onion
2 tablespoons margarine
6 cups water
6 chicken bouillon cubes
8 ounces fine egg noodles
1 teaspoon salt

2 (10-ounce) packages frozen
chopped broccoli
½ teaspoon garlic powder
6 cups milk
1 pound Velveeta cheese,
cubed
1 teaspoon pepper

Sauté onion in margarine. In large pot, put 6 cups water and bouillon cubes. Bring to a boil. Add noodles and salt. Cook for 3-4 minutes until noodles are tender. Remove from heat and stop boiling. Add onions, broccoli and garlic powder.

Cook for 3 minutes more and remove from heat again. Add milk, cheese, and pepper. Stir until cheese melts. Makes 4 quarts or approximately 12 servings. Can be made ahead and frozen for 1 month.

*USO's Salute to the Troops Cookbook*

# RT's Tangy Bachelor Vegetable Soup

2 beef shanks (or soup
bones)
2 medium shallots
2 stalks celery
2 carrots
2 potatoes
Frozen peas
Green beans

Any other leftover
vegetables in the
refrigerator
¼ cup barley
Pinch basil
2½ cups of any bottled
Bloody Mary mix
Tabasco sauce (optional)

Chop your vegetables into bite-size pieces and place all of the above ingredients in any order into a large pot about ⅔ full of water. Pour 1½ cups of Bloody Mary mix into soup. Take remaining cup and make yourself a Bloody Mary and watch the football game. Cook soup for 3 hours, or so, until meat falls off the bones.

*Gourmet Garden*

# Hearty Clam Chowder

4 slices bacon, cut in small
  pieces
3 green onions and tops,
  chopped
1 carrot, finely chopped
1 stalk celery, thinly
  sliced
2 tablespoons chopped green
  pepper
1 clove garlic, minced
5 medium potatoes, peeled
  and cut in ½-inch cubes

2 cups water
1 teaspoon Worcestershire
  sauce
1 teaspoon salt
½ teaspoon freshly ground
  pepper
½ teaspoon thyme
4 drops Tabasco
2 (8-ounce) cans minced
  clams, undrained
2 cups light cream

Sauté bacon until crisp in large soup pot. Drain bacon; pour off all but 1 tablespoon fat. Add green onions and tops, carrot, celery, green pepper, and garlic. Sauté briefly until soft. Add potatoes, pour in water and season with Worcestershire sauce, salt, pepper, thyme, and Tabasco. Cover pan and simmer 15 minutes, or until potatoes are tender.

Mash mixture slightly with a potato masher. Add clams and cream. Stir well. Heat until piping hot, but do not boil. Serves 4-6.

*Cooking for Applause*

# Cioppino

1 large onion chopped
(1 cup)
1 medium green pepper
(chopped)
½ cup celery (sliced)
1 carrot, pared and shredded
3 cloves of garlic, minced
3 tablespoons olive oil
2 (1-pound) cans tomatoes
1 (8-ounce) can tomato sauce
1 teaspoon leaf basil,
crumbled
1 bay leaf

1 teaspoon salt
¼ teaspoon pepper
1 pound fresh or frozen
swordfish or halibut steak
1 dozen mussels or clams in
shell
1½ cups dry white wine
1 (8-ounce) package shrimp
½ pound fresh or frozen
scallops
1 pound crab legs (optional)
2 tablespoons parsley,
minced

Sauté onion, green pepper, celery, carrot, and garlic in olive oil until soft. Stir in tomatoes, tomato sauce, basil, bay leaf, salt and pepper; heat to boiling. Reduce heat, cover and simmer for 2 hours. Discard bay leaf.

While sauce simmers, clean fish and clams. Stir in wine and add fish, shrimp, scallops, and crab legs. Simmer for 10 minutes. Add clams and cover. Steam 10 minutes or until done.

Ladle into soup bowl, sprinkle with parsley. Serve with sour dough bread or crusty French bread.

***Recipes From Missouri...With Love***

# Herbed Black Bean Soup with Smoked Chicken

¼ cup (½-stick)
unsalted butter
1 cup peeled, diced broccoli
stems
½ cup chopped carrot
½ cup chopped onion
½ cup chopped celery
1 tablespoon dried thyme,
crumbled
1 teaspoon Cajun seasoning
1 tablespoon dried oregano
1 tablespoon dried basil,
crumbled
½ cup dry white wine

4 cups chicken stock or
canned broth
2 cups broccoli florets
1 (16-ounce) can black
beans, rinsed and drained
8 ounces smoked chicken,
shredded and chopped
1 tablespoon Worcestershire
sauce
½ teaspoon hot pepper
sauce
2 cups heavy cream
Salt and freshly ground
pepper, to taste

In a sauté pan, melt butter over medium heat. Add broccoli stems, carrot, onion, and celery and sauté for 5 minutes. Add thyme, Cajun seasoning, oregano, and basil and sauté for 5 minutes more. Pour in wine and bring mixture to a boil. Add stock and cook until liquid is reduced by half, stirring occasionally (approximately 12 minutes).

Stir broccoli florets, beans, chicken, Worcestershire sauce, and hot pepper sauce into soup and simmer for 5 minutes, stirring occasionally. Add cream and simmer for 5 minutes more. Season with salt and pepper and serve. Serves 6.

*Note:* A smoky, spicy soup that's even better when prepared a day in advance. Garnish with cilantro, broccoli florets, pimiento, curled carrots, or homemade croutons.

*Above & Beyond Parsley*

The New Madrid earthquake of 1811 was so violent that it was said the course of the Mississippi River flowed north rather than south!

# Jack's Chili Con Carne

3½ pounds top round
  steak, cut into ½-inch
  cubes
5 tablespoons vegetable oil
2 cups coarsely chopped
  onion
4 cloves garlic, minced
4 tablespoons chili powder
1½ teaspoons oregano
1½ teaspoons cumin
1 teaspoon crushed red
  pepper

2 cups beef broth
1 (19-ounce) can whole
  tomatoes with juice
1 (6-ounce) can tomato paste
1 tablespoon salt
1 teaspoon sugar
3 (16-ounce) cans kidney or
  chili beans
1-2 tablespoons yellow corn
  meal

Pat the meat dry with paper towels. Heat 3 tablespoons of the oil in a large, heavy Dutch oven. When hot, add the meat. Sear until all pieces are lightly browned, 3-4 minutes. Drain off fat and transfer to a bowl. Set aside. Add remaining 2 tablespoons oil to the Dutch oven and sauté onion and garlic until onion is wilted but not browned. Stir in chili powder, oregano, cumin, and red pepper. Add broth, canned tomatoes with juice, tomato paste, salt, and sugar, mixing well and breaking up tomatoes. Add seared meat. Cover and simmer 40-50 minutes. Add beans and heat through. Thicken with corn meal to desired consistency. Serves 4-6.

    This recipe was contributed by Missouri US Senator John C. Danforth.

*Sassafras!*

Harry Truman served as US president from 1945 through 1953, first taking office after the death of Franklin Roosevelt. Truman is perhaps best known for his down-home style; his desk bore the sign, "The Buck Stops Here," and he was often quoted as saying, "If you can't stand the heat, get out of the kitchen." Truman was born in 1884 in Lamar and grew up near Independence.

# Ed's Bachelor Chili

5 pounds ground beef
1 large onion, chopped
3 (31-ounce) cans
  chili beans
6 (16-ounce) cans stewed
  tomatoes
2 (16-ounce) cans whole
  potatoes, quartered
1 (8-ounce) can tomato sauce
1 (16-ounce) jar mild taco
  sauce
1 (8-ounce) jar hot taco
  sauce

1 (heaping) tablespoon
  Grey Poupon (mustard)
½ teaspoon cayenne pepper
1 teaspoon chili powder
Generous sprinkle of dill
  weed, garlic powder, and
  coarse ground pepper
2 small Hershey bars
1 large green pepper,
  chopped

Sauté meat; drain. Add remaining ingredients, except Hershey bars and green pepper. Cover and simmer 1 hour and 50 minutes. Add chocolate and green pepper; simmer an additional hour. Yield: 12-14 servings.

*Sing for Your Supper*

# Lentil and Frankfurter Soup

A trim-the-tree favorite. Make ahead—freezes well.

1 (16-ounce) package
frankfurters (can use
turkey franks if preferred)
1 tablespoon olive oil or
corn oil
1 cup celery, chopped
½ cup green pepper chopped
1 cup carrots, chopped
1 clove garlic, pressed or
finely minced
1 (16-ounce) package navy
beans, rinsed

2 (14½-ounce) cans
Swansons Beef Broth
6 cups hot water
1 (16-ounce) can rotel
tomatoes (optional, add if
you want soup to be fairly
spicy)
¼ teaspoon coarsely
ground black pepper
3 whole bay leaves

Slice franks ¼-inch thick in pieces. Heat oil in a 4-quart pan and brown franks on all sides. Remove and refrigerate until ready to use.

Put celery, green pepper, carrots, and garlic in same pan. Sauté for 10 minutes, stirring. Remove from heat. Add beans, beef broth, water, tomatoes (optional), pepper, and bay leaves to pan with vegetables. Cover and cook 2 hours on medium low or until beans are soft. Add franks. Remove bay leaves and serve warm or put into airtight containers and freeze until ready to serve. Serves 8.

**Note:** The word "lentil" is used in reference to the navy beans in this recipe; it contains no lentils.

*It's Christmas!*

Molly Brown, who became the subject of *The Unsinkable Molly Brown* on Broadway stage and on screen, originally hailed from Missouri. The hillbilly heroine moved west to Denver, where she married into unexpected wealth. Returning from Europe on the ill-fated *Titanic*, she became known for her bravery in trying to save other passengers.

# Salads

The lovely Missouri Governor's Mansion in Jefferson City is one of
the oldest governor's residences in the United States.

# Hot Baked Potato Salad

| | |
|---|---|
| 1 chopped onion | ½ teaspoon salt seasoning |
| ¾ cup salad oil | ½ cup water |
| ¼ cup diced bell pepper | ¼ cup vinegar |
| 1 tablespoon flour | 6 cups cubed cooked |
| 1 teaspoon sugar | potatoes |
| ¼ teaspoon paprika | 1 chopped pimento |
| ½ teaspoon dry mustard | Grated cheese |
| 1 teaspoon salt | |

Cook onion and bell pepper in salad oil until tender. Remove from heat. Add flour, sugar, paprika, mustard, salt, salt seasoning, water, and vinegar. Cook until thickened. Add 6 cups cubed cooked potatoes and 1 chopped pimento. Pour into 9x9-inch casserole. Arrange grated cheese on top and a few pieces of pimento for color. Bake long enough to melt cheese at 350°.

*Cooking on the Road*

# German Potato Salad

This was made along with wine in many a home in Hermann.

| | |
|---|---|
| 12 slices bacon | ½ teaspoon celery seed |
| 1 medium onion, peeled and | ¾ cup water |
| diced | ⅓ cup wine vinegar |
| 2 tablespoons flour | 3 pounds red potatoes, about |
| 4 tablespoons sugar | 6 large, boiled, peeled and |
| 2 teaspoons salt | sliced |
| ½ teaspoon pepper | |

Dice bacon and fry until crisp. Remove bacon and cook onion in bacon grease until transparent. Stir in flour, sugar, salt, and pepper and celery seed. Cook over low heat, add water and vinegar, boil for 1 minute. Add bacon and potatoes, stirring gently to coat potatoes. Serve warm, with Missouri country ham.

*Recipes From Missouri...With Love*

# Red Potato Salad
# with Caraway Seeds

3 pounds small red potatoes, unpeeled
¼ cup tarragon vinegar
2 tablespoons sugar
¼ teaspoon paprika
Salt and freshly ground pepper to taste
⅓ cup chopped green pepper

¼ cup chopped green onions
1 teaspoon caraway seeds, crushed
¼ teaspoon celery seed
½ cup sour cream
½ cup mayonnaise
Large Boston lettuce leaves
Chopped fresh chives

Boil potatoes until tender. Drain and pat dry. Cool slightly. Cut into ½-inch slices.

Combine vinegar, sugar, paprika, salt, and pepper in a large bowl. Stir in warm potatoes. Marinate 45 minutes. Gently stir in green pepper, onions, caraway and celery seeds. Combine sour cream and mayonnaise and mix into salad. Cover and chill overnight. When ready to serve, line a serving bowl with lettuce leaves. Sprinkle fresh chives over salad if desired. Doubles easily.

This potato salad is lighter than most with a refreshing flavor. Serves 6.

*Gateways*

# Fresh Snow Pea Salad

4 cups fresh snow peas
1 cup whole red seedless
grapes
1 cup mandarin oranges
1 cup fresh grapefruit
sections

1 small red onion, thinly
sliced
1 green bell pepper, cut
into thin slices
½ cup dry roasted
sunflower seeds

Snip and discard ends of snow peas. In a large bowl combine snow peas, grapes, oranges, grapefruit, red onion, bell pepper and sunflower seeds. Toss with Poppy Seed Dressing. Serves 8.

*Variation:* Add 2 cups of fresh cooked chicken breast, cut into bite-size pieces.

**POPPY SEED DRESSING:**
2 cups sugar
1¼ cups white vinegar
3⅓ cups oil
2 teaspoons dry mustard

1 tablespoon salt
3 tablespoons poppy seeds
¼ cup dried onion flakes

Mix all the above ingredients together in a blender, except the poppy seeds and onion flakes. Add poppy seeds and onion flakes. Blend for a second or two. Store in refrigerator until ready to use. Dressing will keep for up to 3 weeks. Yields 6 cups.

*Luncheon Favorites*

# St. Louis Favorite Salad

1 head romaine lettuce, torn into pieces
1 head iceberg lettuce, torn into pieces
1 (10-ounce) jar artichoke hearts, drained and cut into pieces
1 (4-ounce) jar pimientos
Red onion slices
¼ cup grated Parmesan cheese
Hearts of palm (optional)
½ cup oil
⅓ cup white vinegar

Wash and tear lettuces into bite-size pieces. Cut artichoke hearts and pimientos into pieces. Combine with thinly sliced red onion in a large salad bowl. Add cheese. In a separate container, combine vinegar and oil. Just before serving, add hearts of palm, if desired; pour oil mixture over salad and toss until well coated. Serves 10-12.

*From Generation to Generation*

# Spinach Salad
# with Anchovy Dressing

DRESSING:
2 cups mayonnaise
1 clove garlic, crushed
4 anchovy fillets, diced
1 tablespoon onion, chopped
2½ teaspoons chives, chopped
¼ teaspoon tarragon
2 teaspoons tarragon vinegar

SALAD:
6-7 cups fresh spinach, torn
3-4 cups romaine, torn to bite-size pieces
3 hard cooked eggs, sliced
8 slices bacon, cooked and crumbled
1 avocado, peeled and sliced
½ cup Roquefort cheese, crumbled

Make anchovy dressing by combining all dressing ingredients. Cover and refrigerate at least 4 hours. Toss dressing with all salad ingredients 15 minutes ahead of serving time. Serves 12.

*Gourmet Garden*

# Trees and Raisins

An unusual, make-ahead broccoli salad.

1 large head broccoli, cut
  into small flowerets
10-12 strips bacon, fried
  crisp and crumbled
½ cup raisins

¼ cup chopped red onion
1 cup mayonnaise
½ cup sugar
2 tablespoons vinegar

Combine broccoli, bacon, raisins, and onion in a large bowl. Blend together mayonnaise, sugar, and vinegar. Pour over broccoli mixture. Stir to coat well. Cover and marinate at least 1 hour. Serves 6.

*Sassafras!*

# Gourmet Salad

½ pound bacon
1 bunch romaine lettuce
7½ ounces canned hearts
  of palm

8½ ounces canned
  artichoke hearts
4 ounces Gorgonzola cheese,
  crumbled

Cook the bacon until crisp. Drain and crumble. Tear the lettuce into bite-size pieces. Drain and quarter the hearts o palm and artichoke hearts. Combine the lettuce, hearts of palm, artichoke hearts, and bacon in a large salad bowl. Toss with the dressing to taste. Sprinkle with cheese. Serves 8.

DRESSING:

2 tablespoons onion, chopped
3 tablespoons cider vinegar
2 teaspoons spicy brown
  mustard

½ teaspoon sugar
½ teaspoon salt
¼ teaspoon pepper
1 cup vegetable oil

Add to the bowl of a food processor the onion, vinegar, mustard, sugar, salt, and pepper. Process 5 seconds. Gradually add the oil in a thin steady stream, processing continuously.

*Bouquet Garni*

# Greek Salad

**DRESSING:**

½ cup olive oil (or ¼ cup olive oil and ¼ cup vegetable oil)

2-3 tablespoons red wine vinegar

4-6 anchovy filets, rinsed and chopped

1 teaspoon Dijon mustard

¼ teaspoon salt

⅛ teaspoon pepper

1 cup (4 ounces) feta cheese, crumbled

1 tablespoon capers, drained

Prepare day before so that all seasonings blend well. Combine all ingredients together in jar with a lid. Shake and refrigerate.

**SALAD:**

1 medium tomato, cut into small wedges

1 medium cucumber, thinly sliced

1 medium onion, sliced

1 medium-size head romaine lettuce

1 medium-size head iceberg lettuce

Place in a large bowl first the tomato, cucumber, and onion. Break up lettuces on top. When ready to serve, pour dressing over, toss and serve. Yield: 4-6 servings.

*The Art of Hellenic Cuisine*

# Tangy Apricot Salad Mold

1 cup orange juice
1 (6-ounce) or 2 (3-ounce) packages apricot Jello
2 (16-ounce) cans apricot halves, drained
2 cups buttermilk

1 (15¼-ounce) can crushed pineapple, drained
1 cup broken pecan pieces
1 (6-ounce) bottle green Maraschino cherries

Heat orange juice in saucepan until hot. Add Jello to hot orange juice. Stir until dissolved. Set aside. Cut 1 can drained apricot halves into fourths. Reserve second can of apricots for garnish. Add to orange juice-Jello mixture. Stir in 2 cups buttermilk. Fold in drained crushed pineapple and nuts. Pour into oiled mold and chill until firm.

To serve, unmold on bed of lettuce, surrounded with second can of drained apricot halves and green cherries placed in center of each apricot half. Serve with Cream Cheese Dressing. Preparation time: 12 minutes. Makes 10 individual molds or 1 (½-quart) mold.

**CREAM CHEESE DRESSING:**

1 (3-ounce) package cream cheese, softened
½ cup mayonnaise (no substitutes)

1 tablespoon milk
Salt to taste
1 teaspoon bottled lemon juice (optional)

Mix cream cheese, mayonnaise, and milk together until well blended. Add dash of salt and lemon juice. Beat by hand until light and fluffy. Refrigerate until ready to serve. Preparation time: 6 minutes. Makes 1 cup.

*Rush Hour Superchef!*

Nicknamed "The Cave State," Missouri has more than 5,000 known caves, providing plenty of challenges for daring spelunkers. More than 20 caves have safely guided tours; on foot, from your seat in a Jeep-drawn tram, or in a boat on an underground lake.

# Heavenly Peach Salad

1 (3-ounce) package peach
   Jello
1 (15-ounce) can fruit
   cocktail, drained
1 cup sour cream

1 cup chopped pecans
1 cup miniature marsh-
   mallows
1 (9-ounce) carton Cool Whip

Sprinkle Jello over drained fruit cocktail. Let stand about 2 hours. Add sour cream, pecans and marshmallows. Refrigerate. Before serving, stir in Cool Whip.

*Kitchen Prescriptions*

# Mandarin Salad

¼ cup sliced almonds
1 tablespoon plus 1 teaspoon
   sugar
¼ head lettuce, torn into
   bite-size pieces
¼ bunch romaine, torn into
   bite-size pieces

2 medium stalks celery,
   chopped
2 green onions (with tops),
   thinly sliced
Sweet Sour Dressing
1 (11-ounce) can mandarin
   orange segments, drained

Cook almonds and sugar over low heat, stirring constantly until sugar is melted and almonds are coated. Cool and break apart. Place lettuce and romaine in plastic bag; add celery and onions. Pour dressing into bag. Add orange segments. Close bag tightly and shake until well coated. Add almonds and shake. Refrigerate till ready to serve.

**SWEET-SOUR DRESSING:**
¼ cup vegetable oil
2 tablespoons sugar
2 tablespoons vinegar
1 tablespoon snipped parsley

½ teaspoon salt
Dash of pepper
Dash of red pepper sauce

Shake all ingredients in tightly covered jar. Refrigerate.

*Variation:* Pineapple Salad: Substitute 1 (13¼-ounce) can pineapple chunks, drained, for orange segments, and snipped mint leaves for the parsley.

*Blue Ridge Christian Church Cookbook*

# Green Gage Plum Salad

1 (No. 2½) can green gage
plums or Kadota figs,
drained, save juice

1 (3-ounce) package lemon
Jello

1 (3-ounce) package lime
Jello

1 cup finely chopped celery

1 (3-ounce) package cream
cheese

3 tablespoons light cream

1 tablespoon mayonnaise

Chop plums very fine in medium bowl. In a medium sauce-pan, add enough water to plum liquid to make 3½ cups. Heat to boiling. Remove from heat. Add Jellos. Stir to dissolve. Add the plums. Chill till partially set.

Add celery. Turn into an 8-inch square pan. Blend cream cheese, cream, and mayonnaise till smooth. Spread on top of salad. Take a table knife and make 2 or 3 figure 8's through to marbleize. Cut in 9 or 12 squares after completely set. Serve on lettuce lined plates.

*From Granny, With Love*

# Red Hot Jello Salad

¼ cup cinnamon red hots
½ cup water
3 ounces cherry Jello
1 cup boiling water

2 cups apples, peeled and
chopped
½ cup celery, chopped
½ cup pecans, chopped

Soak red hots in water overnight. Dissolve Jello in boiling water. Add red hot liquid. Chill until partially set. Stir in apples, celery, and chopped nuts. Chill until firm. Serves 6.

*Company's Coming*

Part of the Watkins Mill State Historic Site in Clay County, the Franklin School, an interesting octagonal building, was built in 1872.

# Frog Eye Salad

1 cup Acini de Pepe Macaroni
   Tapioca
1 cup sugar
2 tablespoons flour
3 eggs
1 (20-ounce) can crushed
   pineapple

1 (11-ounce) can mandarin
   oranges
1 cup mini marshmallows
1 (8-ounce) tub Cool Whip
Maraschino cherries
   (optional)

Cook macaroni tapioca 10 minutes. Drain, rinse, set aside. Cook together sugar, flour, eggs, and juice from both cans of fruit. Cook over medium heat, stirring constantly until thickened. Let cool. Mix cooked mixture with macaroni, fruits, marshmallows, and Cool Whip. Makes a very large salad for a crowd. Can be frozen. Maraschino cherries, chopped, may be added for color.

*Remembering the Past—Planning for the Future*

# Cranberry Salad

1 package lemon Jello
1 cup boiling water
1 cup sugar
1 cup ground cranberries
¼ cup cut grapes
   (optional)

1 small can crushed pine-
   apple (juice and all)
1 cup ground red apples
   (unpeeled)
¼ cup nuts (optional)

Pour boiling water over Jello and sugar; stir until dissolved. Chill slightly. Add all other ingredients. Let set until firm.

My family says it tastes like strawberries. Other flavors of Jello may be used. Combine 1 package each lemon or orange or lemon and any red Jello for a double recipe.

*Heavenly Delights*

# Gooseberry Salad

1 (16-ounce) can
   gooseberries or 2 cups
   ground fresh or frozen
   berries
1 (3-ounce) package
   orange-flavored gelatin
1½ cups boiling water

1 cup sugar
½ cup chopped nuts
1 cup celery, finely chopped
1 cup longhorn cheese,
   grated
1 large red apple, cored and
   chopped

Dissolve the gelatin in the boiling water. Add sugar and stir until dissolved. Add the rest of the ingredients after the gelatin has begun to set. Pour into lightly oiled mold or 9x13-inch pan. Makes a large salad; keeps well.

(If you use the canned gooseberries, ¾ cup of sugar will be sufficient.)

*Apples, Apples, Apples*

The state's largest Amish community is in northwest Missouri, near Jamesport, where visitors can tour the Amish farmlands and sample Amish-style country cooking.

# Hot Fruit Salad

1 (17-ounce) can fruit for salad, drained
1 (17-ounce) can apricots, drained
1 (16-ounce) can applesauce
½ cup light brown sugar
3 tablespoons butter or margarine

Slightly stir above ingredients and place in 350° oven for about 1 hour. Delicious with meats.

*Kitchen Prescriptions*

# Frozen Fruit Salad

This is a popular community supper dish.

1 (3-ounce) package cream cheese
1 cup mayonnaise
1 cup drained, crushed pineapple
1 cup ripe peaches
1 tablespoon lemon juice
½ cup maraschino cherries
1 cup cream, whipped

Blend cheese and mayonnaise. Add fruit. Fold in whipped cream. Serve on crisp salad greens or freeze: pack salad mixture in a mold, rinsed out in cold water, then place in the freezing compartment of the refrigerator. When firm, cut salad in cubes and serve on crisp salad greens.

*Treasured Recipes Book I*

# Horseradish Yogurt Salad

1 small (3-ounce) package lemon gelatin
1 cup very hot water
1 cup (8-ounce container) lemon-flavored yogurt
½ cup mayonnaise
1 small flat can crushed pineapple
1 cup cottage cheese
1½ tablespoons (or more) prepared horseradish

Mix gelatin and hot water. Cool and add remaining ingredients. Mold. Keeps well. Good with chicken or pork.

*Talk About Good*

# Apricot Soufflé Ring
# with Chicken Salad

**SOUFFLÉ RING:**

1 cup apricot juice (from can of apricots)
1 cup apricot nectar
6 ounces lemon Jello

2 cups heavy cream, whipped
Fresh mint leaves for garnish
Paprika

Bring apricot juice and apricot nectar to a boil. Add Jello and stir until dissolved. Chill until mixture is consistency of honey. (Check after 45 minutes.) Fold into whipped cream and chill in 6-cup ring mold.

**CHICKEN SALAD:**

1 large onion, sliced
4 stalks celery with leaves, sliced
Salt and pepper
4 whole chicken breasts
8 hard-boiled eggs, chopped

3-4 stalks celery, chopped
½ cup white grapes (optional)
¼ cup chopped pecans (optional)
¾ cup mayonnaise

Place onion, celery, salt, and pepper in large kettle of water. Bring to boil and add chicken breasts. Simmer 1 hour, or until tender. Remove breasts and chill.

Skin and bone chicken and cut into cubes. Add eggs, celery, grapes, and nuts. Add only enough mayonnaise to mix thoroughly, but not to saturate.

Dip soufflé ring very quickly in hot water and unmold on round serving platter. Mound chicken salad in center of ring. Dust with paprika and garnish with fresh mint leaves. Serves 8-10.

*Company's Coming*

A monument in Plattsburg honors Missouri's "President for a Day." David Rice Atchison was president pro tem of the Senate in 1849 when President-elect Zachary Taylor, a religious man, refused to take the presidential oath on Sunday, the day President James K. Polk's term expired.

# Green Pasta Salad with Crabmeat and Roasted Bell Pepper Vinaigrette

4 red bell peppers
2 tablespoons red wine vinegar
1 teaspoon sugar
Pinch cayenne
2 tablespoons olive oil

1 pound green pasta (basil, if available)
¼ pound crabmeat, fresh cooked (lobster or scallops may be used)
Fresh basil for garnish

Roast bell peppers over open flame or under broiler till blackened. Peel skin off under cold running water. Remove seeds. Blend peppers, vinegar, sugar, cayenne, and olive oil in food processor or blender till completely puréed.

Bring 4 quarts water to boil; cook pasta. Drain and rinse with cold water.

To serve, pour vinaigrette on individual plates, arrange pasta on top, and garnish with crab and basil.

*St. Ambrose "On the Hill" Cookbook*

# Chicken Pasta Primavera

This delicious entrée salad is glorious to behold and well suited for informal summertime entertaining.

1 tablespoon vegetable oil
¾ pound uncooked fettuccine, preferably freshly made
1 bunch broccoli, separated into flowerets
2 medium zucchini, cut into ¼-inch slices
1 bunch scallions, thinly sliced
1 sweet red pepper, cut into 1-inch slices
1 (6-ounce) can pitted black olives, drained and sliced
1 (2-ounce) jar pimientos, drained and sliced
2 cups cubed cooked chicken breast
Basil Sauce
⅔ cup freshly grated Parmesan cheese, divided
Salt and freshly ground pepper to taste

Add oil to 3 quarts boiling salted water. Cook fresh pasta 2 to 3 minutes (if packaged is used, cook 8-10 minutes), stirring occasionally. Caution: Do not overcook. Rinse with cold water, drain.

Combine vegetables and chicken with pasta. Fold in ⅔ of the Basil Sauce and ⅓ cup cheese. Season with salt and pepper. (Dish may now be refrigerated for 24 hours.)

To serve, add remaining Basil Sauce, taste and adjust seasoning and sprinkle with remaining cheese.

BASIL SAUCE:
¼ cup minced fresh basil
1 garlic clove
2 eggs
½ teaspoon dry mustard
1 tablespoon tarragon vinegar
½ teaspoon lemon juice
½ teaspoon salt
1½ cups vegetable oil
½ cup sour cream

Basil Sauce may be prepared in advance.

Place basil and garlic in a food processor or blender, process until minced. Add eggs, mustard, vinegar, lemon juice and salt, mix well. With machine running, add oil in a thin stream until thoroughly incorporated. If added too fast, sauce

CONTINUED

may separate. Caution: Use only enough oil to produce a medium-thick mayonnaise. Add sour cream, process 2 or 3 seconds. Refrigerate until ready to use. Serves 8.

*PAST & REPAST*

# Mooney's Grilled Teriyaki Chicken Salad

**4 large chicken breasts**　　　**Mayonnaise**
**Celery**　　　　　　　　　　　**Lemon pepper to taste**

**MARINADE:**
**4-6 cloves garlic, sliced**　　　**2 tablespoons sugar**
**½ cup soy sauce**　　　　　　　**2 teaspoons dry mustard**
**¼ cup sake or dry sherry**

Clean chicken breasts thoroughly. In a glass dish, combine marinade ingredients. Add chicken to this mixture and refrigerate 4-6 hours, turning several times.

Grill over medium coals for approximately 35-45 minutes. (It's okay if skin becomes blackened, but don't allow chicken to overcook and become dry.)

Remove chicken from heat and allow to cool. Skin and debone the breasts, then coarsely chop the meat. In a bowl, combine chopped chicken, celery, mayonnaise, and lemon pepper.

Serve on lettuce plate with sliced tomatoes and hardtack or good-quality wheat crackers. Garnish with lemon wedge and fresh dill weed. Serves 4.

*The Passion of Barbeque*

# Cashew Shrimp Salad

Shrimp salad with a touch of the Orient.

1 (10-ounce) package
  tiny frozen peas
1 pound shrimp, steamed,
  peeled, deveined and
  chopped into bite-size
  pieces
2 cups chopped celery
1 cup mayonnaise

1 tablespoon fresh lemon
  juice
1 teaspoon curry powder
Garlic salt to taste
1 cup unsalted cashews
1 (5-ounce) can chow mein
  noodles

Combine the first 7 ingredients in a large bowl and toss well. Cover and chill at least 30 minutes. Add cashews and noodles and toss again. Serve on lettuce leaves. Serves 6.

*Gateways*

---

Hannibal is the setting for many favorite stories and novels of Missouri writer Samuel Langhorne Clemens, who wrote under the pen name Mark Twain. When a US newspaper mistakenly published the humorist's obituary, Mark Twain cabled, "The reports of my death are greatly exaggerated." He was born in Florida, Missouri, in 1835.

---

# Shrimp Salad
# with Apricot Mayonnaise

| | |
|---|---|
| 6 cups water | 16 large mushrooms, thinly |
| 1 small onion, sliced | sliced |
| 1 bay leaf | 3 tablespoons finely minced |
| 3 cloves | red onion |
| 1 cup dry white wine | 8 or more lettuce leaves |
| 1 teaspoon salt | plus additional chopped |
| 1½ pounds medium to large | lettuce |
| shrimp, shelled and | 8 fresh or canned apricots, |
| deveined | sliced, to garnish |
| 16 snow pea pods | |

In large pot, combine water, onion, bay leaf, cloves, white wine, and salt. Bring to a boil. Add shrimp and cook until pink. Remove shrimp and refrigerate.

Blanch snow peas for 2 minutes in boiling, salted water. Drain well and pat dry. Cut each into 3 pieces. Slice shrimp diagonally into small pieces, reserving 8 largest shrimp (or 1-2 shrimp per person) for garnish. Combine sliced shrimp with snow peas, mushrooms, and red onion. Toss with Apricot Mayonnaise.

**APRICOT MAYONNAISE:**

| | |
|---|---|
| ¾ cup mayonnaise | ½-⅓ cup apricot |
| | preserves |

Whisk mayonnaise and apricot preserves in a medium bowl to blend well. Cover and refrigerate. (May be prepared 2-3 days in advance.)

To serve, line each plate with a lettuce leaf and top with a small layer of chopped lettuce. Mound salad on top and garnish with whole shrimp and sliced apricots. Serves 8.

*Note:* The pale pinks and oranges in this salad look beautiful garnished with nasturtiums, variegated sage, or mint leaves.

*Above & Beyond Parsley*

93

# Soy Tomato Aspic

My grandmother used to make this often. I've replaced the gelatin she used (non-vegetarian) with agar, which works just as well. Stays solid at room temperature. Good with Tofu Mayonnaise.

½ teaspoon chopped fresh
 basil or dill
½ teaspoon chopped fresh
 parsley
½ pound tofu (kneaded
 until smoothly crumbled)
4 tablespoons finely minced
 peppers

1 cup tomato juice (or V8)
¼ teaspoon lemon juice
1 tablespoon tamari
½ tablespoon granulated
 agar

Mix herbs, tofu and peppers together; set aside. Combine liquids and agar in a saucepan and allow to sit for a few minutes. Bring it to a boil, stirring constantly. Continue stirring and boil for 3 minutes. Cool, stir in herb/tofu mix; pour into a mold and refrigerate until set.

**TOFU MAYONNAISE:**
1½ pounds tofu
2 tablespoons tahini
1 teaspoon dill seed
¼ cup vinegar
2 tablespoons prepared
 mustard

½ teaspoon turmeric
 (optional)
¼ cup honey
⅓ cup oil
Salt to taste

Whiz all ingredients in blender. Add milk if needed to desired consistency. Adjust the seasonings to suit your taste.

The oil can be left out of this recipe to make it low in fat. It has plenty of protein on a whole grain bread, so I often make sandwiches simply of sliced vegetables and Tofu Mayonnaise.

***Variation:*** For spicy Tofu Mayonnaise, add ⅛ cup wasabi powder, 1 drop chili oil, and a few drops tamari to each ¼ cup Tofu Mayonnaise.

*The Vegetarian Lunchbasket*

# Clamato Aspic Salad

Artichokes in a zesty aspic...Terrific!

1 (3-ounce) package lemon
  gelatin
1½ cups Clamato juice,
  heated
1 teaspoon lemon juice
Salt and pepper to taste
1 (7-ounce) can artichoke
  hearts, drained and cut in
  half

½ cup green pepper,
  chopped fine
½ cup avocado, chopped
  fine
1 head Boston lettuce

Dissolve gelatin in hot Clamato juice. Add lemon juice, salt, and pepper. Cool slightly. Grease a 6-cup muffin pan. Place 1 tablespoon gelatin mixture in each cup. Place half an artichoke heart in each cup. Chill until firm. Chill remaining mixture until partially thickened. Add the green pepper and avocado. Fill muffin cups with this mixture and chill thoroughly. Unmold on cups made from Boston lettuce.

***Finely Tuned Foods***

# Reuben Salad

**DRESSING:**

1 cup sour cream
¼ cup chili sauce
1 tablespoon sugar

½ teaspoon salt
½ teaspoon dill weed

**SALAD:**

6 cups torn lettuce
1 (1-pound) can sauerkraut, well drained
1 pound corned beef, cut in strips
⅓ cup chopped dill pickle

¼ cup sliced green onions
1½ cups Swiss cheese, cut in strips
3 slices rye bread, buttered, then toasted and cut in cubes

Combine dressing ingredients and set aside. Toast buttered bread and cut into croutons.

Layer: half of lettuce, sauerkraut, corned beef, dill pickle, onion, and cheese. Top with remaining lettuce. Chill till ready to serve. Just before serving, spoon dressing over salad. Top with croutons and toss.

*Sing for Your Supper*

# Cabbage Slaw

By all means, try this new slant on slaw!

1 head cabbage, chopped
8 green onions, chopped
2 (3-ounce) packages uncooked Ramen noodles
2-3 tablespoons butter or margarine
½ cup sesame seeds

½ cup slivered almonds
4 tablespoons sugar
1 cup vegetable oil
1 teaspoon freshly ground pepper
2 teaspoons salt
6 tablespoons rice vinegar

Toss cabbage, onions, and noodles (broken) together. Do not add seasoning packet to noodles. In a small skillet, melt butter and stir in sesame seeds and almonds. Sauté until lightly browned. Toss with the cabbage mixture.

Combine sugar, oil, pepper, salt, and rice vinegar in a blender. Mix well. Pour dressing over cabbage mixture and toss. Chill, stirring frequently. Can be made 2 or 3 days in advance. Serves 12.

*Gateways*

# Varesé Salad

A meal in itself.

1 large head iceberg lettuce
1 box cherry tomatoes, washed and cut in half
1 (14-ounce) can artichoke hearts, drained and cut in half
1 (6-ounce) can pitted black olives, drained and cut in halves

2 small red onions, thinly sliced
3 stalks of celery, chopped
10-12 fresh mushrooms, sliced
1 (10-ounce) package spaghetti, cooked and cooled
Romano cheese, grated

Tear up lettuce. Mix with all other vegetables and spaghetti. Toss with dressing. Top with Romano cheese.

**DRESSING:**

1 (8-ounce) bottle Wishbone Italian Dressing

1 package dry Hidden Valley Ranch Dressing

Mix Italian dressing with ranch dressing. Shake well. Serves 8.

*Finely Tuned Foods*

# Great Grandmother's French Dressing

This recipe came from my husband's grandmother who was born in 1874.

1 cup sugar
Heaping teaspoon salt
Generous shaking of pepper
3 good-sized whole cloves
  garlic

Cider vinegar
Paprika
Salad oil

Funnel sugar into a 1-quart bottle. Add salt, pepper, garlic cloves. Fill bottle two-thirds full of cider vinegar. Shake well. Add generous shake of paprika. Fill remaining one-third of bottle with salad oil. Let stand one week, remove garlic. Shake well before each use.

*Kitchen Prescriptions*

# Feta Cheese Dressing

1 cup crumbled feta cheese
  (4-6 ounces)
1 cup mayonnaise
½ clove garlic, minced
¼ cup red wine vinegar

½ teaspoon salad herbs
½ teaspoon oregano
½ tablespoon Worces-
  tershire sauce
1 tablespoon olive oil

Combine all ingredients in a blender and mix until smooth. This will keep for weeks in the refrigerator.

*Note:* Add ⅓ cup additional crumbled feta if a lumpy texture is desired. Yields 1 pint.

*Adventures in Greek Cooking*

# Vegetables

A very scenic area in the southwest corner of Missouri,
The Noel Bluffs overhang the highway along the Elk River.

# Asparagus Raspberry

Fabulous! Expensive but worth it!

1½ pounds fresh asparagus
2 tablespoons raspberry
  vinegar
1 heaping teaspoon Dijon
  mustard
¾ teaspoon salt
½ teaspoon freshly-ground
  black pepper

6 tablespoons safflower oil
3 tablespoons extra virgin
  olive oil
¼ cup fresh raspberries
2 tablespoons pecans,
  toasted and coarsely
  chopped

Cut all asparagus stalks to same length. Remove woody portion; peel the ends about an inch. Place in a steamer and cook covered over simmering water until tender-crisp. (It is better to have them underdone.)

Mix together vinegar, mustard, salt, and pepper. Whisk in oils. Add berries and mash slightly.

To serve, spoon vinaigrette over individual plates of asparagus and sprinkle with a few toasted pecans.

**Note:** To toast pecans, heat small dry skillet over very low heat, add pecans, toast 3-5 minutes, stirring until golden brown.

*Finely Tuned Foods*

# Creole Asparagus

⅓ cup butter
½ cup flour
Salt
Pepper
2 cans canned asparagus
Milk

1 tablespoon chopped green
  pepper
4 hard cooked eggs, sliced
⅓ cup buttered bread
  crumbs
½ cup grated cheese

Heat oven to 450°. Melt butter. Stir in flour, salt and pepper. Drain liquid from asparagus. Add milk to asparagus liquid to make 2 cups. Add to flour mixture. Cook, stirring constantly, until thick. Layer asparagus, green pepper, eggs, and sauce in 1½-quart casserole. Sprinkle bread crumbs and cheese on top. Bake about 30 minutes.
  Yield: 4-6 servings.

*Sing for Your Supper*

# Frittata of Asparagus

1 bunch (1 - 1½ pounds)
  asparagus
3 eggs
3 tablespoons Parmesan
  cheese

4 tablespoons olive oil
Salt
Pepper

Boil asparagus in salt water till tender; drain. In a skillet, sauté asparagus in olive oil for a few minutes. In a bowl, beat eggs with Parmesan cheese, and salt and pepper to taste. Pour this mixture over asparagus, let it fry without mixing. As egg mixture sets, lift slightly with spatula to allow uncooked portion to flow underneath. When bottom of frittata is golden brown, place a large dish as big as the skillet over the frittata and flip it over and let the other side get golden brown. Serves 4.

*St. Ambrose "On the Hill" Cookbook*

# Pork and Beans

The first thing necessary when about to cook pork and beans is a bean pot of the right shape; an ordinary pudding dish will not cook them so as to get the right color. The mouth of the pot must be small. Take medium sized beans and soak overnight, pour the water off next morning, adding more water and boiling for a few moments. Remove from fire and drain, pouring them into the bean pot, seasoning with salt and pepper and about one tablespoonful of molasses. Score the salt pork and place on top of beans. Nearly cover with water and place in slow oven, cooking about 5-6 hours. Watch carefully that they do not get dry—you may need to add water once or twice.

*Turn of the Century Cookbook*

# Bean Medley

2 medium onions, chopped
   fine
½ pound bacon, chopped
   fine
¾ cup brown sugar
⅓ cup cider vinegar

2 tablespoons prepared
   mustard
Salt and pepper to taste
2 small cans pork & beans
1 regular can kidney beans
1 regular can lima beans
1 regular can butter beans

Brown onions and bacon together. Add brown sugar, vinegar, mustard, salt and pepper and blend. Mix with beans and bake in ovenproof casserole for 1½ hours at 350°.

*Recipes From Missouri...With Love*

---

Marionville is noted for its unusual inhabitants—hundreds of white albino squirrels. So rare and beautiful are these little creatures that in 1990, Governor John Ashcroft proclaimed September 23-29 as White Squirrel Week in Missouri.

---

# K.C. Masterpiece Barbequed Baked Beans

2 (16-ounce) cans pork and
    beans, drained
1 ounce golden raisins
½ cup brown sugar
1 tart apple (such as
    Jonathan), peeled, cored,
    and chopped

1 medium onion, chopped
¾ cup K.C. Masterpiece
    Original Sauce
3 strips uncooked bacon, cut
    in half (or substitute 2
    tablespoons butter or
    margarine)

Preheat oven to 350°. Mix all ingredients except bacon in a
2-quart baking dish. Top with uncooked bacon (or butter).
Bake uncovered for 1 hour.

*Kansas City BBQ*

# Old Settler's Baked Beans

½ pound ground beef
½ pound bacon, chopped
1 medium onion, chopped
Salt and pepper to taste
1 can red kidney beans
1 can pork and beans
1 can butter beans

⅓ cup brown sugar
½ cup white sugar
¼ cup barbecue sauce
¼ cup catsup
½ teaspoon chili powder
1 tablespoon mustard
2 tablespoons molasses

Brown together in large skillet ground beef, chopped bacon,
and onion, along with salt and pepper; drain fat. Add beans.
Mix sugars, barbecue sauce, molasses, and spices together
and add to meat-bean mixture. Pour into large baking dish
and bake at 350° for approximately 1 hour. This may be
frozen before or after baking. Serves 10-12.

*Silver Dollar City's Recipes*

Soybeans have become the number one cash crop in Missouri.
Half of all soybeans raised in Missouri are exported.

# Broccoli Swiss Bake

Nice colors!

1½ cups summer squash
(½-inch pieces)
3 cups fresh broccoli
½ cup butter or margarine
1 egg, beaten
½ cup shredded Swiss
cheese

¼ cup milk
¼ teaspoon dry mustard
1 teaspoon salt
Pepper and cayenne to taste
½ cup Parmesan cheese
2 tablespoons toasted
sesame seeds

Steam squash and broccoli so they are crisp tender. Layer in casserole. Melt butter and mix with egg, Swiss cheese, milk, and seasonings. Pour over broccoli and squash. Top with Parmesan cheese and sesame seeds. Bake 20 minutes at 350°. Serve immediately.

*With Hands & Heart Cookbook*

# Pasta Con Broccoli

1 (16-ounce) package
cavatelli noodles
1 quart half-and-half
4 ounces butter
1 teaspoon garlic
4 ounces tomato sauce
(spaghetti sauce)

4 ounces broccoli (usually
add more)
4 ounces mushrooms (could
add more)
Salt and pepper
1 cup Parmesan cheese
(could add more)

Cook noodles until half done. Drain off water; put back in pot. Add cream, butter, garlic, tomato sauce, and cut broccoli. Bring to a hard boil. When noodles are cooked, add mushrooms. Remove from heat; add salt and pepper to taste, and cheese.

Will feed one hungry Italian or a family of 5-6.

*St. Ambrose "On the Hill" Cookbook*

# Broccoli with Pine Nuts and Capers

Fresh broccoli is available year-round at reasonable prices in most markets and is far superior to the frozen.

3 pounds fresh broccoli
⅓ cup butter
⅓ cup pine nuts
2 garlic cloves, minced
½ cup water

3 tablespoons capers, well
   drained
Salt and freshly ground
   pepper to taste

Remove and separate broccoli flowerets from stems. Peel stems, halve lengthwise if thick, cut crosswise into ½-inch slices. (Yield should be 8 cups flowerets and stems.) Drop broccoli into a 4-quart saucepan filled with boiling salted water, cook 4 minutes. Rinse under cold water, drain and pat dry.

Melt butter in a large skillet, add pine nuts and garlic. Sauté 30 seconds, remove mixture, set aside. Add broccoli to skillet, toss over moderate heat for 2 minutes. Add water, cover, cook over high heat for 6 minutes or until tender-crisp. Add pine nut mixture and capers, season with salt and pepper. Cook uncovered over high heat 1 minute. Taste and adjust seasoning. Serve hot. Serves 8-10.

*PAST & REPAST*

# Crunchy Broccoli Casserole

1 small jar sliced mushrooms
1 can sliced water
   chestnuts, drained
1 envelope onion soup mix
2 tablespoons oleo

2 packages frozen broccoli,
   cooked and drained
¼ cup bread crumbs
½ cup grated cheese

Sauté mushrooms and water chestnuts with soup mix in oleo in skillet. Mix with broccoli in casserole. Top with bread crumbs and cheese. Bake at 325° for 20-25 minutes, or until bubbly. Yield: 6 servings.

*Blue Ridge Christian Church Cookbook*

# English Pea Casserole

1 stick oleo, melted
1 medium onion, chopped
½ bell pepper, chopped
2 cans tiny English peas,
  drained (LeSueur is our
  choice)

1 small can water
  chestnuts (with half
  of liquid)
3 tablespoons pimento
1 can celery soup,
  undiluted

Cook oleo, onion, and bell pepper slowly until soft but not brown. Add English peas and water chestnuts. Add pimento and celery soup. Mix well; top with bread crumbs. Bake in 350° oven until bubbly and crumbs are brown. Bake in medium Pyrex casserole.

*Cooking on the Road*

# Tangy Green Beans

4 slices bacon, cut into
  ½-inch pieces
½ cup chopped onion
2 (16-ounce) cans whole
  green beans, drained
¾ cup water

3 tablespoons white
  vinegar
1 beef flavored bouillon
  cube
¼ teaspoon pepper

Cook bacon in a large skillet until lightly browned. Stir in onion and cook until tender. Add beans and remaining ingredients; cook until thoroughly heated.

*St. Ambrose "On the Hill" Cookbook*

 Born in St. Louis in 1850, Eugene Field was a humorist and verse writer. His most famous work is the children's lullaby favorite, "Wynken, Blynken, and Nod."

# Company Vegetable Casserole

1 bag frozen California
blend vegetables
(cauliflower, broccoli and
carrot slices)
1 (8-ounce) box Brussels
sprouts (optional)
½ cup Minute rice

1 small can mushrooms,
drained
1 can cream of mushroom
soup
1 small jar Cheez Whiz
1 tablespoon onion flakes
1 teaspoon seasoned salt
¾ cup milk

Place frozen vegetables in 2½-quart casserole. (Do not cook.) Mix rice (uncooked) and mushrooms with vegetables. Combine mushroom soup, Cheez Whiz, onion flakes, seasoned salt, and milk. Place in saucepan and heat until cheese melts. Pour cheese sauce over vegetables (may not cover completely). Bake at 350° for 1 hour. Serves 10.

*Blue Ridge Christian Church Cookbook*

# Swiss Vegetable Medley

1 (16-ounce) bag frozen
broccoli, carrots, and
cauliflower combination,
thawed and drained
1 (10¾-ounce) can
condensed cream of
mushroom soup

1 cup shredded Swiss cheese
⅓ cup sour cream
¼ teaspoon ground black
pepper
1 (2.8-ounce) can Durkee
French fried onions

Combine vegetables, soup, ½ cup cheese, sour cream, pepper, and ½ can fried onions. Pour into a 1-quart casserole. Bake, covered at 350° for 30 minutes. Remove from oven and top with remaining cheese and onions. Bake uncovered 5 minutes longer.

*Luncheon Favorites*

# Baked Onions

6 medium onions, peeled
   and sliced in half
6 slices bacon (optional)
¼ cup tomato juice or
   ketchup
2 tablespoons brown sugar

½ teaspoons salt
¼ teaspoon pepper
¼ teaspoon paprika
½ teaspoon dill or celery
   seed
Chopped parsley

Place cut onions in greased casserole, 10x6x2-inches. Fry
bacon crisp and crumble. Combine tomato juice, brown
sugar, and spices. Pour over onions and cover. Bake about
1 hour at 350°. Baste occasionally. Good with frozen broccoli or green beans, also roast chicken and rice.

*Talk About Good*

# Baked Tarragon/Honey Onions

4 medium onions, peeled
4 pats butter
2 tablespoons honey

6 tablespoons fresh
   tarragon, finely diced

Place onion on sheet of foil large enough so that the onions
may be wrapped completely in it. In the center of each onion,
place a pat of butter and then pour ½ tablespoon honey over
each. Sprinkle each onion with 1½ tablespoons of the diced
tarragon. Wrap in foil and bake in 350° oven for 20 minutes
or until onion is transparent. Serves 4. (Yellow onions are
better for this recipe.)

*From Seed to Serve*

---

Mushroom hunting is a favorite outing for many Ozarkians
during the early spring. There are several edible mushrooms,
but unless you are very knowledgeable and able to tell the
"good" ones from the "bad" ones, it is wise to stick to morels. They look
like wrinkled light brown cedar trees.

---

# Mushroom Pie

Excellent when served with steak or roast beef.

| | |
|---|---|
| 1 (9-inch) unbaked pie shell | 1½ teaspoons salt |
| 4 tablespoons butter | 1 teaspoon lemon juice |
| 2 tablespoons minced shallots or whites of green onions | 4 eggs |
| | 1 cup heavy cream |
| | ⅛ teaspoon pepper |
| 1 pound mushrooms, thinly sliced | ⅛ teaspoon nutmeg |
| | ½ cup grated Swiss cheese |

Prebake pie shell 8-10 minutes in 450° oven. In skillet, sauté shallots in butter and add mushrooms, salt, and lemon juice. Cover, and simmer 10 minutes. Uncover, increase heat, and cook rapidly until liquid has evaporated, stirring occasionally.

Beat eggs with cream, pepper, and nutmeg. Combine with mushrooms. Pour into partially cooked pie shell and sprinkle grated cheese over top. Dot with butter and bake in preheated 350° oven for about 35 minutes until puffed and slightly firm when you jiggle the pan. Serves 6-8.

*The Cook Book*

# Spinach and Artichoke Casserole

3 (10-ounce) packages frozen
chopped spinach
1 (8-ounce) package cream
cheese
½ cup margarine
2 (8½-ounce) cans
artichoke hearts, sliced
in half

Salt and pepper to taste
½ teaspoon Worcestershire
sauce
2 shakes Tabasco sauce
1 cup Pepperidge Farm
Cornbread Stuffing

Cook chopped spinach and drain well. Mix with cream cheese and margarine while hot; season. Place a layer of spinach in a 2-quart casserole, then layer of artichokes. Season with salt, pepper, Worcestershire sauce and Tabasco. Sprinkle a small amount of cornbread stuffing on top. Repeat and cover with rest of stuffing.

If you like, sprinkle small amount of Romano cheese on stuffing. Can be done ahead to this point. Bake at 350° for 30 minutes. Serves 8-10.

*Gourmet Garden*

# Spanakopita
## (Spinach Pie)

1½ - 2 pounds spinach, fresh
½ pound feta cheese, crumbled
½ pound cottage cheese, large curd
Salt and white pepper to taste

1 bunch green onions
5-6 eggs
3-4 sticks melted butter
½ pound filo dough (or more if preferred)

In a small pot, sauté the green onions in a little butter and set aside. Rinse, chop, and drain the spinach and place in a large mixing bowl. Add the sautéed green onions, the feta and cottage cheeses, and the salt and pepper. Then slowly fold the beaten eggs into the spinach mixture and set aside. Butter a 9x13-inch baking pan, and one at a time, layer about 7 filo sheets in the bottom of the pan, brushing each one with melted butter. Spread the spinach mixture evenly over the pastry sheets. Top with about 7 more individually buttered filo sheets, and be certain to thoroughly butter the last filo sheet. Refrigerate the pita an hour or two, and then score into squares with the tip of a sharp knife. Do not cut all the way down through the pita. Bake the pita in a preheated 350° oven about 1 hour or until a light golden color.

After baking place on a wire rack to cool and cut into squares before serving. Do not cover the pita while cooling because it will get soggy.

*Note:* 3 (10-ounce) packages of frozen chopped spinach may be substituted for the fresh spinach. Be sure the frozen spinach is completely thawed and well drained before adding to the other ingredients.

If time does not permit refrigeration before baking and scoring the pita, it may be baked immediately after preparation. It will be a little more difficult to score, but this should be done before baking.

*Adventures in Greek Cooking*

# Okra-Tomato Supreme

A really delicious okra recipe—a meal in itself.

1½ cups fresh okra (cut in ½-inch pieces)
½ cup chopped onions
½ cup chopped green peppers
2 tablespoons salad oil

1 tablespoon sugar
1 teaspoon flour
¾ teaspoon salt
1 pint to 1 quart cooked tomatoes

Cook okra gently in small amount of water. Drain well and pour cold water over to rinse. Cook onions and green pepper in salad oil until tender, not brown. Blend sugar, flour, and salt and stir in tomatoes and okra. Heat until hot through. Stir as little as possible to prevent breaking okra.

Variations of this recipe can be made by adding hamburger, browned and drained. Add onions, peppers, and tomatoes. Place thick raw slices of okra on top and let simmer and steam until okra is tender.

*Treasured Recipes Book II*

# Sherried Tomatoes

Fresh tomatoes

FOR EACH TOMATO:
1 tablespoon sherry
⅛ teaspoon dill weed
⅛ teaspoon or 2 twists black pepper

1 tablespoon mayonnaise
1 tablespoon finely grated cheddar cheese

Remove core from each tomato and slice tomato in half. Place cut side up on a cookie sheet. Pierce each tomato several times with a fork. Sprinkle each half with sherry, dill weed, and pepper. Broil for 2-3 minutes. (May be prepared to this point 1 hour before serving.) Top each half with a mixture of mayonnaise and cheese. Broil for 2-3 minutes or until bubbly and slightly browned. Serve immediately.

*Beyond Parsley*

# Italian Stuffed Tomatoes

8 medium tomatoes
Salt
3 tablespoons olive oil
6 green onions, finely
  sliced
1 pint fresh mushrooms,
  finely sliced
1 (8½-ounce) can
  artichokes, drained and
  coarsely chopped

2 cloves garlic, minced
1 teaspoon Italian seasoning
1 teaspoon basil
1 teaspoon soy sauce
½ teaspoon salt
¼ teaspoon sugar
¼ cup dry bread crumbs
¼ cup grated Parmesan
  cheese

Slice off tops of tomatoes. Scoop out pulp; drain and reserve pulp. Lightly salt the tomato cups and drain on paper towels for 30 minutes.

In a large skillet heat olive oil to medium-high heat. Add green onions, reserved tomato pulp, mushrooms, artichokes, and garlic to skillet and sauté 3-4 minutes. Add Italian seasoning, basil, soy sauce, salt, and sugar and continue to sauté until liquid evaporates. Spoon vegetable mixture into drained tomato cups. Top with combined bread crumbs and Parmesan cheese. Bake in preheated 400° oven for 10 minutes, or until hot and bubbly. Do ahead. Serves 8.

*Cooking in Clover*

# Fettuccine with Fresh Tomatoes and Brie

A perfect merger.

2 tablespoons olive oil
4 large tomatoes, peeled, seeded and chopped
1 clove garlic, crushed
1 bunch fresh basil, trimmed

Salt and freshly ground pepper to taste
6 ounces Brie cheese rimmed and cubed
1 pound fettuccine

Heat olive oil and quickly sauté tomatoes, garlic, basil, salt, and pepper. Add Brie and cook until mixture is creamy, stirring constantly. Cook fettuccine according to package directions and drain. Pour sauce over fettuccine and toss. Serve immediately. Egg or spinach fettuccine can be used. Fresh is best. Serves 4-6.

The word basil is derived from the Greek word for king, basileias. It was once used to make royal perfumes and medicines. Today, basil is one of the most popular herbs used with over 50 varieties available.

*Gateways*

# Zucchini Casserole

Different, with zip!

8 slices Pepperidge Farm Bread, trimmed
¼ cup butter (scant)
1 (1-pound) can whole corn, drained
2 cups zucchini, thinly sliced
1 (4-ounce) can green chilies, seeded and chopped

½ pound Monterey Jack cheese, shredded (2 cups)
½ cup sharp cheddar cheese, shredded
4 eggs
2 cups milk
1 teaspoon salt
⅛ teaspoon pepper

Butter the bread and put in a 9x13-inch flat casserole, buttered side down. Cover bread with layered corn, zucchini, chilies, and both cheeses. Mix eggs, milk, salt, and pepper together. Pour over the vegetables. Let set 4 hours. Bake at 375° for 25 minutes. Let rest 10 minutes before serving. Easy. Do ahead. Serves 8.

*With Hands & Heart Cookbook*

# Pasta with Vodka Sauce and Sun-Dried Tomatoes

1 pound penne or other
  tubular pasta
5 tablespoons unsalted
  butter
½ cup julienned sun-dried
  tomatoes
⅔ cup vodka, preferably
  Polish or Russian
¼ teaspoon hot red pepper
  flakes

1 (16-ounce) can Roma
  tomatoes, drained, seeded,
  and puréed
¾ cup heavy cream
½ teaspoon salt
¾ cup freshly grated
  Parmesan cheese

In a large pot of boiling, salted water, cook pasta until al dente (tender but still firm), 8-10 minutes. Meanwhile melt butter in a large, non-corrodible skillet over moderate heat. Add sun-dried tomatoes and sauté 3-5 minutes. Add vodka and pepper flakes and simmer for 2 minutes. Add puréed tomatoes and cream, simmering for 5 minutes longer. Season with salt. When pasta is done, drain well and add to skillet with the hot sauce. Reduce heat to low, add the cheese, and mix thoroughly. Pour into a heated bowl and serve at once. Serves 4.

*Kansas City Cuisine (Trattoria Marco Polo)*

# Butternut Squash Casserole

1 (2½ - 3-pound) butternut
  squash
¼ cup butter or margarine
1 tablespoon brown sugar
¼ teaspoon salt
Pinch of white pepper

1½ tablespoons shortening
1½ quarts sliced Jonathan
  or Granny Smith apples
  (about 2 pounds) unpeeled
¼ cup sugar

Cut squash in half lengthwise. Scrape out seeds and steam 30 minutes, or bake on foil, cut-side-down, in 350° oven until tender. Scrape out pulp and mash or beat in mixer or processor until smooth. Add butter, brown sugar, salt and pepper; set aside. In skillet, melt shortening and add apples. Sprinkle with sugar and cover, simmering until barely tender. Spread in an 8- or 9-inch casserole and spoon squash mixture evenly over apples.

**TOPPING:**

3 cups corn flakes, coarsely
  crushed
½ cup chopped pecans

2 tablespoons melted butter
½ cup brown sugar

Spread topping over squash and bake in 325° oven for 12-15 minutes, or till lightly browned. Serves 8.

*Tasty Palette*

# Baked Corn

½ cup chopped onion
½ cup chopped green pepper
1 stick butter
1 small package corn muffin
  mix
1 can kernel corn, undrained

1 can creamy corn
2 eggs, beaten
1 cup sour cream
1 teaspoon salt
4 ounces shredded cheese

Sauté onion and green pepper in butter. Combine all ingredients, except cheese. Bake in a 350° oven for 1 hour. Use 9x13-inch pan. Sprinkle cheese on top. Serves 15-18.

*Recipes Old and New*

# Company Corn

¼ - ½ pound bacon, fried
   crisp and crumbled
2 tablespoons bacon
   drippings
2 tablespoons butter

2 tablespoons chopped onion
4 tablespoons flour
1 cup dairy sour cream
2 (16-ounce) cans whole
   kernel corn, drain 1 can

In a large skillet, sauté onion in bacon drippings and butter
until tender. Add flour and mix well. Stir in sour cream. Mix
in corn and cook over low heat until mixture begins to thicken.
Stir in bacon, saving some to use as garnish. Pour into a
serving dish and garnish with reserved bacon; serve immediately. Serves 8.

***Sassafras!***

# Super Brussels Sprouts
### *(Low-cal)*

1 (11-ounce) can mandarin
   oranges (undrained)
2 pounds fresh Brussels
   sprouts
1½ cups water
¼ teaspoon salt
¼ teaspoon white pepper

2 tablespoons lemon juice
2 teaspoons cornstarch
½ teaspoon dried whole
   basil
1 (8-ounce) can sliced water
   chestnuts, drained

Drain oranges, saving liquid; set both aside. Wash Brussels
sprouts; remove dry or discolored leaves. Cut off stem ends
and slash bottom of each sprout with a shallow X. Combine
sprouts, water, salt, and pepper in a saucepan; bring to a
boil. Cover; reduce heat. Simmer 10 minutes or until tender; drain.

Combine reserved liquid from oranges with lemon juice,
cornstarch, and basil in small saucepan, stirring until cornstarch is dissolved. Bring to a boil; boil 1 minute, stirring
constantly. Pour sauce over Brussels sprouts. Add oranges
and water chestnuts and toss. Makes 8 servings.

***Tasty Palette***

# Latkes

3 cups potatoes, unpeeled,
  scrubbed and cut into
  chunks
1 egg
1 small onion, quartered

2 tablespoons flour
1 tablespoon soft butter
½ teaspoon sugar
½ teaspoon salt
Dash pepper

Blend three-fourths of potatoes in a food processor, using steel knife. Add rest of ingredients. Using shredder, process rest of potatoes, mix well. Pour by spoonfuls onto hot well-greased griddle. Turn when edges are brown.

*Gourmet Garden*

# Fried Potatoes and Onions

A late 1800s method that is still popular in the Ozarks. Vegetable oil was usually substituted by the mid 1900s.

Peel and cut the potatoes and onions into thin slices, as nearly the same size as possible; "make some butter or drippings quite hot" in a frying-pan; add the potatoes and onions. Fry them on both sides until nicely browned. When they are crisp and done, take them up, "place them on a cloth before the fire" to drain the excess grease from them. Serve very hot after sprinkling them with salt.

*á la Rose*

# Spicy Potatoes

3 pounds potatoes, unpeeled
3 tablespoons oil
¾ teaspoon salt
½ teaspoon dried oregano
½ teaspoon paprika
¼ teaspoon garlic, crushed
¼ teaspoon freshly ground
  pepper
¼ cup grated Parmesan
  cheese

Preheat oven to 450°. Grease a cookie sheet. Wash potatoes and cut each into 8 or 10 wedges; drain. Put them in a bowl and toss lightly with oil. Combine remaining ingredients. Sprinkle half of the cheese mixture over potatoes and toss. Add remaining cheese and toss. Place potatoes on the cookie sheets in a single layer and bake 25-30 minutes, flipping potatoes if necessary. Leftovers can be reheated. Easy. Can do ahead. Serves 6.

*Cooking in Clover II*

# Creamy Grilled Potatoes

5 medium potatoes, peeled
  and thinly sliced
1 medium onion, sliced
6 tablespoons butter or
  margarine
⅓ cup Cheddar cheese,
  shredded
2 tablespoons parsley,
  minced
2 tablespoons Worcestershire
  sauce
Salt and pepper to taste
⅓ cup chicken broth
2 tablespoons bacon bits

Place sliced potatoes and onion on 22x18-inch piece of heavy-duty foil. Dot with butter. Sprinkle with cheese, parsley, Worcestershire sauce, salt, and pepper. Fold up foil around potatoes; add chicken broth. Sprinkle with bacon bits. Seal edges tightly. Grill packet on covered grill over medium-hot Kingsford briquets about 35 minutes or until potatoes are tender. Serves 6.

*The Never Ending Season*

# Swedish Potatoes

| | |
|---|---|
| 2 tablespoons butter | 1 teaspoon salt |
| 1 cup chopped onions | ⅛ teaspoon pepper |
| 1 package frozen fancy fries | ½ cup sour cream |
| 1 cup shredded cheddar cheese | 2 eggs slightly beaten |

Melt butter in large skillet. Add onions and potatoes, heat and stir until onions are wilted and potatoes are hot; remove from heat. Stir in cheese, salt and pepper. Pour into shallow baking dish. Mix sour cream and eggs together and pour over potatoes. Bake for 20 minutes at 350°. A good companion for pork chops.

*Lavender and Lace*

# Potato Puffs

| | |
|---|---|
| 4½ cups diced potatoes | 1½ cups all-purpose flour |
| 2 teaspoons salt | 6 eggs |
| 1½ cups water | Salad oil |
| 6 tablespoons butter | |

Boil potatoes in water to which 1 teaspoon salt has been added. Cook until potatoes are soft. Drain well; mash with potato ricer. Do not add the usual butter or milk.

In a saucepan, heat 1½ cups water, remaining teaspoon salt and the butter until water boils and butter melts. Reduce heat. Add flour all at once and stir until batter is firm and leaves sides of pan. Remove from heat. Turn batter into bowl of electric mixer. Add eggs, one by one, beating well after each addition. Add potatoes and mix until well blended. Heat 1-inch oil in electric skillet to 370°. Drop potato mixture by teaspoons into hot oil. Fry until puffed and golden brown. Drain on paper toweling. Sprinkle with salt.

Puffs may be made ahead of time by frying only to a light brown. Place in a single layer on cookie sheet and place in freezer. At serving time, bake in preheated 450° oven, uncovered, 8-10 minutes, or until medium brown. Sprinkle with salt. Serves 8-12. Recipe may be reduced to one-half.

*Talk About Good*

# Confetti Potatoes

Exceptionally tasty and wonderful for buffets.

**15 medium-sized potatoes
with jackets**
**½ cup margarine, melted**
**1 small jar pimentos with
juice, chopped**
**1 green pepper, diced**

**1 large onion, finely
chopped**
**¾ pound American cheese,
diced**
**2 cups cornflakes, crushed**

Cook, peel and cube potatoes. To melted butter, add pimento juice, and combine all ingredients except cornflakes. Place in a buttered 2½-quart casserole dish, top with crumbs and bake at 350° for 30 minutes. Serves 10-16.

*Finely Tuned Foods*

# Mashed Potatoes

It hardly seems necessary to give directions for preparing this simple dish, but many cooks spoil it by using cold milk instead of hot. Boil peeled, sliced potatoes, drain, and when are quite dry add the boiling milk and a little butter, pepper and salt to taste. Beat and whisk until light and very white. No one who has not tried it can realize the difference the hot milk makes.

*Turn of the Century Cookbook*

# Sweet Potatoes and Apples

This is a good "fix ahead" dish to serve with pork or fowl. When your oven is going, bake 3 or 4 sweet potatoes or pierce and cook in the microwave, then peel, cube and refrigerate a day or two until ready to use. For 4 servings:

| | |
|---|---|
| 2 tablespoons margarine | 2 teaspoons lemon juice |
| 4 apples, peeled and cubed | 1/4 teaspoon cinnamon |
| 1/4 cup onion, minced | Dash of allspice |
| 2 tablespoons brown sugar, firmly packed | 3 or 4 cooked sweet potatoes, cut in cubes |

Heat margarine in skillet; add apples and onions. Cook 4 or 5 minutes until apples are soft. Stir in sugar, juice, and seasonings, stirring until sugar is melted; add sweet potatoes and cook until thoroughly heated.

*Apples, Apples, Apples*

# Sweet Potato-Carrot TZimmes

Sukkot—Rosh Hashana.

| | |
|---|---|
| 8 large carrots, peeled | 3/4 cup honey |
| 2 large sweet potatoes, peeled | 1 tablespoon lemon juice |
| Water | 3 tablespoons margarine |
| 1/2 teaspoon salt | 3 tablespoons flour |

Slice carrots 1/4-inch thick. Cut sweet potatoes into small pieces. Place in heavy saucepan; add cold water to cover. Cook until tender. Add salt, honey and lemon juice; simmer gently 20 minutes. Melt margarine in small skillet; blend in flour. Stir into carrots and sweet potatoes, stirring until mixed. Serves 6-8.

*From Generation to Generation*

# Rice Casserole

1 cup margarine (8 ounces)
½ pound fine noodles
2 cups minute rice, uncooked
2 cans chicken broth (don't add water)
1 can sliced water chestnuts

1 teaspoon soy sauce
2 cans onion soup or equivalent pareve powdered mix
1 (4-ounce) can mushrooms (optional)

Melt margarine in large pan. Add raw noodles and keep turning until lightly browned. Add rest of ingredients. Stir through and put in 3-quart casserole or 9x12-inch pan.

Bake at 350° for 20 minutes, covered, 25 minutes uncovered. Place under broiler for a few minutes for more of a crust. Serves 12.

*From Generation to Generation*

# Macaroni and Cheese Bake

1 (16-ounce) box macaroni (long is best)*
½ stick butter
Approximately 36 Ritz or Hi-Ho crackers**

1 (1-pound or more) packages American cheese (mild cheddar is good)
Salt and pepper to taste
Approximately 1 cup milk

Cook macaroni in boiling salted water, about 12-15 minutes. Drain and blanch with cold water. Rub butter on bottom and sides of large casserole bowl. Layer cheese, macaroni, and crumbled crackers and dot with butter; continue layering until bowl is ¾ full, having cheese on top.

Pour milk over all with bowl about half full of milk. Cover and bake 1 hour at 350° or until top is golden brown. Serves about 8 people.

**Note:** I always put Reynolds Wrap on bottom of oven under bowl to catch any boil-over.

*You can also use elbow.
**Plain saltines can be used, but others are better.

*USO's Salute to the Troops Cookbook*

# Homemade Noodles

½ - 1 cup flour
1 egg and 1 egg yolk
½ teaspoon salt
¼ cup water

1 drop of yellow food
coloring (place on
toothpick to keep from
getting too much)

Place ½ cup flour in bowl. Add beaten egg and yolk, salt, water and food color; mix. Add more flour, as needed, to make a very thick dough. Fold over or knead just enough to hold shape on top of well floured board. Too much kneading makes noodles tough. Roll out to ⅛-inch thick. Let stand for an hour or two. Cut into strips. Cook in simmering broth for about 20 minutes or until tender. Do not remove lid during cooking time.

Mother would roll out the batter all over the table where it would dry until it would be cut into strips. The boys liked to eat the batter raw, so many times we would find holes along the edges.

*Kohler Family Kookbook*

# Pasta Primavera

½ cup unsalted butter
1 medium onion, minced
1 large clove garlic, minced
1 pound thin asparagus, tough ends trimmed, cut into ¼-inch slices
½ pound mushrooms, thinly sliced
6 ounces cauliflower, broken into florets
1 medium zucchini, cut into ¼-inch slices
1 small carrot, halved lengthwise, cut into ⅛-inch diagonal slices
1 cup heavy cream

½ cup chicken broth
2 tablespoons chopped fresh basil
1 cup frozen small peas, thawed
2 ounces prosciutto or cooked ham, chopped
5 green onions, chopped
Salt and freshly ground pepper to taste
1 pound fettuccini or linguini, cooked al dente, thoroughly drained
1 cup freshly grated Parmesan cheese

CONTINUED

Heat large skillet over medium-high heat. Add butter, onion and garlic, and sauté until onion is softened, about 2 minutes. Add asparagus, mushrooms, cauliflower, zucchini, and carrot, and stir fry for 2 minutes. Remove vegetables and set aside.

Increase heat to high. Add cream, broth, and basil, and boil until liquid is reduced, about 3 minutes. Stir in peas, ham, and green onion, and cook 1 minute more. Season with salt and pepper to taste. Add pasta and cheese, tossing until thoroughly combined and pasta is heated through. Turn onto large platter and garnish with reserved vegetables. Serves 4-6.

*Cooking for Applause*

# Manicotti

¾ pound ricotta cheese
6 ounces mozzarella cheese, grated
2 tablespoons grated Parmesan cheese
2 tablespoons granulated sugar

1 lightly beaten egg
6-8 manicotti noodles (uncooked)
Salt and pepper to taste
1 (32-ounce) jar of your favorite spaghetti sauce

Combine all ingredients except noodles and sauce and 2 tablespoons mozzarella cheese. Mix well. Fill uncooked manicotti using a teaspoon or a small rounded knife. Pour a generous amount of spaghetti sauce in the bottom of a greased 9x13-inch pan. Arrange filled manicotti in a single layer side-by-side. Cover baking dish with foil crimping edges to seal tightly. Place in a preheated 400° oven for 40 minutes. After 40 minutes, remove foil, add a little more sauce over manicotti. Sprinkle with grated mozzarella and Parmesan cheese. Allow to bake an additional 5-10 minutes with foil removed. Serves 4.

*From Generation to Generation*

# Beet Pickles

1 can beets
½ cup water
¾ teaspoon cinnamon
¼ teaspoon allspice

½ cup sugar
½ cup vinegar
¼ teaspoon cloves

Combine and simmer for 15 minutes.

*Heavenly Delights*

# Red Beet Eggs

1 (1-pound) can small whole
   beets (do not drain)
1 cup cider vinegar
⅓ cup sugar

¾ teaspoon salt
¼ cup water (about)
8 hard cooked eggs, shelled

Empty beets and their liquid into a small saucepan; add vinegar, sugar, and salt and heat just until sugar dissolves. Cool to room temperature. Place eggs in a bowl or a half gallon jar. Pour in beet mixture and add just enough water so that liquid covers eggs. Cover and refrigerate, allowing eggs to marinate a couple of days. Stir now and then or invert jar of eggs and beets gently a few times so that all eggs redden evenly. Spoon beets, eggs and some of the liquid into a serving bowl and serve. Red beet eggs make excellent picnic fare.

*Lavender and Lace*

# Pepper Relish

24 green peppers
24 red peppers
12 large onions

1 quart vinegar
3 tablespoons salt
4 cups sugar

Grind peppers and onions through food chopper (today we would use a food processor); cover all with boiling water and let stand 10 minutes. Drain well. Add vinegar, salt and sugar and boil for 20 minutes. Place in sterile jars and seal. Great in tuna salad and in salad dressing for sandwich spread.

*Recipes & Stories of Early-Day Settlers*

# Pesto

1 cup torn fresh basil
  leaves
1 cup parsley
½ cup walnuts
½ cup olive oil
⅓ cup Parmesan cheese
2 tablespoons dill weed

2 tablespoons chives
2 tablespoons rosemary,
  oregano or thyme
1 tablespoons lemon juice
1 clove garlic, quartered
¼ teaspoon pepper

Blend all ingredients in food processor or blender.  Stores 2 weeks in refrigerator or several months in freezer.

*Hint:* Make in ice cube trays for easy-use cubes.

*Recipes Old and New*

# Horseradish Mousse

This piquant mousse adds a touch of refinement to barbecued brisket or chicken.  Attractive garnished with a selection of pickles and olives.

1 tablespoon unflavored
  gelatin
¼ cup cold water
2 cups low-calorie cottage
  cheese
1 tablespoon grated onion

3 tablespoons prepared
  horseradish
¼ cup skim milk
Few drops of Tabasco sauce
Salt and freshly ground
  pepper to taste

Soften gelatin in water.  Combine cheese, onion and horseradish in a food processor or blender, process until smooth.

Heat milk in a small saucepan, add gelatin, stir over low heat until dissolved.  Add to cheese mixture.  Stir in Tabasco, season with salt and pepper.  Spoon into a lightly oiled 1-pint mold, refrigerate.  Unmold and serve with barbecued brisket.  Makes 2 cups.

*PAST & REPAST*

# Peach Butter
## (Spicy)

10 cups ripe peaches
2½ - 3 cups water
2 teaspoons cinnamon

1 teaspoon nutmeg
1 teaspoon powdered cloves
4 cups honey

Cook peeled, cut peaches and water over low heat until smooth and turning brown, 4-5 hours. Stir occasionally to prevent sticking. Add spices and honey. Cool butter and press through a sieve. Pour into sterilized canning jars. Close tightly.

*Heavenly Delights*

# Show Me Preserves

An unusual taste combination of Missouri's backyard produce—strawberries and black walnuts.

3 pints fresh strawberries,
   hulled, or 1 quart frozen
   unsweetened strawberries
3 cups sugar

½ cup fresh lemon juice
2 tablespoons kirsch or
   curaçao
¾ cup black walnut pieces

Combine strawberries, sugar, lemon juice, and kirsch in a large, heavy saucepan. Cook over low heat 5 minutes or until sugar dissolves. Increase the heat and boil 30 minutes, stirring frequently. Remove from heat and stir in walnuts. Pour immediately into hot sterilized ½-pint jars leaving ½-inch head space. Seal jars and process in boiling water bath 10 minutes. Makes eight ½-pint jars.

*Sassafras!*

---

The "Show-me" nickname has been around for a long time, but it gained fame in 1899 when Congressman Willard Vandiver of Cape Girardeau County said in a Philadelphia speech: "Gentlemen, frothy eloquence neither convinces nor satisfies me. I'm from Missouri; you've got to show me."

THE PONY EXPRESS
St. JOSEPH, MISSOURI

Meats

St. Joseph was the eastern starting point of The Pony Express. This statue memorializes the 400 riders and horses who carried the mail.

# Foolproof Standing Rib Roast

This is lusciously browned on outside and rare on inside, regardless of size.

Allow roast to stand at room temperature for 1 hour. In the morning, preheat oven to 375°. Rub roast with seasoning salt, pepper, and garlic. Place on rack in pan rib-side-down (fatty-side-up) and roast for 1 hour; turn off oven. Leave roast in oven but do not open oven.

Before serving time, turn oven on again to 375° and reheat roast 30-40 minutes (30 minutes is for rare, 40 minutes is for medium rare). Do not remove roast or open oven from time roast is put in until finished cooking. Remove immediately. Let stand 15 minutes before carving.

*Gourmet Garden*

# Hickory-Smoked Brisket

| | |
|---|---|
| 1 whole brisket, 4-6 pounds | ¼ cup bottled steak sauce |
| Salt | ¼ cup prepared mustard |
| Dampened hickory chips or | 1 tablespoon celery seed |
| liquid smoke | 2 tablespoons Worcestershire |
| 1½ cups ketchup | sauce |
| ¾ cup brown sugar | 1 clove garlic, minced |
| ¾ cup chili sauce | Dash Tabasco sauce |
| ½ cup white wine vinegar | Freshly ground pepper |
| ¾ cup water | to taste |
| ½ cup lemon juice | |

Salt brisket and place on grill away from hot coals. Add dampened hickory chips, or brush meat with liquid smoke and close hood. Barbeque slowly for 4 hours, or until meat is tender. Cool and slice very thin across grain. Line up slices in shallow pan. Combine remaining ingredients and simmer 30 minutes; pour over meat. Heat 1 hour on grill or in 200° oven. Serves 8-12.

*Company's Coming*

# Winter Steak with Tarragon Butter

1 (2-inch thick) sirloin
  steak, second or third cut
Salt and pepper to taste

1½ tablespoons butter
1½ tablespoons oil

Pat steak dry. Salt and pepper steak on both sides. Sear in butter and oil for 2-4 minutes on each side or until dark brown. Transfer meat to large baking dish and bake at 350° for 25 minutes for medium rare. Transfer to a warm platter. Makes 4-6 servings.

*Note:* Top each serving of beef with a pat of Tarragon Butter and garnish with sprigs of fresh tarragon.

TARRAGON BUTTER:

2 medium shallots
2½ tablespoons chopped
  fresh parsley
4 teaspoons tarragon vinegar
1½ teaspoons fresh
  tarragon or ½ teaspoon
  dried

½ teaspoon freshly ground
  pepper
½ cup butter, well chilled
  and cut into small pieces

Mince shallots in food processor, using steel blade. Add parsley, vinegar, tarragon, and pepper; process briefly. Add butter and blend well. Transfer to waxed paper and form a roll. Refrigerate or freeze until firm.

*Beyond Parsley*

# Steak Round-Up

2 pounds beef round steak
Salt and pepper to taste
1 teaspoon mustard

¾ cup barbecue sauce
4½ ounces Kraft processed
Swiss cheese

Lay steak out flat and season with salt and pepper. Spread with mustard, then with barbecue sauce. Arrange cheese slices to cover meat, and then roll up (like a jelly roll). Secure with 2-6 toothpicks and place in glass casserole dish. Cover and bake at 325° for 60-90 minutes until tender. Serves 8.

*The Never Ending Season*

# Sukiyaki

1 pound (chuck) beef strips
¼ cup margarine
1 (4-ounce) can mushrooms
and juice or 4 ounces fresh,
sliced plus 4 tablespoons
water
2 rounded tablespoons sugar
1 teaspoon salt
1 teaspoon seasoned salt

2 tablespoons soy sauce
1 cup celery, sliced in
3-inch strips
1 cup sliced onions
1½ cups bamboo shoots or
water chestnuts
½ cup green onions, sliced
in 3-inch strips

Cut beef into thin strips, about ½ inch by 3 inches; melt margarine in large skillet or wok and brown beef for about 3 minutes; add juice or water, sugar, salt, seasoned salt, and soy sauce; cover and simmer 20 minutes. Add mushrooms, celery, and sliced onions. Cook covered for 5 minutes. Add drained bamboo shoots or water chestnuts and green onions, and cook uncovered for 5 minutes more. Serve immediately over rice. After simmering, you may add a little more water. Serves 3-4.

*From Generation to Generation*

# Beef Marsala

½ cup butter
1 small onion, chopped
1 pound mushrooms, sliced
1 green pepper, sliced
1 large tomato, chopped
1 cup Marsala wine
1½ cups beef bouillon
1 tablespoon salt

1 teaspoon black pepper
1 cup vegetable oil
8 (6-ounce) beef filets or
   chicken or veal
½ cup flour
2 tablespoons chopped
   parsley

In large skillet, melt butter. Add onion and cook over medium heat until transparent. Add mushrooms, green pepper, and tomato; cook about 5 minutes. Add wine; cook about 3 minutes. Add bouillon, salt and pepper; cook covered over low heat for 10 minutes. In second skillet, heat oil. Dredge filets in flour. Cook in oil to desired doneness. Drain excess oil and add Marsala wine sauce; cook for 5 minutes. Serve garnished with parsley. Serves 8.

*Tasty Palette*

# Spanish Rice and Meat

2 tablespoons oil
1 pound lean chopped beef
2 large onions, chopped
1 large green pepper,
   chopped
3 stalks celery, chopped

1 clove garlic, minced
½ cup raw brown rice
1 cup water
Salt and pepper to taste
1 pint tomatoes (2 cups)

Pour oil in heavy skillet or Dutch oven. Brown meat and vegetables. Add rice and water; simmer for 30 minutes. Add tomatoes and seasonings. Continue cooking for about 30 minutes until rice is tender, adding more liquid if necessary. Serves 4-6.

*Heavenly Delights*

# Zucchini Moussaka

2 tablespoons vegetable oil
3 zucchini, cut in ¼-inch
  slices
1 onion, sliced
1 pound lean ground beef
1 (8-ounce) can tomato sauce
1 clove garlic, minced
½ teaspoon salt
¼ teaspoon cinnamon

1 egg, slightly beaten
1 cup small curd cottage
  cheese
¼ cup freshly grated
  Parmesan cheese or feta
  cheese
Cinnamon
Nutmeg

Put oil in skillet, add zucchini and onion, and lightly brown.
Remove from skillet and place in a shallow 1½-2-quart baking dish.

Brown ground beef in same skillet. Drain fat. Stir in tomato sauce, garlic, salt, and cinnamon. Spoon mixture over zucchini and onion in baking dish. Blend egg and cottage cheese. Spoon over meat. Sprinkle Parmesan or feta over cottage cheese mixture. Sprinkle cinnamon and nutmeg over top. Bake at 350° for 30 minutes. Serves 6.

*Cooking for Applause*

# Moussaka

1½ pounds ground beef
1 onion, chopped
1 teaspoon garlic powder
1 tablespoon oregano
½ teaspoon each, salt
 and pepper
1 (8-ounce) can tomato
 sauce
½ can water

3 medium potatoes,
 peeled
Vegetable oil
2 small eggplants
¾ stick margarine
½ cup flour
2 cups milk
1 cup grated Parmesan
 cheese

Brown meat and onion. Drain excess fat. Add seasonings, tomato sauce, and water. Simmer 10 minutes. Set aside until needed.

Cut potatoes into ½-inch slices. Place on towel and pat dry. Heat ½ inch oil in skillet on high. Brown potatoes quickly on both sides—do not have to cook through. Drain on paper towel.

Prepare eggplant. Wash and cut off tips. Peel strips of skin off, leaving rows of skin, alternating with peeled part. Cut into ½-inch slices. Lay slices on large cookie sheet and brush generously with olive oil on both sides. Broil about 5 minutes until lightly browned. Turn and repeat—withered appearance is desired.

Start sauce while eggplant is in oven: melt margarine and stir in flour. Stir until roux bubbles. Slowly pour milk in thin stream, stirring constantly. Bring gently to boil and remove from heat. Add cheese and stir.

To assemble casserole, use a 9x12x2-inch pan. Layer eggplant, potato (sparingly), meat, potato, eggplant, then sauce. Bake 45-60 minutes at 350° until top is browned.

Before serving, set aside for 15-20 minutes. Serves 8.

*Adventures in Greek Cooking*

# Beefsteak and Kidney Pie

| | |
|---|---|
| 1 pound round steak | Salt and pepper to taste |
| 1 large beef kidney | ¼ teaspoon thyme |
| ¼ cup bacon drippings | 3 cups water |
| 2 medium onions, sliced | 2 tablespoons sherry |
| 6 tablespoons flour | ½ receipt standard pastry |

Cut the steak into 1-inch cubes. Soak the kidney in salt water for 30 minutes, then drain and slice after removing the thin outer skin. Cut each slice in half and trim out fat and tubes. Heat the bacon fat in a heavy frying pan; add steak and onions and sauté until brown.

Stir in the flour and seasonings; brown well. Add the water, stirring constantly over low heat, until the mixture thickens and boils. Add the kidney slices and cook for about 10 minutes. Pour into a buttered 2-quart casserole; cover and bake at 350° for 2 hours.

Now remove from the oven, stir in the sherry, and cover with the rolled pastry. Make several slits in the pastry, then bake at 450° until brown—about 15 minutes. This serves 6; can be made in advance, adding new pastry for the reheating the next day. Serves 4.

Mrs. Trent reminds us that the guests must wait for the Yorkshire pudding—never the pudding for the guests!

**YORKSHIRE PUDDING:**

| | |
|---|---|
| 2 eggs | 3 cups milk |
| A pinch of salt | 12 tablespoons hot beef |
| 1 cup flour | drippings |

Beat the eggs with the salt until thick, light and fluffy; add the flour and milk alternately, beating all the time to assure an air-filled batter. Have 2 muffin tins heating in the oven; pull out and measure a tablespoon of hot drippings from the beef roast into each muffin cup. Fill each cup half full of batter, then bake at 450° for 20-30 minutes. Serves 12 as an accompaniment for roast beef.

*The Shaw House Cook Book*

# Beef and Zucchini Pasta in Wok

4 ounces linguini
3-4 quarts water
2⅛ teaspoons vegetable
  oil
3-4 small zucchini
  (approximately 1 pound)
1 small garlic clove,
  crushed
½ pound lean ground beef
1 (16-ounce) can whole
  peeled tomatoes, slightly
  chopped

¼ cup packed chopped
  fresh basil or 1 table-
  spoon dried leaf basil
⅛ teaspoon dried leaf
  thyme
⅛ teaspoon dried leaf
  oregano
½ teaspoon salt
⅛ teaspoon freshly ground
  black pepper
1 tablespoon grated
  Parmesan cheese

Break linguini into 2-inch pieces. In a large saucepan, bring 3-4 quarts of water to a boil. Add ⅛ teaspoon oil and linguini; cook according to package directions until tender, but firm.

While pasta cooks, cut zucchini lengthwise in thin slices. Stack slices and cut in lengthwise julienne strips. Place wok over high heat; add remaining 2 teaspoons oil. When hot, add meat and garlic. Remove and discard garlic, add ground beef to wok, stir-fry, breaking up meat, until lightly browned. Stir in zucchini strips; stir-fry 1 minute. Add tomatoes with juice, basil, thyme, oregano, salt and pepper. Drain cooked pasta; stir cooked pasta and cheese into wok. Stir-fry until mixture is bubbly hot. Serves 4.

*Sing for Your Supper*

# Hearty Short Ribs

3½ - 4 pounds beef short
  ribs
1 can condensed beef broth
6 peeled potatoes, quartered
3 tablespoons soft butter
⅓ cup flour

1 clove garlic, finely
  chopped
¼ cup Missouri sherry or
  red wine
1 teaspoon salt
Freshly cracked pepper to
  taste

Brown the short ribs in a shallow pan (such as a 9x13-inch cake pan) in a hot oven (550°) for approximately 15 minutes. Drain excess fat. Lower oven temperature to 325°, add the beef broth to the ribs and cover. Bake for 2 hours or until meat is tender. During the last ½ hour, add the potatoes.

To make the gravy, melt the butter in a skillet, add the flour and slowly brown. Stir this paste into the meat juices—about 1½ cups. If not enough, add some beef broth. Add garlic and cook over medium heat until thickened. Stir in sherry and salt and pepper. Combine ribs and gravy and cook about 15 minutes. Serve ribs and potatoes with cooked and buttered carrots, green beans or vegetable of your choice.

***Recipes From Missouri...With Love***

# German Sauerkraut & Country Ribs

Just good, plain, fattening food. Do serve with mashed potatoes, and chew slowly to enjoy every swallow!

3 pounds country pork or
  spare ribs
1 large can or 2 pounds bulk
  kraut
1 teaspoon caraway seeds

1 teaspoon celery seeds
½ cup barley (old-fashioned
  pearl, if you can find it)
Dash of pepper

Wash and cut pork into serving size pieces. Mix all ingredients together. *Do not* rinse kraut. Simmer slowly about 2 hours, adding a bit of water as needed. Serves 4—maybe—depends on the size of your appetite.

***Treasured Recipes Book I***

# Best Bar-B-Que

I have never seen this recipe in any recipe book. I have had it for 35 years and enjoy it every time we have a party or have a number of guests.

| | |
|---|---|
| **2 pounds beef roast (no fat, no bone)** | **2 pounds pork roast (no fat, no bone)** |

Boil together or in separate containers until very tender. Remove from broth. Let cool. Save broth. Do not cut meat, but tear apart with fingers or forks or both when cool. In separate pan, mix:

| | |
|---|---|
| **1 medium bottle tomato catsup** | **1 cup diced celery** |
| **1 medium jar India relish** | **1 cup diced bell pepper** |
| **1 cup onions, diced finely** | **Salt and pepper to taste** |

Mix ingredients with meat. Simmer (do not boil) for 1½ - 2 hours. Add some broth, just enough to make moist. (This can be served as sandwiches.) Makes a large amount for about 20 people.

*Cooking on the Road*

# Chicken Fried Steak and Cream Gravy

Tenderize steaks by pounding with a meat tenderizing mallet. Dredge each side in seasoned flour. Heat butter or lard in a heavy skillet. Add flour-coated meat; brown on first side then turn over to brown the second side. Remove the meat from the skillet to a hot serving platter. Make cream gravy by pouring some of the fat from the skillet, leaving about 2 tablespoons. Stir in about 2 tablespoons of flour. Cook until bubbly, then stir in about a cup or so of hot liquid: cream, milk, potato water, water, or a combination.

*á la Rose*

# Smoke-House Spaghetti

¼ pound bacon, cut in
   1-inch pieces
1 medium onion, chopped
1 pound ground beef
2 (8-ounce) cans tomato
   sauce or tomato soup
Salt to taste
⅛ teaspoon pepper
½ teaspoon oregano

½ teaspoon garlic salt
1 (4-ounce) can mushrooms
¾ pound spaghetti
¼ pound shredded provolone
   cheese or mozzarella
   (about 1 cup)
¼ pound shredded cheddar
   cheese

Sauté bacon in skillet; add onion and ground beef. Brown. Stir in tomato sauce, salt, pepper, oregano, garlic salt, and mushrooms. Simmer 15 minutes.

Break spaghetti in half and cook, then stir into sauce. Place half the mixture in a 2-quart baking dish. Top with half of the cheeses. Repeat layers. Bake in a 375° oven 20-25 minutes. Serves 6-8. Will freeze.

*Wanda's Favorite Recipes Book*

# Italian Meatballs
# and Spaghetti Sauce

If you are having company with small children, on a tight budget, and want to serve an elegant meal, this is great!

**SAUCE:**

1 cup minced onion
2 tablespoons fat or salad oil
1 pound ground chuck
2 minced cloves garlic
2 tablespoons snipped parsley
1 minced medium green pepper

1 (No. 2) can tomatoes (2½ cups)
2 (6-ounce) cans tomato paste
1½ cups water
1 tablespoon salt
⅛ teaspoon pepper
1 teaspoon sage
¼ teaspoon thyme
2 bay leaves (this makes it)

In large kettle, sauté onions in fat until tender. Add chuck; cook stirring often till meat loses red color. Add remaining ingredients; simmer uncovered 1½ hours or until desired thickness, stirring occasionally. Meanwhile, prepare meat balls and spaghetti.

¼ pound ground chuck
½ cup fine dried bread crumbs
¾ teaspoon cornstarch
1 egg, beaten

½ cup light cream
¾ teaspoon salt
2 tablespoons salad oil
¾ - 1 pound spaghetti

Combine first 6 ingredients; form into small balls. In skillet, heat oil; brown balls on all sides about 20 minutes before sauce is done; add meat balls. Also, cook spaghetti as package directs, drain. Serve sauce over hot spaghetti. Makes 6 generous servings.

If you wish, make sauce day before; also shape balls; refrigerate both. To serve, cook spaghetti, reheat sauce, brown balls, drop into sauce; cook 15-20 minutes.

*A Collection of Recipes from the Best Cooks*
*in the Midwest*

# Spaghetti Pie

**CRUST:**

6 ounces thin
  spaghetti (vermicelli),
  cooked and drained
½ clove garlic, minced
¼ cup butter

½ cup grated Parmesan
  cheese
1 large egg, beaten
1 tablespoon fresh basil or
  1 teaspoon dried

Combine vermicelli with other ingredients. Chop mixture with a knife and press mixture into a 10-inch pie plate.

**FILLING:**

½ pound ground beef
¾ pound Italian sausage
½ cup chopped onion
1 (15-ounce) can tomato
  sauce

1 (6-ounce) can tomato paste
1 teaspoon sugar
1 teaspoon dried basil
1 teaspoon dried oregano
¼ cup white wine

Cook ground beef, Italian sausage and onion together. Drain fat. Stir in remaining ingredients. Heat thoroughly.

1 cup ricotta cheese or
  sour cream

6 ounces mozzarella cheese,
  shredded

Spread ricotta cheese or sour cream on Crust. Top with Filling and cover with mozzarella cheese. Bake at 350° for 30 minutes or until golden brown. Makes 6-8 servings.

*Note:* Spaghetti Pie is the solution to many menu dilemmas. Its rich Italian flavor has universal appeal. Prepare two at a time and freeze one. Just for fun, try making bird's nest size individual pies, using 5-inch tart pans.

***Beyond Parsley***

 Winston Churchill gave his famous "Iron Curtain" speech, which officially opened the Cold War, at tiny Westminster College in Fulton in 1946.

# Pizza Spaghetti Pie

**MEAT LAYER:**

1 pound lean ground beef
½ cup fine dry bread
   crumbs
½ cup chopped onion

1 teaspoon salt
Dash of pepper
1 (5.3-ounce) can evaporated
   milk (⅔ cup)

Combine and press mixture firmly onto bottom and side of a 9-inch pie plate. Bake in preheated 350° oven 35-40 minutes. Spoon off drippings.

**SPAGHETTI LAYER:**

4 ounces spaghetti, cooked
   and drained
1 egg, beaten

¼ cup grated Parmesan
   cheese
2 tablespoons butter

Combine and spread in baked meat shell.

**TOPPING:**

1 (8-ounce) can pizza sauce
½ teaspoon oregano
Green pepper rings

1 cup shredded mozzarella
   cheese (4 ounces)

Combine topping ingredients and spread on spaghetti layer. Bake an additional 10 minutes. Let stand 5 minutes before cutting into wedges. Yield: 6 servings.

*Delicious Reading*

# Meatloaf with Zesty Topping

1½ pounds ground beef
¼ medium onion, minced
2 slices dry toast, cubed
¾ cup applesauce
1 teaspoon salt
¼ teaspoon pepper

2 tablespoons catsup
2 tablespoons brown sugar
1 teaspoon dry mustard
1 teaspoon prepared
  horseradish

Mix together thoroughly the ground beef, onion, dry bread cubes, applesauce and seasonings. Pack into 9x5x3-inch greased loaf pan. Combine catsup, brown sugar, mustard, and horseradish and spoon over top of loaf. Bake at 325° for 1 hour. Yield: 6 servings.

*From the Apple Orchard*

# Microwave Lasagna

1½ pounds ground beef
1 (15-ounce) can tomato
  sauce
1 (6-ounce) can tomato paste
½ cup chopped onion
1 teaspoon salt (or
  substitute and garlic)
½ teaspoon pepper
2 teaspoon Italian spice

¾ - 1 pound ricotta cheese
  (to taste)
3 eggs
¾ cup Parmesan cheese
6 lasagna noodles, prepared
  per package instructions
8 ounces shredded mozza-
  rella cheese

Combine beef, sauce, paste, onion, salt, pepper, and spices in 2-quart microwave safe casserole. Microwave in HIGH for 10-12 minutes, turning and stirring twice. Drain excess grease when finished. Set aside.

Blend ricotta and eggs. Add Parmesan cheese. Mix well. In a 12x8-inch baking dish, place 3 prepared noodles on bottom. Layer ⅓ of meat mixture. Top with ½ of cheese mixture. Sprinkle with ⅓ of mozzarella cheese. Repeat 1 time. Sprinkle remaining meat mixture on top. Add rest of mozzarella. Bake on HIGH for 15-18 minutes. Let stand 5-10 minutes before serving. Serves 6.

*Delicious Reading*

# Mexican Lasagne

This is really good. May be fixed and set in refrigerator until close to baking time. If cold, suggest baking longer than 20 minutes.

1½ pounds ground chuck
1 medium onion, chopped
1 (1-pound, #303) can
  tomatoes, with juice
1 (10-ounce) can enchilada
  sauce
1 (1¼-ounce) can sliced
  ripe olives, drained
1 teaspoon salt
¼ teaspoon each garlic
  powder and pepper
¼ cup salad oil

5-8 corn tortillas
1 cup small curd cottage
  cheese
1 egg
½ pound Jack cheese,
  thinly sliced
½ cup shredded cheddar
  cheese
½ cup finely crushed,
  packed tortilla or corn
  chips

Brown ground chuck and onion in a large fry pan. Blend in tomatoes, enchilada sauce, ripe olives, salt, garlic powder, and pepper. Bring to a boil, then reduce heat and simmer, uncovered 20 minutes.

Meanwhile, sauté tortillas in hot salad oil a few seconds on each side until softened. Drain tortillas on paper towels, then cut in half. Beat cottage cheese with egg.

Spread ⅓ of meat sauce in greased, shallow 3-quart casserole or 9x13-inch pan. Top with half of Jack cheese and half cottage cheese mixture, then half of tortilla halves, smoothing each in even layer. Repeat layering, placing final ⅓ of meat sauce across top. Sprinkle cheddar cheese and crushed chips over meat sauce. Bake, uncovered, in 350° oven 20 minutes. Cut into squares to serve. Best with green salad. Serves 6-8.

*A Collection of Recipes from the Best Cooks*
*in the Midwest*

 Missouri borders eight states: Arkansas, Oklahoma, Kansas, Nebraska, Iowa, Illinois, Kentucky, and Tennessee.

# Fiesta Enchiladas

1½ pounds lean ground
  beef
1 (16-ounce) can tomato
  sauce
2 packages enchilada
  seasoning mix
2½ cups water
1 pinch sugar
1 tablespoon dried minced
  onion
⅛ teaspoon garlic powder

12 corn tortillas
2 cups grated sharp cheddar
  cheese (8 ounces)
1 (8-ounce) carton sour
  cream
3 ripe avocados, cut into
  slivers
3 ripe tomatoes, minced and
  drained
Toothpicks

Brown beef in skillet and drain well. While beef is browning, combine tomato sauce, seasoning mix, water, sugar, onion, and garlic powder in saucepan. Bring to a boil, reduce heat, and simmer 8-10 minutes.

Soften corn tortillas. Put in steamer or in colander over simmering water until soft enough to roll—only takes a minute or two. Do not let water touch tortillas. Combine browned and drained ground beef, ¾ cup of grated cheese, and 2 cups sauce in mixing bowl. Stir until well mixed. Spoon meat mixture into tortillas; roll up and secure with a toothpick or place seam-side-down in baking dish. Pour rest of sauce evenly over rolled tortillas. Sprinkle with remaining cheese.

Bake at 350° 15 minutes. Remove from oven and spread 1 cup sour cream (room temperature) over enchiladas. Sprinkle avocado slivers and minced tomatoes over entire top. Serve.

Preparation time 20 minutes; cooking time 15 minutes. Makes 12.

*Note:* Enchiladas can be made ahead and refrigerated or frozen. Let come to room temperature before baking. To prepare avocados and minced tomatoes in advance—sprinkle avocados with lemon juice and cover tightly; salt and pepper minced tomatoes and wrap in paper towel. Refrigerate until ready to use.

*Rush Hour Superchef!*

# Swedish Cabbage Casserole

1 pound lean ground beef or
1 pound ground turkey
½ cup chopped onion
1 (16-ounce) can tomatoes
½ cup instant rice
1 (8-ounce) can tomato
sauce

½ cup cubed cheese (American or Monterey Jack)
1 tablespoon Worcestershire sauce
½ teaspoon salt (optional)
¼ teaspoon garlic powder
3 cups shredded cabbage

Brown beef or turkey and onion until onion is tender; drain. Add tomatoes and rice, stirring to blend tomatoes. Blend thoroughly. Bring to a boil. Cover and turn off heat. Let stand for 10 minutes.

Stir in next 5 ingredients and heat till cheese is melted. Arrange cabbage in the bottom of an 11x7x2-inch pan. Spread meat mixture over cabbage. Cover. Bake at 350° for 30 minutes. Makes 6 servings, 240 calories per serving.

*Blue Ridge Christian Church Cookbook*

# Margaret Kohler's Goulash

2 pounds ground beef
½ package Williams Chili
  Seasoning
Salt to taste
1 large can tomatoes

2 large potatoes, diced
3 large carrots, diced
1 large onion, diced
3 stalks celery, diced

Brown beef in small amount of oil, then add chili seasoning, salt, and tomatoes. Mix other vegetables and cook until almost tender in a small amount of water. Add to meat and cook in oven at 350° until tender (about 1½ hours). Serve with corn bread.

Margaret made this up in a large turkey roaster and took it to the family reunions in the early 1940s. The men thought it was great and Margaret always took home an empty pan.

*Kohler Family Kookbook*

# Plenty More in the Kitchen

4 ounces egg noodles
1 medium onion, chopped
1 clove garlic, minced

1 tablespoon oil
1 pound ground beef

Cook noodles. Fry onions and garlic in oil. Brown meat. Add following ingredients:

1 (16-ounce) can corn
1 teaspoon brown sugar
1 teaspoon chili powder
¼ teaspoon thyme
¼ cup shredded cheddar
  cheese

1 (4-ounce) can mushrooms
1 teaspoon salt
Dash of pepper
1 teaspoon Worcestershire
  sauce
1 small can tomato sauce

Simmer for about 15 minutes. Mix in noodles and put in casserole dish. Top with more cheddar cheese. Bake at 350° for 35-45 minutes.

*Covered Bridge Neighbors Cookbook*

# Hungry Jack Beef Casserole

1 pound ground beef
¼ cup onion, chopped
¾ cup barbecue sauce
1 tablespoon brown sugar
1 (16-ounce) can pork and
  beans

1 (10-ounce) package flaky
  biscuits
¾ cup cheddar cheese,
  shredded

Heat oven to 375°. In skillet, brown ground beef and onion; drain. Stir in barbecue sauce, brown sugar, and beans; heat until bubbly. Pour into 2-quart casserole.

Separate dough into 10 biscuits; cut each biscuit in half crosswise. Place biscuits, cut-side-down, in spoke fashion around edge of casserole. Sprinkle cheese over biscuits. Bake at 375° for 22-27 minutes or until golden brown.

***Delicious Reading***

# Silver Dollar City's Meatball Sandwiches

2 slightly beaten eggs
3 tablespoons milk
½ cup fine, dry bread
  crumbs
¾ teaspoon salt and pepper
1 pound ground beef
½ pound bulk Italian pork
  sausage
½ cup chopped onion
½ cup chopped green pepper

1 (8-ounce) can tomato sauce
1 (6-ounce) can tomato paste
2 teaspoons sugar
1 teaspoon garlic salt
½ teaspoon dried oregano,
  crushed
¼ teaspoon dried parsley
  flakes, crushed
1 cup water
8 individual French rolls

Combine eggs, milk, crumbs, salt and pepper to taste. Add beef and mix well. Form into 24 (1½-inch) meatballs. Brown in hot skillet. Remove meatballs.

In same skillet, combine sausage, onion, and green pepper. Cook until sausage is browned. Drain fat. Stir in tomato sauce, tomato paste, sugar, garlic salt, oregano, parsley, and 1 cup water. Return meatballs to skillet. Cover and simmer for 15 minutes, stirring once or twice. Cut thin slice from tops of rolls and hollow out, leaving ¼-inch wall. Fill each roll with 3 meatballs and some sauce.

*Silver Dollar City's Recipes*

# Hamburger Boats

¾ pound ground chuck
¾ pound ground round
½ cup chopped onion
½ cup ketchup
1 egg

2 tablespoons seasoned
  bread crumbs
Salt and pepper to taste
3 French rolls (each 5½
  inches long)

Combine ground chuck, ground round, chopped onion, ketchup, egg, bread crumbs, salt, and pepper. Mix until ingredients are thoroughly blended.

Cut rolls in half. Scrape soft bread from centers of each half to make cavity. Spread cavity with either ketchup or mustard or combination of the two. Divide meat mixture into 6 equal parts and mound over cavities of each roll. Bake in 350° oven for 30 minutes uncovered. Easy. Do ahead. Serves 4-5.

*Cooking in Clover*

# Bavarian Super Sandwich

1 pound bulk pork sausage
2 cups chopped onions
2 cups package biscuit mix

2 tablespoons poppy seed
¾ cup milk
1 egg

Fry sausage until done. Remove sausage and reserve 2 tablespoons fat. Cook onions in reserved fat until tender but not brown.

Combine biscuit mix, poppy seed, milk, and egg. Beat vigorously for 30 seconds. Spread batter in greased 9-inch square pan. Top with sausage; then onions. Bake at 400° for 15 minutes.

**TOPPING:**

1 cup sour cream
1 egg, beaten

¾ teaspoon salt
¼ teaspoon pepper

Mix ingredients and spoon over bread. Bake 10 minutes longer. Dash with paprika. Cut in 9 squares and serve hot.

*Covered Bridge Neighbors Cookbook*

# Crispy Corn Dogs

You will be a hit with your family when you make home-made corn dogs. Use up the remaining batter by dipping onion rings and frying them last—a great combination.

1 cup all-purpose flour
¾ cup yellow cornmeal
2 tablespoons sugar
1 tablespoon dry mustard
2 teaspoons baking powder
1 teaspoon salt
1 cup milk

1 egg, sightly beaten
2 tablespoons shortening, melted
12 hot dogs
12 skewers
Vegetable oil for deep-fat frying

Combine flour, cornmeal, sugar, mustard, baking powder, and salt. Add milk, egg, and shortening. Mix until smooth. Pour mixture into a tall glass. Put hot dogs on skewers and dip, one at a time, in cornmeal batter. Fry until golden brown in vegetable oil heated to 375°. Drain on paper towels. Yield: 12 corn dogs.

*Variation:* To make bite-size corn dogs: Cut each hot dog into 10 pieces. Dip hot dog sections into batter, covering completely. (Wooden picks work well for dipping.) Drop in hot oil and cook until golden, turning once; drain on paper towels. Insert party picks and serve immediately. Serve with mustard or catsup if desired.

***From the Ozarks' Oven...***

# Barbeque Rub

2 cups sugar
¼ cup paprika
2 teaspoons chili powder
½ teaspoon cayenne pepper

½ cup salt
2 teaspoons black pepper
1 teaspoon garlic powder

Combine all ingredients and use as a rub for any barbeque meat. Yields about 3 cups.

***The Passion of Barbeque***

# Barbecued Pork Burgers

2 pounds ground pork
¼ cup buttermilk
2 teaspoons seasoned salt
1 teaspoon black pepper
¼ teaspoon garlic powder
¼ teaspoon ground oregano
¼ cup minced onion

Combine all ingredients. Mix thoroughly and form into ¼-pound patties.

Sear patties on the grill, then reduce flame and cook over direct heat for about 10 minutes on each side. Serves 4-6.

*Kansas City BBQ*

# Barbequed Pork Loin
# Baby Back Ribs

1 slab pork loin baby back ribs

MARINADE:
½ cup chicken stock
½ cup soy sauce
¼ cup oil
¼ cup vinegar
6 tablespoons sugar
2 cloves garlic, minced

Combine marinade ingredients and marinate ribs in refrigerator for 2 hours to overnight.

Remove ribs from marinade and sprinkle with dry barbeque seasoning. Cook over medium coals (225°) until internal temperature registers 160° on a meat thermometer. Baste with marinade or sprinkle lightly with dry seasoning every 30 minutes during cooking process. Serves 2-3.

*The Passion of Barbeque*

Called "The City of Fountains," beautiful fountains are everywhere in Kansas City! Rome, Italy, is the only city in the world with more fountains than Kansas City.

# Clinton County Pork Chops with Sour Cream Sauce

6 loin pork chops
½ cup water
2 tablespoons brown sugar
2 tablespoons finely
chopped onion
2 tablespoons ketchup
1 garlic clove, minced

1 beef bouillon cube or 1
teaspoon instant beef
bouillon
2 tablespoons flour
¼ cup water
½ cup sour cream

In a large skillet, brown pork chops. Add ½ cup water, brown sugar, onion, ketchup, garlic, and bouillon cube. Cover and simmer 30-40 minutes until tender. Remove chops to serving platter. Keep warm. In a small bowl, combine flour with ¼ cup water. Slowly add to cooking liquid, stirring constantly. Stir in sour cream; heat thoroughly. Do not boil. Serve sauce over chops. Yields 6 servings.

***Remembering the Past—Planning for the Future***

# Pork Medallions with Mustard Cream Sauce

24 (1-inch) medallions from
  2 pork tenderloins
Garlic powder
Onion powder
Salt and pepper
1 cup flour
3 tablespoons butter
⅓ cup wine vinegar

8 crushed peppercorns
2 cups heavy cream, room
  temperature
½ cup Dijon mustard
2 tablespoons butter
½ teaspoon salt
Chopped fresh parsley

Flatten pork medallions between 2 pieces of waxed paper to between ¼ - ½-inch thickness. Combine garlic powder, onion powder, salt and pepper to taste, and flour. Dredge the pork medallions in seasoned flour.

In a large skillet melt 3 tablespoons butter over medium-high heat. Sauté pork medallions for 2 minutes on each side. Transfer to 12x8x2-inch baking dish, and keep warm in 150° oven. Add to the skillet wine vinegar and crushed peppercorns, and boil the mixture, stirring in brown bits that cling to pan, until it is reduced by two-thirds.

Add heavy cream and simmer the mixture 5 minutes or until it thickens some. Remove pan from heat and swirl in Dijon mustard and 2 tablespoons butter. Season sauce with salt to taste and pour over pork medallions. Bake uncovered in 250° oven for 2 hours, basting meat with sauce several times. Sprinkle chopped fresh parsley over top and serve. Will hold in oven covered at 150° for 1 hour. Serves 6-8.

*Cooking in Clover*

 Known as "Black Jack," General John J. Pershing commanded American troops in the Spanish-American War, in the Phillipines, and in World War I. His home is in Laclede.

# Mushroom Stuffed Pork Chops

2 (1¼-inch) pork loin rib
chops
1 (2-ounce) can chopped
mushrooms, drained
1 tablespoon (snipped
parsley)
1 tablespoon finely chopped
onion
¼ teaspoon salt
Dash of pepper

1 slice Swiss cheese,
torn up
1 slightly beaten egg
¼ cup fine dry bread
crumbs
1 tablespoon cooking oil
⅓ cup water
¼ cup dry white wine
1 tablespoon cornstarch
1 tablespoon cold water

Trim excess fat from chops; sprinkle meat with little salt and
pepper. Cut pocket in fat side of each chop. Combine mushrooms, parsley, onion, salt and pepper. Place cheese in pockets of chops; stuff with mushroom mixture. Reserve any leftover mushroom mix for the sauce. Dip chops in beaten egg,
then in bread crumbs.

In an 8-inch skillet, slowly brown chops in hot oil. Add the
⅓ cup water and the wine. Cover and simmer about 1 hour
or until meat is tender. Place meat on serving platter and
keep warm.

For sauce, blend cornstarch and 1 tablespoon cold water.
Stir into wine mixture in skillet. Cook and stir until thickened and bubbly. Stir in any reserved mushroom mix; beat
through. Serve over meat. For more than 2 servings, double
the recipe.

*Delicious Reading*

# Stuffed Pork Tenderloin

¼ pound ground pork
¼ cup chopped onion
3 slices rye bread, crumbled
¼ teaspoon nutmeg
1 (15½-ounce) can cream
of mushroom soup
1 egg, beaten

2 (1½-pound) pork
tenderloins
6 strips bacon
½ cup beef broth
Fresh parsley and spiced
apple rings for garnish

Preheat oven to 450°. Brown ground pork with onion in a small skillet; drain. Stir in bread, nutmeg, half the soup, and egg. Split each tenderloin lengthwise almost through to ends and bottom, forming a pocket.

Fill cavities with stuffing mixture. With split sides together, tie or skewer tenderloins; arrange bacon strips on top of meat. Place in a lightly greased 9x13-inch baking dish. Bake 10-15 minutes to cook bacon. Reduce oven to 350°. Dilute the remaining soup with broth; spoon over tenderloins. Bake 40-45 minutes per pound or to 170° on a meat thermometer. Garnish and serve hot. Serves 4-6.

*Sassafras!*

# Mabel's Ham Loaf

1 pound ground ham
1 pound ground pork
½ cup milk
1 egg

½ cup fresh white bread,
rolled between hands
until it crumbles
½ cup brown sugar
½ teaspoon cloves

Grind ham and pork together. Mix in milk, egg, and bread. Make into a loaf. Mix brown sugar and cloves. Pat on top of loaf. Bake in slow oven at 275° for 1 hour.

*USO's Salute to the Troops Cookbook*

# Broccoli and Ham Quiche

1 (10-inch) unbaked pie crust

1 (10-ounce) package frozen chopped broccoli, cooked and well drained

2 cups chopped ham

⅓ cup minced onion

½ cup shredded Swiss cheese

½ cup shredded cheddar cheese

4 eggs, slightly beaten

2 cups whipping cream

¾ teaspoon salt

¼ teaspoon sugar

Preheat oven to 425°. Sprinkle broccoli and ham, onion, and cheeses in pie crust. Blend eggs and cream. Add salt and sugar. Pour over mixture in crust. Bake 15 minutes at 425°. Reduce heat to 300° for 35-40 minutes. Let stand for 10 minutes before serving. Serves 6.

*Luncheon Favorites*

# Souvlakia

## (Shish-ke-bob)

Leg of lamb (or beef, or pork)

1 cup olive oil

⅓ cup lemon juice

½ cup wine

1 or 2 cloves garlic, chopped

Salt, pepper, and oregano to taste

1 or 2 bay leaves

1 or 2 tomatoes, quartered

1 large onion, cut into chunks

1 large green pepper, cut into chunks

Mushrooms

Cut meat into 1-inch cubes. Place meat in a container with a lid. Cover meat with marinade of olive oil, lemon juice, wine, and garlic. Sprinkle with salt, pepper, and oregano. Add bay leaves. Place vegetables on top of meat. Weigh down with heavy plate. Cover and refrigerate 24-48 hours.

Skewer meat and vegetables. Place on broiler pan and bake at 350 for 25-30 minutes or (broil) to desired doneness. Or cooked over glowing charcoal for approximately 20-30 minutes, while basting with marinade. Yield: 8 servings.

*The Art of Hellenic Cuisine*

# Sausage with Vegetables and Fettuccine

1 (12-ounce) roll sausage
1 garlic clove, minced
1 medium onion, chopped
1 green pepper, chopped
2 cups fresh mushrooms, sliced
1 medium zucchini, sliced, (about 3 cups)

1 (14-ounce) can whole tomatoes, coarsely chopped
1 teaspoon basil, dried
1 teaspoon thyme, dried
½ teaspoon oregano, dried
¼ teaspoon black pepper, ground
12 ounces fettuccine
¼ cup Parmesan cheese

In large nonstick skillet, brown crumbled sausage. Remove from skillet and drain. Remove all but 1 tablespoon of fat from skillet. Add garlic, onion, green pepper, mushrooms and zucchini. Sauté 5 minutes. Add tomatoes, with liquid, along with basil, thyme, oregano, pepper and sausage. Stir thoroughly.

Cover and simmer 10 minutes. Cook fettuccine in 4 quarts water, 6-8 minutes. Cook, uncovered, 6-8 minutes, or just until tender, stirring occasionally.

Drain; rinse with warm water. Toss pasta and sausage with vegetable mixture gently. Sprinkle with Parmesan cheese. Serves 6.

*The Never Ending Season*

# Deer Cordon Bleu

1½ - 2 pounds deer loin or
round (¼-inch thick)
½ pound ham (thin sliced)
½ pound shredded cheese
(Swiss, American, cheddar)
1 cup flour

¾ cup milk
1 egg
1 teaspoon salt
1 teaspoon pepper
Cracker crumbs
Vegetable oil for frying

Pound deer with meat mallet until about ⅛-inch thick. Cut tenderized meat into 5- or 6-inch squares. Cut ham slices to fit inside edges of deer meat. Put about 2 tablespoons cheese on ham. Roll deer (keeping ham and cheese inside). Fold in edges of deer while rolling to seal cheese.

Make a batter by mixing flour, milk, egg, salt and pepper. Beat until smooth. Dip rolls in batter. Coat with crumbs. Deep fry at 365°-370° until golden brown. Drain on a rack.

*The Sportsman's Dish*

# Quick and Spicy Deer Sausage

5 pounds deer burger (ground
fine with suet)
5 tablespoons Morton's
Tender Quick
2 tablespoons coarse black
pepper
2 tablespoons mustard seed
1 tablespoon brown sugar

1 tablespoon garlic powder
1 tablespoon cayenne
1 tablespoon ground red
pepper
1 tablespoon liquid smoke
1 cup dry quick oats
3 cups warm water

Mix deer burger, spices, oats, and 2 cups water thoroughly until combined. Cover, let stand 1 hour at room temperature. Mix in third cup of water, let stand 30 minutes. Stuff into casings or roll into 2x10-inch rolls and wrap in aluminum foil. Punch small holes in casings or foil to allow drainage during cooking.

Place on rack in foil-lined pan. Bake 70 minutes at 350°, turning once after 35 minutes. After cooling slightly, wrap in paper towels to absorb excess liquid. Cool before slicing. Wrap excess rolls in foil. Place in plastic bags and freeze.

*The Sportsman's Dish*

# Mustard Mousse

½ cup sugar
2 tablespoons dry mustard
1 tablespoon unflavored
  gelatin
¾ teaspoon ground turmeric
1 teaspoon celery salt
4 large eggs, room
  temperature

1 cup water
½ cup white wine vinegar
  or cider vinegar
1 cup heavy cream, whipped
  until it holds a soft shape;
  do not overbeat

In top of a double boiler, combine dry ingredients. Stir to break up mustard lumps. Beat in eggs with wire whisk until thoroughly combined, then add water and vinegar. Place pan over boiling water on low heat; whisk constantly until gelatin dissolves and mixture thickens slightly. Be careful it does not curdle.

Transfer mixture to a bowl and chill until it mounds slightly when dropped from spoon. (If it gets too firm, liquefy over warm water).

Fold cream into mustard mixture and pour into greased 5- to 6-cup ring mold. Chill several hours until set. Makes 16 servings.

*Note:* For a buffet, surround mousse with thinly sliced baked ham or smoked turkey. Tuck fresh flowers, parsley, and lemon roses in appropriate places to complete the picture.

**Beyond Parsley**

# The Best of the Best Bearnaise Sauce

Prepare ahead. Will keep a week or two in refrigerator. Also freezes well. If frozen, do not cook to thicken until ready to use.

**PART I:**

2 tablespoons chicken broth
³⁄₄ teaspoon bottled lemon
  juice or 1 tablespoon
  fresh lemon juice

3 tablespoons chopped green
  onions (tops included)
2 tablespoons tarragon
  vinegar

**PART II:**

3 egg yolks
½ cup butter (1 stick),
  softened
2 sprays celery leaves
2 sprigs parsley

½ teaspoon salt
⅛ teaspoon coarsely ground
  black pepper
¼ teaspoon Tabasco

Bring all ingredients in Part I to a boil. Place all ingredients in Part II in blender and run at medium speed. Slowly pour hot mixture (Part I) into blender while running. Mix well. Cook over hot water until sauce thickens—about 3-4 minutes, stirring constantly. Makes 1 cup.

*It's Christmas!*

# Onion Marmalade

½ cup butter
6 medium red onions (about
  2½ pounds), sliced
1 bunch scallions, white
  parts only

3 tablespoons sugar
¼ cup red wine vinegar or
  balsamic vinegar
1 cup dry red wine

In a medium skillet, melt butter. Add onions and scallions; cook over medium high heat, stirring, 15 minutes or until tender. Add sugar and cook 1 minute, stirring constantly. Add remaining ingredients and continue cooking, stirring until liquid is absorbed, about 15 minutes. Easy. Can do ahead—may freeze. Yields 2½ cups.

    Good with roasted meat or poultry.

*Cooking in Clover II*

# Poultry

*The George Washington Carver statue at Diamond,
where Carver spent his boyhood.*

# Roast Chicken

1 chicken, cut into quarters
1 teaspoon salt
¼ teaspoon pepper
2 tablespoons oregano

4 tablespoons butter or
 margarine
½ cup lemon juice
1 cup tomatoes, chopped

After cutting chicken into quarters, sprinkle with salt, pepper, and oregano on all sides. Melt butter in a baking pan. Place chicken in pan. Pour lemon juice all over. Arrange chopped tomatoes on top. Bake in 350° oven until golden brown on both sides. If so desired, potatoes can be placed around chicken and cooked along with chicken.

*The Art of Hellenic Cuisine*

# My Old-Fashioned Dressing

1 medium onion, diced
1 cup celery, diced (include
 some tops)
1 large apple, cored and
 chopped
Liver from chicken or
 turkey, cooked
10 cups (2 or 3 day-old)
 bread, cubed or broken
½ pound pork sausage,
 cooked

1 (10-ounce) can cream of
 celery soup
2 eggs, beaten
½ cup raisins
Dash of garlic powder
Salt and pepper to taste
⅓ cup margarine, melted
1-2 teaspoons rubbed sage
1 cup milk or broth

Dice or chop onion, celery, apple and cooked chicken liver. Break or cube bread. Mix all ingredients in large bowl. (I use a large Tupperware salad bowl. If I do not have pork sausage, or for a change, we like oysters in place of the sausage.) More moisture may be needed; the secret of good dressing is to have it very moist, but not soupy. Stuff turkey or chicken, if that's the way you like it. More often than not, I bake it in a greased 9x13-inch pan at 350° for 35-40 minutes; either way, my son-in-law thinks it is great.

*Apples, Apples, Apples*

# Baked Chicken Breasts

4 large chicken breasts
4 tablespoons butter
¼ cup flour
¾ cup milk
¾ cup chicken broth
⅓ cup dry white wine
¼ cup chopped onion
1 (7½-ounce) can crab
 meat, drained

1 (3-ounce) can chopped
 mushrooms, drained
½ cup cracker crumbs (10)
2 tablespoons parsley
½ teaspoon salt
Pepper
1 cup (4 ounces) shredded
 Swiss cheese
1/2 teaspoon paprika

Bone and skin chicken breasts, pound out to ⅛-inch thick. In saucepan, melt 3 tablespoons butter; blend in flour. Add milk, chicken broth and wine all at once. Cook, stirring, till thick and bubbly. Set aside.

In skillet cook onion in remaining butter till tender, but not brown. Stir in crab, mushrooms, crumbs, parsley, salt and pepper. Mix in 2 tablespoons of the first mixture from saucepan. Top each breast with ¼ cup of this crab mixture. Fold sides in. Roll up. Place seam-side-down in 12x7x2-inch baking dish. Pour sauce from pan over. Bake covered for 1 hour at 350°. Uncover, sprinkle with cheese and paprika. Bake 2 or 3 minutes longer. Serves 8.

*Treasured Recipes Book I*

# Chicken Camille

A real palate pleaser—decidedly different!

4 chicken breasts
Salt and pepper (approx-
    imately ⅛ teaspoon
    per chicken breast)
1 clove garlic, crushed

4 tablespoons butter or
    margarine
2 (8-ounce) cartons sour
    cream
4 ounces crumbled
    Roquefort cheese

Sprinkle each chicken breast lightly with salt and pepper. Rub skillet with crushed garlic clove and discard. Melt 4 tablespoons butter over moderately high heat and place chicken breasts in skillet. Brown on both sides in melted butter and remove to baking dish when browned, about 10-12 minutes.

While chicken is browning, preheat oven to 350°. Mix sour cream and Roquefort together. Pour over chicken breasts. Cover baking dish and bake 30 minutes. *Do not overcook* or sour cream will separate. Place chicken breasts on individual plates, spooning ample amount of sauce over each. Sprinkle with paprika and garnish with parsley. Pass remaining sauce at table. Preparation time: 15 minutes. Cooking time: 30 minutes. Serves 4.

*Rush Hour Superchef!*

# Deb's Lip-Lickin' Chicken

4 chicken breasts
Seasoned salt to taste
Lemon pepper to taste

Minced garlic to taste
½ cup soy sauce
½ cup Worcestershire sauce

Wash chicken breasts and pat dry. Rub with spices and place on the grill, meat-side-down, searing for 5 minutes. Flip to bone-side-down and sear for 5 more minutes. Lower firebox to ⅔ down position and, with heat deflector in place, cook for 1 hour and 15 minutes.

Put soy sauce and Worcestershire in a spray bottle and use to baste meat frequently (every 20 minutes). Serves 4-6.

*Kansas City BBQ*

# Herbed Parmesan Chicken

3 pounds chicken breasts,
skinned and boned
¼ teaspoon garlic powder
¼ teaspoon paprika
⅛ teaspoon dried thyme
¼ cup freshly grated
Parmesan cheese

1 tablespoon minced
fresh parsley
⅓ cup fine bread crumbs
1 tablespoon vegetable oil
2 tablespoons margarine
⅓ cup Marsala wine

Cut chicken breasts into pieces 1½ to 2-inches wide. Combine next 6 ingredients in a paper bag. Coat chicken with mixture a few pieces at a time by shaking the bag. Place chicken in a baking dish and press any remaining seasonings into chicken. Sprinkle chicken with oil and melted margarine. Bake, uncovered, at 350° for 30 minutes. Pour wine over chicken and cover with foil. Reduce heat to 325°; bake 15 additional minutes. Remove foil, raise heat to 350° and bake 10 minutes. Serves 6-8.

This is a lowfat recipe that can be prepared ahead, frozen, and reheated in the microwave.

*Gateways*

# Herb Cheese Chicken Florentine

4 chicken breast halves,
boned and skinned
1 bunch fresh spinach
8 ounces garlic herb cream
cheese

½ cup buttermilk dressing
1 cup bread crumbs
¼ cup Parmesan cheese

Spray 11x13-inch baking pan with non-stick vegetable oil. Place chicken breast between two sheets of waxed paper and pound to flatten.

Wash spinach and remove stems. Steam in microwave for 2 minutes. Drain well. Cover each chicken breast with drained spinach leaves. Portion 2 ounces herb cheese on spinach and roll up. Secure with toothpick if necessary. Dip into buttermilk dressing and roll in bread crumbs mixed with Parmesan cheese. Bake in 350° oven 45 minutes. Serves 4.

*The Never Ending Season*

# Chicken Dijonnaise Strudel

Excellent entrée for an elegant dinner!

**4 chicken breasts (1¾
pounds) skinned and
boned**
**½ cup butter**
**2 cups celery chopped**
**2 large onions, chopped**
**¼ cup Chablis Blanc**
**½ cup parsley**

**½ cup whipping cream**
**8 ounces Dijon mustard**
**1 pound Swiss cheese, grated**
**1 pound sweet butter**
**1 package phyllo dough**
**3 cups seasoned bread
crumbs**

Skin and slice boned breasts into narrow stirps. Sauté in heavy bottomed skillet over medium heat in salted butter for 2 minutes or just until meat is no longer pink on the inside. Lift meat out with a spatula and reserve in a 4-quart bowl.

Sauté the celery and onions in the butter remaining in the skillet until vegetables are tender crisp. Add wine and reduce sauce. Add parsley, then add vegetable mixture to chicken. Add cream to empty skillet with mustard. As the cream reduces, add grated cheese. Stir and boil until quite thick, reducing cream by half. Stir into chicken and vegetable mixture; refrigerate.

Melt unsalted butter over low heat. Unwrap phyllo dough leaves, 5 at a time; keep remaining phyllo dough covered. Place 5 sheets on waxed paper. Fold in half and open 1 leaf at a time, brushing the unfolded sheets with butter and sprinkling with crumbs. When center is reached, turn dough over and start at the back toward the center. Brush the final open surface with butter and sprinkle with crumbs. Arrange ⅓ of the filling lengthwise along edge of phyllo.

Roll into a long narrow tube, pressing the filling into place (placing waxed paper underneath helps). Pinch ends in and slide onto greased cookie sheet. Brush with more butter and sprinkle with crumbs on top. Repeat with remaining 2 strudels. Refrigerate finished strudels until all are complete.

Bake in 350° oven until tops are browned and crisp, about 25-30 minutes. Serve warm. Makes 3 strudels, each yield-

CONTINUED

ing 12 (1-inch) thick slices. Serve with green beans almondine, salad, and a good white wine. Serves 12.

*Note:* Strudel can be frozen. Brush with butter. Do not add crumbs until ready to bake.

**With Hands & Heart Cookbook**

# Chicken Imperial

6 large boned chicken breasts, halved
1 cup dry sherry
1 cup seasoned dry bread crumbs
1 cup grated Parmesan cheese
1 cup chopped or slivered almonds

¼ cup finely chopped parsley
1 teaspoon garlic powder
1 teaspoon salt
½ teaspoon pepper
¾ cup melted butter or margarine

Marinate chicken in dry sherry, 2-3 hours. Combine bread crumbs, Parmesan cheese, ¾ cup almonds, parsley, garlic powder, salt and pepper. Dip chicken pieces in butter and roll in bread crumb mixture. Arrange in 13x9-inch baking pan and sprinkle with remaining almonds. Bake uncovered in preheated 350° oven for one hour.

Easy. Do ahead. Serves 6.

**Cooking in Clover**

# Chicken Sicilian

4 chicken breasts, boned and
   skinned
¼ cup olive oil
2 tablespoons minced garlic
2 tablespoons chopped
   shallots
1 cup diced tomatoes
1 cup whole black olives
2 cups julienned red bell
   pepper

2 cups julienned green bell
   pepper
2 tablespoons chopped fresh
   thyme
2 tablespoons chopped fresh
   basil
¼ cup chicken broth
1 pound linguini, cooked

Grill or broil chicken breasts. While chicken is cooking, heat oil in a large sauté pan. Add garlic and shallots, and cook until soft. Add diced tomatoes, black olives, julienned peppers, and herbs, and sauté until hot but still crisp. Pour vegetables into a bowl and set aside until ready to serve. In the same pan, pour in chicken broth and add cooked linguini. Heat thoroughly.

Divide linguini equally among 4 plates. Place a chicken breast on top of pasta, then divide vegetables equally over each breast. Serves 4.

Round out this creation with a salad or side dish.

*Kansas City Cuisine (Coyote Grill)*

# Chicken and Asparagus Casserole

6 whole chicken breasts
(12 halves)
1 medium onion, chopped
½ cup butter
1 (8-ounce) can mushrooms,
drained
1 (10½-ounce) can cream
of chicken soup
1 (5⅓-ounce) can
evaporated milk
1/2 pound sharp cheddar
cheese, grated

¼ teaspoon Tabasco
2 teaspoons soy sauce
1 teaspoon salt
½ teaspoon pepper
1 teaspoon Accent
2 tablespoons pimento,
chopped
2 (15-ounce) cans green tip
long asparagus
½ cup slivered almonds

Cook chicken breasts until tender either in water, steamed, or microwave. Cool. Debone and tear into bite-size pieces. Set aside.

Sauté onion in butter and add remaining ingredients, except asparagus and almonds. Simmer sauce until cheese melts and sauce is smooth. Grease a 15x9x2-inch casserole and layer chicken, then asparagus, sauce, and repeat layers, ending with sauce. Top with almonds. Bake in 350° oven until heated through and bubbly, about 25-30 minutes. Serves 12. Also freezes well. Wonderful company dish.

*Tasty Palette*

# Ozark Chicken Casserole

2 cups cooked diced chicken
1 cup cooked rice
1 tablespoon lemon juice
1 cup chopped celery
1 medium onion, chopped
½ cup mayonnaise

3 hard-boiled eggs, chopped
1 can cream of chicken soup
Salt and pepper to taste
½ stick butter, melted
2 cups Pepperidge Farm
Herb-Seasoned Stuffing
Mix

Combine chicken, rice, juice, celery, onion, mayonnaise, eggs, soup, and seasoning thoroughly and place in greased casserole. Mix butter and stuffing and sprinkle over top. Bake at 350° for about 30 minutes.

*Talk About Good*

# Tandoori Chicken

1 medium onion, chopped
5 tablespoons vegetable oil
2 garlic cloves
¼ cup yogurt
2 tablespoons lemon juice
1 tablespoon freshly minced
  ginger or 1 teaspoon ginger
  powder
1½ teaspoons salt

2 teaspoons ground
  coriander
1 teaspoon sugar
½ teaspoon turmeric
½ teaspoon ground cumin
¼ teaspoon cayenne pepper
5 pounds chicken pieces
2 medium onions, sliced

Place chopped onion in blender or food processor with 3 tablespoons oil and remaining ingredients, except oil, chicken and onion slices; process on high speed until puréed. Pour marinade into a 9x13-inch baking dish or large plastic bag. Add chicken and coat well. Refrigerate for at least 4 hours or overnight.

Preheat broiler, remove chicken from marinade; broil skin-side-down 7-9 inches from heat source for 15-20 minutes. Turn over and broil another 10-15 minutes, basting with marinade. Meanwhile in a saucepan, heat remaining 2 tablespoons oil, and cook the sliced onions until tender, about 15 minutes. To serve, place chicken on platter and top with onions. Must do ahead. Serves 8.

*Cooking in Clover II*

# Wild Rice Chicken Supreme

1 (6-ounce) package Uncle
  Ben's Long Grain and Wild
  Rice
¼ cup butter or margarine
⅓ cup chopped onion
⅓ cup flour
1 teaspoon salt
Dash of black pepper

1 cup half-and-half
1 cup chicken broth
2 cups cubed, cooked
  chicken
⅓ cup diced pimento
⅓ cup chopped parsley
¼ cup chopped, slivered
  almonds

Cook contents of rice and seasonings packets according to package directions. While rice is cooking, melt butter in a large pan. Add onion and cook over low heat until tender. Stir in flour, salt and pepper. Gradually stir in half-and-half and chicken broth. Cook, stirring constantly, until thickened. Stir in chicken, pimento, parsley, almonds, and cooked rice. Pour into greased 2-quart casserole. Bake, uncovered, at 400° for 30 minutes. Makes 6-8 servings.

*Delicious Reading*

# Cassoulet

1 pound white beans
4½ cups water
2 cans chicken broth
3 medium chopped onions
4 quartered carrots
1 spiked onion (stick 4
  whole cloves and 1 bay leaf
  into a whole onion)

1 teaspoon thyme
1 teaspoon marjoram
¼ cup celery leaves
½ pound bacon
1 cut-up chicken, skinned
4 pieces Polish sausage

Soak beans in 4½ cups water for 1½ hours. Add broth, chopped onions, 1 quartered carrot, spiked onion, thyme, marjoram, and celery leaves. Simmer for 1 hour.

Brown bacon. Drain. In bacon grease, slightly brown chicken. Add bacon, chicken, remaining carrots, and Polish sausage to bean mixture. Bake at 350° in a covered casserole dish for 1½ hours.

*Recipes Old and New*

# Chicken á la King in Toast Cups

1 (4-ounce) can mushrooms, drained
¼ cup chopped green pepper
¼ cup butter
¼ cup flour
1 teaspoon salt
⅛ teaspoon pepper
1 cup chicken broth
1 cup milk
1 cup diced cooked chicken
¼ cup chopped pimento

Sauté mushrooms and green pepper in butter. Blend in flour, salt, and pepper. Let bubble. Slowly stir in chicken broth and milk; bring to boiling over low heat, stirring constantly. Boil 1 minute. Add chicken and pimento; heat through. Serve in Toast Cups. Serves 6.

**TOAST CUPS:**
Cut crusts from day-old bread; brush lightly with melted butter. Press into muffin pan or custard cups. Toast in oven (350°) for 15-30 minutes.

*Talk About Good*

# Chicken Squares with Mushroom Sauce

3 cups diced chicken
1 cup cooked rice
2 cups soft bread crumbs
⅓ cup diced celery
¼ cup chopped pimento
4 eggs, beaten
2 teaspoons salt (or to taste)
½ teaspoon poultry seasoning
2 cups chicken broth

Combine first 5 ingredients. Beat together the last 4 ingredients. Add to first mixture. Pour into 8-inch square pan and bake at 350° for 1 hour. Top with Mushroom Sauce and serve.

**MUSHROOM SAUCE:**
1 (10½-ounce) can mushroom soup
⅔ (12-ounce) can milk
1 (3-ounce) can drained mushrooms

Heat. Good luncheon dish!

*Heavenly Delights*

# Huntington Chicken

2 tablespoons butter
3 tablespoons flour
1 cup cream
1 teaspoon salt
¼ teaspoon celery salt
⅛ teaspoon pepper
1 cup cold, cooked chicken
or fowl

½ cup cooked macaroni
½ cup sliced fresh
mushrooms
⅓ cup grated Parmesan
cheese
Buttered bread or cracker
crumbs

Melt butter; add flour and stir until well blended; then pour on gradually, while stirring constantly, one cupful of thin cream. Bring to the boiling point and season with salt, celery salt and pepper; then add cold, cooked chicken or fowl, cut in small strips or cubes, macaroni, cut in small pieces, sliced fresh mushrooms, and grated Parmesan cheese. Fill buttered ramekin-dishes with mixture, cover with buttered bread or cracker crumbs and bake brown. A good way to use remnants of cold fowl.

*Turn of the Century Cookbook*

# Chicken Marco Polo

This is a festive way to use up leftover chicken, turkey, or ham.

2 slices bacon
½ cup onion, diced
½ cup celery, sliced
1 (2-ounce) jar pimentos,
chopped
1 can water chestnuts,
drained and sliced
1 can mushroom soup

6-8 ounces sharp cheddar
cheese, cubed
½ cup almonds, slivered
1 pound fine spaghetti,
cooked
2-3 cups cubed chicken or
other meat

Sauté bacon (remove from pan). In bacon drippings, sauté onion and celery for 5 minutes. Add all other ingredients to cooked spaghetti. Toss lightly and carefully with 2 forks. Put in a buttered casserole. Bake 350° for 45 minutes. If soupy, serve on chow mein noodles.

*Treasured Recipes Book I*

# Plucky Enchiladas

A novel after-Thanksgiving recipe for leftover turkey!

2 (4-ounce) cans whole green
chilies
1 large garlic clove, minced
½ cup and 2 tablespoons
vegetable oil (Puritan oil
may be used)
1 (1-pound, 12-ounce) can
whole tomatoes
2 cups onions, chopped

1 teaspoon salt
½ teaspoon oregano
3 cups turkey or chicken,
cooked and shredded
2 cups sour cream
½ pound Cheddar cheese,
grated
12-16 corn tortillas

Rinse seeds from chilies and chop. Sauté chilies and garlic in 2 tablespoons oil. Drain tomatoes and reserve ½ cup liquid. Break up tomatoes and add with onions, salt, oregano, and reserved tomato liquid to sautéed chilies and garlic. Simmer slowly, uncovered, until thick, about 30 minutes. Set aside.

Combine turkey or chicken with sour cream and cheese. Heat ½ cup oil and fry the tortillas until limp. Drain from oil. Fill each tortilla with the meat mixture and roll. Place seam down in an ungreased casserole and pour chili sauce combination over the top. Bake at 350° for 20 minutes. Do ahead. Freeze.

*With Hands & Heart Cookbook*

# Country Fried Chicken

Chicken, cut into serving
  pieces
Milk, buttermilk, beer or
  salted water
3 tablespoons brown sugar
3 tablespoons parsley flakes
2 tablespoons garlic salt
2 tablespoons onion salt
1 tablespoon rosemary
1 tablespoon sage
1 tablespoon oregano
1 tablespoon ginger
1 tablespoon paprika
1½ teaspoons thyme
1 teaspoon marjoram
1 teaspoon pepper
Flour
Shortening

Marinate chicken pieces in the refrigerator overnight in milk, buttermilk, beer or salted water. Combine and pulverize seasonings in a blender. Add 2 tablespoons mixed seasonings to 1 cup flour. (Pancake mix, cake flour, or biscuit mix can be substituted for the flour.) Store remaining mixed seasonings in an airtight container. Dredge marinated chicken pieces in seasoned flour. Place on a wire rack to dry 20 minutes. For extra crispy chicken, dip again in buttermilk and seasoned flour and let dry another 20 minutes. Heat ½ inch melted shortening in a heavy skillet. Fry chicken about 10 minutes. Turn and fry an additional 20 minutes. Large pieces may need to be turned again. Turning too often reduces crispness. Drain on paper towels.

*Sassafras!*

# Barbeque Sauce for Chicken

½ cup salad oil
1 cup water
2 tablespoons onion, chopped
1 clove garlic, crushed
1½ teaspoons sugar
1 teaspoon salt
1 teaspoon chili powder
1 teaspoon paprika
1 teaspoon pepper
½ teaspoon dry mustard
Dash cayenne
1 teaspoon Worcestershire
  sauce
1 teaspoon hot sauce
¼ cup lemon juice
1 cup catsup
¼ cup steak sauce
½ green pepper, chopped
1 tablespoon cider vinegar

Combine all ingredients in a saucepan and simmer for 1 hour. Brush onto grilled chicken pieces. Yields about 3 cups.

*The Passion of Barbeque*

# Wild Turkey Kiev

Boneless wild turkey breast
1 stick margarine
Chopped chives (fresh or
  dried)
1 cup flour
¾ cup milk

1 egg
1 teaspoon salt
1 teaspoon pepper
Cracker crumbs
Vegetable oil for frying

Cut larger turkey breast portions into ¼-inch slices, smaller pieces into ½-inch slices. Place between 2 sheets waxed paper. Flatten to ⅛-inch by pounding lightly with the flat edge of meat cleaver or bottom of a skillet.

Place 1 pat of margarine on edge of turkey breast. Add 1 teaspoon chives and roll, folding in edges to seal margarine. Make a batter by mixing flour, milk, egg, salt and pepper. Beat until smooth. Dip turkey rolls in batter, coat with cracker crumbs. Deep fry at 365°-370° until golden brown. Drain on a rack.

*The Sportsman's Dish*

# Ozarks Smoked Turkey

1 onion, minced
½ cup butter
3 tablespoons light brown
  sugar
1 (0.4-ounce) package
  Italian salad dressing mix

1 clove garlic, minced
1 teaspoon salt
Freshly ground pepper
  to taste
¾ cup tarragon vinegar
1 (20-pound) turkey

Combine all ingredients except turkey in a small saucepan. Simmer 3-4 minutes. Stuff turkey, if desired, and truss as usual. Brush generously with herb sauce. Cook in smoker according to manufacturer's directions. One hour before cooking is finished, add damp hickory chips to smoker and baste turkey every 20 minutes with the herb sauce. Serves 16-18.

*Sassafras!*

# Turkey Pot Pie

| | |
|---|---|
| 1 cup frozen peas | 4 cups turkey broth |
| 1 cup diced carrots | ½ cup sifted flour |
| 1 cup diced celery | 1 cup milk |
| 2 medium potatoes, diced | 2 cups diced cooked turkey |
| 1 medium onion, diced | Salt and pepper to taste |

Cook the vegetables just until tender in turkey broth. Remove vegetables and measure broth; add water to make 4 cups. Blend flour with milk and stir until smooth. Stir into the hot broth and cook until thick. Add the vegetables and turkey to the gravy. Season. Pour the mixture into a large (9x13-inch) buttered casserole.

**HOT WATER PASTRY:**

| | |
|---|---|
| ¾ cup shortening | 1 egg, separated |
| 2 cups flour | ½ cup hot water |
| ¾ teaspoon salt | |

Cut shortening into flour and salt. Beat egg yolk and add to it the hot water. Stir egg yolk mixture into flour mixture until a soft dough is formed. Roll to ½-inch thickness; cut to fit top of baking dish. Pierce with fork for steam to escape. Brush dough with beaten egg white. Bake in a 425° oven about 25 minutes.

*Eat Pie First...Life is Uncertain!*

# Stuffed Cranberry-Pepper Game Hens

4 Cornish hens, rinsed and dried
1 large shallot
2 celery stalks, cut into 1-inch pieces
1 medium Granny Smith apple, cored and quartered
1½ cups cranberries
2 tablespoons unsalted butter
1 cup cooked wild rice
⅓ cup pine nuts
2 teaspoons plus 1 tablespoon jalapeño pepper jelly
1 teaspoon salt
½ teaspoon sage
Freshly ground pepper, to taste
Nutmeg, to taste
1 tablespoon vegetable oil
¾ cup water

In a food processor, drop shallot through feed tube and mince finely. Add celery and chop finely. Set aside. Finely chop apple and transfer to a large bowl. Slice cranberries, using medium slicing blade. Reserve ¾ cup and add remainder to apples.

In a skillet, melt butter and sauté celery-shallot mixture until soft (approximately 8 minutes). Add to apple mixture. Stir in rice, pine nuts, 2 teaspoons jelly, ½ teaspoon salt and sage. Season with pepper and nutmeg.

Stuff hens loosely with rice and fruit mixture. Tie legs together and place wings under body. Place in a roasting pan and brush with vegetable oil. Bake hens at 450° for 30 minutes. Reduce temperature to 350° and bake for 15 minutes more.

Meanwhile, cook reserved cranberries and water in a 1½-quart non-aluminum saucepan until very soft. Add 1 tablespoon jelly and stir until dissolved. Remove from heat and strain glaze. Reserve cranberries.

Pour off fat in roasting pan. Brush hens with glaze. Bake for 10 minutes, brushing frequently with glaze.

Preheat broiler. Broil hens until brown (approximately 2-3 minutes), then let stand for 5 minutes.

Mix strained cranberries with pan drippings. To serve, spoon sauce over hens or pass separately. Serves 4.

*Note:* Hot jalapeño and fruit orchestrate a complex, surprising flavor for these game hens.

***Above & Beyond Parsley***

# Marinated Cornish Game Hens

2 Cornish game hens

MARINADE:

| | |
|---|---|
| 2 teaspoons oil | ⅓ cup soy sauce |
| 2 teaspoons brown sugar | 1 teaspoon wine vinegar |
| 1 teaspoon ginger | 1 clove garlic, minced |

Mix marinade ingredients together and marinate birds overnight in refrigerator.

Bring heat in smoker to 200°-225° Cook hens for 1½ hours or until thigh meat is soft when squeezed. Serves 2-4.

*The Passion of Barbeque*

# Roast Quail
# á la Talleyrand

From the handwritten cookbook of Mrs. Adam Lemp, loaned us by her great-granddaughter.

| | |
|---|---|
| ½ pound dried apricots | 1 teaspoon minced onion |
| 1 tablespoon + ½ cup butter | 1 cup bread crumbs |
| | ½ teaspoon salt |
| 2 tablespoons minced celery | 6 quail, plucked and cleaned |
| 1 teaspoon parsley, chopped | ½ cup wine vinegar |

Wash and drain the apricots; cut them into small pieces. Melt 1 tablespoon butter in a saucepan and add celery, parsley, and onion to the butter. Cook for a few minutes. Add to the bread crumbs, salt, and apricots. Stir together until well mixed.

Meanwhile, pluck and clean your quail. Rub with wine vinegar both inside and outside, then fill with the apricot stuffing. Don't fill too full; the birds will burst in cooking if you do. Truss the birds, then place on a rack in a shallow roasting pan. Pour ½ cup melted butter over them; bake at 450° for 5 minutes. Then reduce the heat to 375° and cook for 20 minutes more. Serves 6.

*The Shaw House Cook Book*

# Pheasant Madeira

4 pheasant breasts, boned
   and skinned
2 cups flour
2 eggs
1 cup buttermilk
¼ cup butter
½ cup Madeira

1 cup sliced shitake
   mushrooms
¼ cup sliced artichoke
   bottoms
3 cups chicken stock
1 cup heavy cream
¼ cup halved red grapes

Dredge pheasant breasts in flour. Combine eggs and buttermilk. Dip pheasant into egg mixture. Dredge again. Melt butter and sauté pheasant over medium heat. Cook approximately 4-5 minutes on each side. Place in a warm oven to hold.

Heat wine to boiling in a saucepan and add mushrooms. When wine is reduced by half, add artichoke bottoms, chicken stock, and heavy cream. Reduce by half or until thickened to a creamy consistency. Add grapes to sauce at the last minute.

Place a pheasant breast on each plate and pour about ¼ cup of the sauce over the top of each.

This dish is especially good served with a mixture of white and wild rice seasoned with fresh thyme and diced onions. Carrots that have been steamed and glazed with a mixture of honey and orange juice also go well with this meal. Serve in the fall and winter months when pheasant is usually plentiful. Serves 4.

***Kansas City Cuisine (E.B.T. Restaurant)***

Seafood

Rocky Falls is part of the Ozark National Scenic Riverways.
East of Eminence.

# Psari Plaki
### (Baked Fish and Vegetables)

1 pound cod or orange
  roughy
Salt and pepper to taste
Juice of ½ lemon
3 onions, chopped
¾ cup olive oil
1½ cups canned tomatoes

½ cup parsley, chopped
2 cloves garlic, chopped
2 carrots, sliced
2 ribs celery, sliced
¼ cup raisins, optional
½ cup water
1 cup white wine

Clean fish thoroughly. Rub with salt and pepper. Sprinkle with lemon juice. Sauté onions in oil until golden brown. Add all remaining ingredients and simmer until vegetables are tender. Bake fish at 350° in greased baking pan until done. Remove fish from baking pan onto serving dish. Cover with vegetable sauce. Serve immediately.

In above recipe you may substitute almost any fish of your choice: haddock, bluefish, etc. Yield: 6 servings.

*The Art of Hellenic Cuisine*

# Heavenly Sole

1 - 1½ pounds skinless
  sole filets
2 tablespoons lemon juice
½ cup (2 ounces) freshly
  grated Parmesan cheese
3 tablespoons mayonnaise

3 tablespoons chopped
  green onion
Salt to taste
Dash of Tabasco sauce
¼ cup butter, softened

Place filets in a single layer on well greased bake-and-serve platter. Brush fish with lemon juice and let stand for 10 minutes. Broil filets about 4 inches from heat for 6-8 minutes or until filets flake easily when tested with a fork. Combine remaining ingredients. When removed from heat, spread with cheese mixture. Broil 2-3 minutes longer or until lightly browned. Serves 3-4.

*The Cook Book*

# Sea Shells

1 (7¾-ounce) can red
 salmon
¼ cup soda crackers,
 crumbled
1 egg
¼ teaspoon pepper
12 jumbo macaroni shells,
 cooked in salt water and
 drained

2 tablespoons butter
½ teaspoon salt
2 tablespoons flour
1 cup scalded milk
4 ounces Monterey Jack
 cheese, shredded
3 tablespoons fresh dill
 weed, crumbled

Combine salmon, crackers, egg, and ⅛ teaspoon pepper. Stuff shells with salmon mixture. Melt butter and add salt, ⅛ teaspoon pepper, and flour. Mix until well blended; stir into scalded milk. Add cheese and continue to heat over low heat until cheese is melted. Add dill weed. Place shells in baking dish and pour sauce over top. Heat in 350 oven for 10 minutes and serve immediately. Serves 2-3.

*From Seed to Serve*

# Tuna Asparagus Deluxe Casserole

⅓ cup butter
½ cup celery, chopped
½ cup green pepper,
 chopped
1 small onion, chopped
1 can cream of mushroom
 soup
1 can cream of chicken soup
2 cups flaked tuna

½ cup mayonnaise
½ cup chopped parsley
Cooked noodles
1 can asparagus tips
1 cup grated sharp cheddar
 cheese
Small jar pimento (optional)
Crushed corn flakes
Sliced almonds

Sauté celery, green pepper, and onion in butter (oleo); add soups, tuna, mayonnaise, and parsley. Layer tuna mixture with cooked noodles, asparagus, cheese, pimento, and end with tuna mixture. Top with crushed corn flakes and sliced almonds. Bake at 350° for 45 minutes. Dry noodles or patty shells may be used instead of cooked noodles. Serves 12-14.

May use chicken or turkey in place of tuna. The mayonnaise may be substituted with small tub sour cream.

*Blue Ridge Christian Church Cookbook*

# Filet of Fish Parmesan

1 pound (fresh or frozen) boneless fish filets (any mild tasting fish—flounder, crappie, sole, trout)
3 tablespoons butter
½ teaspoon salt
½ teaspoon coarsely ground black pepper

1 tablespoon bottled lemon juice
1 tablespoon dry white wine
¼ cup Parmesan cheese
Paprika
Parsley
Lemon wedges

Preheat oven to 400°. Cut 3 tablespoons butter into small cubes and place in shallow baking dish in 400° oven. While butter is melting, sprinkle filets on both sides with salt and pepper. Remove melted butter from oven and add lemon juice. Place filets flesh side down in sizzling butter and bake in oven 10 minutes (if fish is thick, cook 15 minutes).

Turn with spatula and baste with juices. Add 1 tablespoon wine, ¼ cup Parmesan, and sprinkle with paprika. Return to oven; bake until done—approximately 5 minutes. Serves 2.

To serve: garnish with parsley and lemon wedges. Preparation time 4 minutes; cooking time 10-15 minutes.

*Note:* You may run fish under broiler if filets are not brown enough.

*Rush Hour Superchef!*

# Baked Fish á la Italianne

2 pounds fish fillet (sole,
scrod or whitefish)
¼ - ½ cup butter or
margarine
3 tablespoons oil
1 teaspoon garlic powder or
minced garlic

1 teaspoon lemon juice
½ teaspoon oregano
⅓ cup white wine
Salt, pepper, paprika to
taste
½ cup bread crumbs

In a small saucepan, melt butter or margarine; add oil, garlic, lemon juice, oregano, wine, salt and pepper. Place fish in a shallow baking pan and sprinkle with paprika. Pour sauce over fish and sprinkle with bread crumbs overall. Bake at 350° 20-30 minutes, until fish flakes. Garnish with lemon wedges and parsley. Serves 4.

*From Generation to Generation*

# Grouper with Dilled Cucumber Sauce

2 (6-ounce) grouper fillets
3 tablespoons butter

1 tablespoon lemon juice
2 sprigs fresh dill

DILLED CUCUMBER SAUCE:
1 cup peeled, seeded and
diced cucumber
¼ cup sliced green onions
¼ cup oil
1 tablespoon lemon juice

2 sprigs fresh dill (or 1
teaspoon dried dill weed)
½ teaspoon salt
Freshly ground pepper to
taste

In an electric blender or food processor, combine all sauce ingredients and purée. Refrigerate.

Melt butter in a small saucepan and add lemon juice. Set aside.

Grill fillets over hot coals for 5 minutes per side. Baste while cooking, using sprigs of dill to brush on lemon butter. Serve with Dilled Cucumber Sauce.

The Dilled Cucumber Sauce is also an excellent accompaniment to grilled or steamed vegetables. Serves 2.

*Hooked on Fish on the Grill*

# Mesquite Grilled Amberjack

4 (6 - 8-ounce) amberjack
  fillets
Olive oil
Freshly ground red, green,
  and black peppercorns
  to taste

8 ounces fresh corn kernels
  (thawed frozen corn may
  be substituted)
¼ cup chopped onion
2 cloves garlic, minced
1 tablespoon chopped

Lightly brush fillets with oil and season to taste with peppers. Soak a handful of mesquite wood chips. When ready to grill fish, throw wood chips on hot coals. Grill fillets for 5 minutes each side. Cover grill for a smokier flavor while fillets are cooking. Serve with Avocado Corn Salsa. Serves 4.

**AVOCADO CORN SALSA:**

2 large ripe avocados
8 ounces fresh corn kernels
  (thawed frozen corn may
  be substituted
Juice from 1 lime
Salt to taste

1 tablespoon chopped
  cilantro
¼ cup chopped onion
2 cloves garlic, minced
¼ teaspoon red pepper
  flakes

Chop avocados into ½-inch cubes. Add the rest of the ingredients and gently stir together. Let sit 1 hour before serving. Makes approximately 3 cups.

*Hooked on Fish on the Grill*

# Savory Salmon Cups

1 (16-ounce) can Red Sockeye
  Salmon
1 large egg
Milk
1 (1⅛-ounce) package dry
  Hollandaise sauce mix
¼ cup Italian seasoned
  bread crumbs
½ teaspoon salt
8 drops Tabasco
1 tablespoon dry onion
  flakes
1 tablespoon dry parsley
  flakes
Pepper to taste

Drain salmon and reserve liquid. Remove bones and flake salmon. Blend in egg. Add enough milk to salmon liquid to measure ¾ cup and stir into salmon. Add remaining ingredients and blend thoroughly. Spoon into well greased muffin tins. Bake in 350° oven for 45 minutes. Easy. Can do ahead. Yield: 12.

*Cooking in Clover*

# Salmon Steaks
# with Soy Marinade

4 salmon steaks
2 tablespoons orange juice
¼ cup soy sauce
1 clove garlic, pressed
1 tablespoon butter
  (optional)

Combine the orange juice, soy sauce, garlic and butter, if desired, over medium-high heat in a small saucepan. Cook until the mixture becomes thick enough to coat the back of a spoon.

Wash and pat dry the salmon steaks. With a spoon, rub the soy marinade on both sides of the fish. Refrigerate 1-2 hours before preparing.

Preheat oven to 450° and bake for 10-15 minutes, until the fish flakes when tested with a fork.

*Note:* The salmon may also be broiled, grilled, or microwaved. Serves 4.

*Bouquet Garni*

# Microwave Mountain Trout

2 (8-ounce) trout
2 tablespoons lemon juice
¼ cup melted butter
2 tablespoons dehydrated
  onions
2 tablespoons slivered
  almonds

2 heaping teaspoons parsley
  flakes
Paprika
Salt
Pepper

Wash fish and pat dry. Sprinkle inside and out with lemon juice. Pour 1 tablespoon butter inside each trout. Place onion, almond, and parsley inside cavities. Season to taste with paprika, salt and pepper. Pin body cavities closed with toothpick and pour remaining butter over fish. Cover properly in baking dish to prevent splatters. Cook on high setting for 4 minutes. Do not overcook.

For more than 2 fish or larger fish, adjust cooking time carefully in proportion to total weight. If more browning is desired, 1 or 2 minutes under broiling element in conventional oven is sufficient. Yield: 2 servings.

*Talk About Good*

# Vodka Steamed Scallops

Irresistible!

1 pound bay scallops
1 tablespoon vodka
½ teaspoon cornstarch
1 tablespoon minced ginger
¼ cup scallions, chopped

1 tablespoon fresh
  coriander, chopped
1 tablespoon peanut oil
2 cloves garlic, crushed
1 tablespoon soy sauce

In a large bowl, toss scallops with vodka and cornstarch. Place scallops in a steaming basket. Top with ginger, scallions and coriander. Steam over boiling water for 5 minutes.

While scallops steam, heat oil in small skillet. Add garlic and reduce heat. Cook until garlic begins to brown. Remove garlic. Add soy sauce to oil, blending well. Pour garlic-and soy-flavored oil over scallops. Serve immediately over hot rice. Serves 4.

*Finely Tuned Foods*

# Scallops Dijonnaise

1 pound sea scallops, halved
1½ tablespoons dry white
  wine
3 tablespoons flour
1 teaspoon salt
Freshly ground pepper to
  taste
3 shallots, minced

1 clove garlic, minced
½ cup clarified butter
½ cup dry white wine
½ cup heavy cream
2 tablespoons Dijon mustard
Salt and freshly ground
  pepper to taste
Minced fresh parsley

Place scallops in medium bowl, add 1½ tablespoons wine, cover and refrigerate for 1 hour. Combine flour, salt and pepper. Drain scallops and pat dry on paper towels. Dust scallops with flour mixture and shake off excess. Sauté shallots and garlic in butter until fragrant. Add scallops and sauté until golden. Transfer to serving dish.

Deglaze skillet with ½ cup wine over high heat. Add cream and mustard and reduce sauce until thickened. Add salt and pepper. Pour over scallops and sprinkle with parsley. Serves 3-4.

*Cooking for Applause*

# Carolina Deviled Crab

Guaranteed to be delicious! Baked in any kind of oven-proof dish, this treasured family recipe, a deep South favorite, becomes a conversation piece when served in its natural habitat, a crab shell! (A good investment which lasts for years, crab shells are inexpensive and have a multitude of uses.)

| | |
|---|---|
| 1 pound crab meat | 1 (8-ounce) carton sour |
| 4 hard-cooked eggs, peeled | cream |
| and finely chopped | 2 tablespoons softened |
| 1 teaspoon Dijon mustard | butter |
| ½ teaspoon salt | 1 cup Saltine cracker crumbs |
| ½ teaspoon Tabasco | 2 tablespoons butter for top |
| 1½ tablespoons bottled | of mixture |
| lemon juice | |

Preheat oven to 350°. Remove carefully any shells from crab meat. Place in large mixing bowl: crab meat, chopped eggs, mustard, salt, Tabasco, lemon juice, sour cream, and 2 tablespoons butter. Mix thoroughly and place in crab shells, ramekins, or baking dish. (If not using immediately, wrap well in aluminum foil or plastic wrap, then in freezer paper, and freeze.) Sprinkle cracker crumbs over top and dot with 2 tablespoons butter divided among the 6 shells. Bake at 350° approximately 20 minutes or until crumbs are brown on top and crab is hot throughout. *Do not overcook!*

Preparation time 20 minutes; cooking time 20 minutes; freezes well. Serves 6.

***Rush Hour Superchef!***

The son of a Baptist minister, J. C. Penney established in 1902 his impressive chain of retail stores that remain strong today. He was born in Hamilton in 1875 one of 12 children. His initials stood for "James Cash."

# Lemon-Basil Basted Shrimp

24 jumbo shrimp (about
  1¼ pounds), shelled
  and deveined

MARINADE:

2 teaspoons finely chopped
  garlic
2 teaspoons finely chopped
  shallots
1½ teaspoons Dijon
  mustard

⅓ cup dry white wine
⅓ cup fresh lemon juice
¼ teaspoon black pepper
½ cup olive oil
⅓ cup finely chopped fresh
  basil

Combine marinade ingredients. Add the shrimp and toss until thoroughly coated. Marinate until coals are ready.

Remove shrimp from marinade and pour remaining liquid into a saucepan. Arrange shrimp on grill topper, keeping them flat. Cook for about 3 minutes or until shrimp can be lifted from grill without sticking. Then turn over and cook for about 2 more minutes.

Bring pan of marinade to a boil and simmer for 2 minutes. Arrange shrimp on a platter and spoon marinade over all. Serve immediately. Serves 4.

*Hooked on Fish on the Grill*

# Garithes Me Pilaf
## *(Shrimp With Rice)*

½ cup olive oil
2 medium onions, chopped
1 (8-ounce) can tomato sauce
1 teaspoon each—salt,
   pepper, and oregano

½ cup parsley, chopped
1 pound raw shrimp, peeled
1 cup rice
2½ cups boiling water

Heat oil and sauté onions. Add tomato sauce, salt, pepper, oregano, and parsley. Cover and cook for 5 minutes. Add shrimp and cook 5 minutes longer. Stir in rice. Pour in boiling water. Stir again. Simmer, covered for 25 minutes. Yield: 4 servings.

*The Art of Hellenic Cuisine*

# Shrimp Fried Rice

3 green onions, tops
   included, chopped
1 onion, chopped
½ cup butter
3 cups cold cooked rice
2 eggs, beaten

4 ounces water chestnuts,
   drained and sliced
Soy sauce to taste
1 (7¾-ounce) can tiny
   shrimp, drained and rinsed

Sauté onions in butter in wok or large frying pan over moderately high heat. Stir in rice, mixing until heated and coated with butter. (Add more butter if necessary.) With wooden spoon, make a path to bottom of pan; pour in eggs and gently scramble. Mix throughout rice. Add water chestnuts and sprinkle liberally with soy sauce to taste. Gently fold in shrimp and heat. Serves 4.

*Company's Coming*

 Big Spring, near Van Buren, is America's largest single-outlet spring. On an average day, it gushes 277 million gallons of water.

# Easy Shrimp Scampi

1 - 2 tablespoons sliced
  green onions
2 - 4 cloves garlic, crushed
½ cup butter
1 pound shrimp, peeled
  and deveined
2 tablespoons dried basil

¼ cup dry white wine
2 tablespoons lemon juice
½ teaspoon grated lemon
  rind (optional)
¼ teaspoon hot sauce
  (Tabasco)
Salt and pepper to taste

Sauté onions and garlic in butter few minutes; turn heat to low and add shrimp. Cook, stirring frequently, about 3 minutes. Add remaining ingredients and simmer another 2-3 minutes, or until shrimp turn pink. Do not overcook or use high heat or shrimp will be tough.

Serve with French bread split in half brushed with olive oil and sprinkled with Parmesan cheese. Heat under broiler 1-2 minutes. Serves 4.

*Tasty Palette*

# Pernod-Buttered Lobster Tails

**PERNOD BUTTER:**
1 stick butter
2 tablespoons Pernod liqueur

2 tablespoons crushed
  tarragon

Make Pernod Butter with these three ingredients.

4 (8-ounce) rock lobster
  tails

4 tablespoons butter, melted
Oil on grill

Cut top membrane from lobster tails and discard. Loosen meat from shell. Brush lobster tails with melted butter.

Put tails on grill, cut-side down and cook 2-3 minutes. Turn tails and cook until done, 7-9 minutes. The shell may char.

Serve lobster tails with Pernod Butter and enjoy. Serves 4.

This recipe appears courtesy of Donnie Morris who says, "This is so good you'll want to slap your grandmaw!"

*Hooked on Fish on the Grill*

# Smoked Oyster and Corn Casserole

1 egg
½ cup milk
1 (#2) can cream style corn
⅛ teaspoon salt

2½ teaspoons soy sauce
1 tablespoon minced onion
1 can smoked oysters, drained

In casserole to be used for baking, beat egg lightly with a fork. Add milk, corn, and seasonings. When mixed, scatter drained oysters over the top. Sprinkle with 4 soda crackers or 6 butter wafers, coarsely crushed. Bake at 325° for 30-35 minutes or until mixture is set. Serves 4-6.

*Treasured Recipes Book II*

**Cakes**

The Winston Churchill Museum and Library are housed in a 16th century church that was bombed out in London. Fulton.

# Lazy Daisy Cake

This cake has been a long-time family favorite. It was always my choice for birthdays and special occasions. We also called it Hot Milk Cake. I remember helping my mother, Hazel Binion, bake the cake and watch the frosting bubble and caramelize during the 1940s.

| | |
|---|---|
| 2 eggs | 1 teaspoon baking powder |
| 1 cup sugar | ½ teaspoon salt |
| 1 teaspoon vanilla | ½ cup milk |
| 1 cup flour | 2 tablespoons butter |

Combine eggs, sugar, vanilla, and beat until thick. Add sifted dry ingredients: flour, baking powder, and salt. Heat milk with butter to boiling point; add to first mixture. Bake in greased 8-inch square pan in a moderate oven (350°) for 30-40 minutes. When done, cool and spread with the following frosting.

**BOILED COCONUT FROSTING:**

| | |
|---|---|
| ½ cup brown sugar | ½ cup shredded coconut |
| 2 tablespoons softened butter | 2 tablespoons cream |

Combine brown sugar, softened butter, shredded coconut, and cream. Spread on cake and place under broiler until browned and bubbly. Watch the frosting carefully, it browns quickly and changes from just right to burned in a matter of seconds!

*Grandma's Ozark Legacy*

# Coconut Sour Cream Cake

1 box white cake mix (Duncan Hines preferred) with no pudding in mix
¼ cup oil
3 eggs
1 (8-ounce) carton sour cream
1 (8.5-ounce) can cream of coconut

Mix all ingredients with an electric mixer as per other cake mix elaborations. Bake in greased 9x12-inch pan at 350° for 30 minutes. Cool cake in pan. Cover with the following icing:

ICING:
1 (8-ounce) package cream cheese
1 box powdered sugar (3.5 cups)
2 tablespoons milk
1 teaspoon vanilla
1 can Angel Flake Coconut

Blend powdered sugar into softened cream cheese; then work in the milk and vanilla. Ice cake. Sprinkle coconut over the iced cake. Can freeze.

*Wanda's Favorite Recipes Book*

# Stir-In-The-Pan Cake

¼ cup Crisco oil
1 box Swiss chocolate cake mix
2 eggs
1¼ cups water
1 small package chocolate instant pudding
1 small package chocolate chips
½ cup chopped pecans

Preheat oven to 350°. Pour oil into 9x13-inch pan. Tilt pan until bottom is covered with oil. Pour cake mix, eggs, water, and pudding into pan. Stir with fork or spoon until blended. Scrape sides and spread batter evenly in pan. Sprinkle on chocolate chips and nuts. Bake at 350° for 35-45 minutes, until toothpick inserted in center comes out clean. Cut and serve directly from pan. Serves 16-20.

*Delicious Reading*

# Beer and Spice Brunch Cake

**CAKE:**

1 (18¼-ounce) package
  yellow cake mix
1 (4-ounce) package vanilla
  or lemon instant pudding
1 cup beer*
½ cup vegetable oil
4 eggs

1 teaspoon ground cinnamon
½ teaspoon ground
  cardamon (optional)
¼ teaspoon ground allspice
½ teaspoon ground cloves
½ teaspoon ground ginger

In a large bowl, blend all ingredients. Beat at medium speed 2 minutes. Pour into a greased and floured 10-inch tube pan. Bake at 350° for 50-60 minutes or until cake springs back in center when done. Cool right-side-up in pan 25 minutes before removing. Frost with Lemon Sugar. Can be frozen. Serves 12.

**LEMON SUGAR:**

1½ cups confectioners'
  sugar
2 tablespoons butter or
  margarine, softened

¼ teaspoon grated lemon
  peel
1-2 tablespoons lemon juice

Combine sugar, butter, lemon peel, and lemon juice and blend well.

*Saint Louisans choose Budweiser, the "King of Beers."

***Gateways***

# Sheet Cake

| | |
|---|---|
| 1 stick oleo | 1 teaspoon vanilla |
| 4 tablespoons cocoa | ½ cup buttermilk |
| 1 cup water | 1 teaspoon soda |
| ½ cup Crisco | Dash cinnamon |
| 2 cups flour | 2 eggs |
| 2 cups sugar | |

In saucepan put oleo, cocoa, water, Crisco. Bring to full boil, then pour over flour and sugar mixture. Add vanilla, buttermilk, soda, a little cinnamon, and 2 eggs, slightly beaten. Pour in large greased cookie sheet and bake at 400° for 15 minutes. Five minutes before cake is done, start frosting.

**FROSTING:**

| | |
|---|---|
| 1 stick oleo | 1 box powdered sugar |
| 4 tablespoons cocoa | 1 teaspoon vanilla |
| 6 tablespoons water | 1 cup nuts, optional |

Bring first 3 ingredients to full boil and then add remaining ingredients.

*A Collection of Recipes from the Best Cooks*
*in the Midwest*

# Egg Replacer for Baking

To replace 2 eggs:

| | |
|---|---|
| ½ pound tofu | ½ teaspoon baking soda |
| 2 tablespoons yogurt | |
| 1 tablespoon cornstarch or arrowroot | |

Process in blender or food processor.

*The Vegetarian Lunchbasket*

---

The Anheuser-Busch Brewery in downtown St. Louis is the world's largest brewery. The Brew House, the Clydesdale Stables, and the main office building have been designated National Historic Landmarks.

# Pineapple Upside Down Cake
### *(And this is the modern version.)*

3 tablespoons butter or
  margarine
1 cup brown sugar
1 large can sliced pineapple
8 maraschino cherries
1½ teaspoons baking
  powder

Pinch salt
3 eggs
1½ cups sugar
½ cup water
1 teaspoon vanilla
1½ cups flour

Put butter and brown sugar in an iron frying pan. Let simmer a couple of minutes and add sliced pineapple. Place a maraschino cherry in center of each pineapple slice. Remove from the heat. Make a batter of the remaining ingredients and pour over pineapple slices. Heat oven to 400°. Put skillet in oven for 10 minutes. Reduce heat to 350° and bake an additional 50 minutes or until cake is done. Turn out of pan on a large platter. Serve plain or with whipped cream.

*Treasured Recipes Book II*

# Missouri Upside Down Cake

3 tablespoons butter or
  margarine
¾ cup brown sugar
2 cooking apples, peeled
  and sliced
¼ teaspoon cinnamon
⅓ cup shortening

⅓ cup sugar
2 eggs
1 teaspoon vanilla
1½ cups flour
2 teaspoons baking powder
½ teaspoon salt
⅔ cup milk

Melt butter in 9-inch round pan. Add brown sugar and stir until melted. Arrange sliced apples on sugar/butter mixture. Sprinkle cinnamon over apples.

Cream shortening and sugar. Blend in eggs and vanilla, beating thoroughly. Add dry ingredients alternately with milk. Pour over apples in pan. Bake at 350° for 40-45 minutes, or until done. Turn out onto serving plate immediately.

Serve with whipped cream or pistachio ice cream. Yield: 6-8 servings.

*From the Apple Orchard*

# Kathy's Apple Cake

2 cups flour
2 cups sugar
2 eggs
1 batch Apple Pie Filling

2 teaspoons soda
1 teaspoon vanilla
1 cup walnuts
1 cup coconut

Mix together the preceding. Bake in greased and floured 15½ x 10½ x 1-inch baking sheet for 35 minutes at 350°.

**APPLE PIE FILLING:**

½ cup brown sugar
2 tablespoons cornstarch
½ teaspoon cinnamon
1 tablespoon lemon juice

1 tablespoon butter or
    margarine
1¼ cups water
6 cups apples, peeled and
    sliced

In saucepan, combine brown sugar, cornstarch, cinnamon, lemon juice, water and butter. Stir in sliced apples and cook until hot, about 10 minutes.

**ICING:**

1¾ cups powdered sugar
1 (8-ounce) package cream
    cheese

1 teaspoon vanilla
½ stick oleo
½ cup chopped nuts

Spread icing on cake while warm.

*Home Cookin'*

In 1925, while working for a St. Louis aircraft corporation, Charles Lindbergh heard that someone was offering a prize of $25,000 to the first pilot to cross the Atlantic non-stop from New York to Paris. On May 20, 1927, history was made as he crossed 3,600 miles of the Atlantic in the "Spirit of St. Louis."

# Rosy Apple Cake

1 cup flour
1 teaspoon baking powder
¼ teaspoon salt
3 tablespoons butter or
    margarine

1 egg beaten with
    1 tablespoon milk
4-5 medium cooking apples
1 (3-ounce) package
    strawberry gelatin
1-2 tablespoons sugar

Mix first three dry ingredients. Cut in butter. Add egg and milk mixture. Mix together thoroughly and press in bottom and up sides of an 8-inch round pan. Peel apples and slice into dough-lined pan. Sprinkle dry gelatin over top of apples. Add 1-2 tablespoons sugar, depending on tartness of apples. Mix the following topping and sprinkle over apples:

**TOPPING:**
¾ cup sugar
¾ cup flour

¾ stick butter or
    margarine

Cut butter into sugar/flour mixture, until crumbly. Sprinkle over top of apples. Bake at 375° for 45 minutes. Yield: 6-8 servings.

*From the Apple Orchard*

# Fresh Apple Cake

1 cup salad oil
2 cups sugar
2 eggs
1 teaspoon vanilla
2½ cups flour
1 teaspoon soda

1 teaspoon salt
1 teaspoon baking powder
1 teaspoon cinnamon
3 cups chopped apples
1 cup raisins
1 cup nuts (if desired)

Beat together the salad oil, sugar and eggs. Add the vanilla. Sift together the flour, soda, salt, baking powder, and cinnamon. Stir the dry ingredients into the oil, sugar and egg mixture. Add the chopped apples, raisins, and nuts. This mixture will be thick like a cookie batter. Bake at 350° for 40-45 minutes or till done. This will be nice and golden brown.

*Heavenly Delights*

# Pumpkin Torte

**STEP 1:**

| | |
|---|---|
| 24 graham cracker squares, crushed | ½ cup butter |
| ⅓ cup brown sugar | ½ cup nuts, chopped |

Mix and pat into bottom of 9x13-inch pan.

**STEP 2:**

| | |
|---|---|
| 1 (8-ounce) package cream cheese | ½ cup sugar |
| | 2 eggs |

Beat together well and pour over crust; bake 15-20 minutes at 350° till set.

**STEP 3:**

| | |
|---|---|
| 1¼ cups pumpkin | 1 teaspoon cinnamon |
| 3 egg yolks (save whites) | 1 envelope Knox Gelatine |
| ⅓ cup brown sugar | ¼ cup warm water |
| 1 teaspoon vanilla | 3 egg whites |
| ½ cup milk (canned) | ¼ cup powdered sugar |
| ½ teaspoon salt | Cool Whip |

Mix first 7 ingredients together and cook, stirring, long enough to cook eggs. Dissolve Knox Gelatine in warm water. Add to pumpkin mixture while still warm. Beat egg whites stiff; add powdered sugar. Fold into pumpkin mixture. Pour over baked layers and refrigerate. Can be made ahead. When ready to serve, cover with layer of Cool Whip.

*Blue Ridge Christian Church Cookbook*

# Bavarian Apple Torte

**CRUST:**

½ cup butter, room
  temperature
⅓ cup sugar

¼ teaspoon vanilla
1 cup all-purpose flour

Cream butter, sugar, and vanilla. Blend in flour. Spread dough on the bottom and 1 inch up the sides of a 9-inch springform pan.

**FILLING:**

12 ounces cream cheese,
  room temperature
¼ cup sugar

1 egg
1 teaspoon vanilla

Beat together cream cheese and sugar. Blend in egg and vanilla. Pour into pastry-lined pan.

**TOPPING:**

⅓ cup sugar
½ teaspoon cinnamon
4 cups peeled and sliced
  tart apples

¼ cup slivered almonds
1 cup heavy cream, whipped
Cinnamon

Combine sugar and cinnamon; toss with apples. Arrange apples in concentric circles over cream cheese layer, avoiding spilling apple juice on pastry. Sprinkle with slivered almonds. Bake at 450° for 10 minutes. Reduce heat to 400° and continue baking for 25 minutes. Cool before removing rim of pan.

Serve with a bountiful amount of whipped cream, laced with cinnamon. Makes 8 servings.

*Beyond Parsley*

Maifest and Oktoberfest are celebrated each year in the Missouri River town of Hermann by residents who are still proud to share their German heritage. The home of several renowned wineries, the whole town of Hermann is a National Historic Site.

# Raspberry Torte

**CRUST:**

| | |
|---|---|
| 1⅓ cups flour | 1 cup ground walnuts |
| 3 tablespoons sugar | 1 egg yolk |
| 11 tablespoons chilled unsalted butter, cut into pieces | ⅔ cup seedless raspberry jam |

Combine the flour and sugar in a food processor. Cut in the butter, using rapid on/off turns, until the mixture resembles coarse meal. Blend in the walnuts. With the machine running, add yolk through the feed tube and mix just until the dough comes together. Gather into a ball and press into the bottom and ⅔ the way up the sides of a 9-inch springform pan. Spread the bottom with half of the jam and chill.

**FILLING:**

| | |
|---|---|
| 1½ cups packed brown sugar | ¼ cup flour |
| 1 egg | ½ teaspoon baking powder |
| 1¼ cups chopped walnuts | ⅛ teaspoon salt |
| ¾ cup shredded coconut | |

Using a mixer, beat the brown sugar and egg in a large bowl for 10 minutes until it is very thick. Mix the remaining ingredients and pour it into the crust.

Preheat oven to 300° and bake for 25-30 minutes, until the filling is set. Cool completely and spread the top with the remaining jam. Serves 10.

*Bouquet Garni*

# Nut Torte
# with Fabulous Frosting

4 eggs, separated
1 cup sugar
2 tablespoons flour
½ teaspoon salt

½ teaspoon baking powder
1 tablespoon orange juice or
 Jamaican rum
2 cups pecans, chopped

Beat egg yolks until thick and light; then beat in sugar. Stir in flour, salt, baking powder, orange juice or Jamaican rum, and chopped pecans (reserve 2 tablespoons for frosting). Beat the egg whites until stiff and fold in. Pour into 2 greased 8-inch layer cake pans. Bake in preheated 350° oven for 25 minutes. Cool. Remove from pans, and 1-3 hours before serving, put layers together with filling and frosting.

**FILLING:**

½ cup whipping cream,
 whipped

1½ teaspoons grated
 orange rind

Mix ingredients and put between layers.

**FROSTING:**

6 ounces semi-sweet
 chocolate, melted

½ cup sour cream
Dash salt

Mix together, spread on torte and garnish with reserved nuts.

*The Cook Book*

# Dirt Cake

2 cups powdered sugar
2 (8-ounce) containers Cool
  Whip
2 (8-ounce) packages cream
  cheese

2 large packages chocolate
  pudding
4 cups milk
1 (20-ounce) package Oreo
  cookies

Mix powdered sugar, Cool Whip, and cream cheese. Set aside. Make pudding with milk, let cool completely. Crush Oreo cookies till they look like dirt. In flower pot, layer cookies, pudding and cream cheese mixture, ending with cookies. Refrigerate. Before serving, add silk flowers.

Instant pudding may be used. Skim milk may be used. Flower pot measures 8½ inches at top.

*USO's Salute to the Troops Cookbook*

# Whipped Cream Chocolate Roll

6 ounces semi-sweet
  chocolate bits
5 tablespoons brewed coffee
6 egg whites
6 egg yolks

1 cup sugar
½ pint heavy cream
1 teaspoon vegetable oil
Lemon or orange rind,
  grated (optional)

Melt chocolate with coffee on stove. Meanwhile, whip egg whites until stiff. In separate bowl whip the egg yolks and gradually add sugar. Add the melted chocolate mixture to the egg yolks and fold into the whites.

Spread half of oil around jelly roll pan and place waxed paper on pan. Spread remaining oil on waxed paper. Pour mixture into pan. Bake 15 minutes at 375° and don't pre-heat oven. Remove from oven and let cool. Then turn over onto a towel. Whip the cream and spread onto cake with optional grated rind, and then roll.

Serve with fresh strawberries.

*Gourmet Garden*

# Christmas Pound Cake

Make well ahead—keeps in freezer for 3 months. Keeps well unrefrigerated for a week to 10 days.

1 (18.25-ounce) box yellow cake mix (Betty Crocker Super Moist Butter Yellow Cake Mix preferred)
1 (3¾-ounce) box vanilla pudding and pie filling mix
3 eggs
⅓ cup corn oil
1 (5½-ounce) can apricot nectar (⅔ cup)
¼ cup apricot brandy
1½ teaspoons pure orange extract

Preheat oven to 325°. Grease and flour a 10-inch Bundt pan (or any pan of equivalent size). In mixing bowl, combine cake mix, pudding mix, eggs, oil, apricot nectar, apricot brandy, and orange extract. Mix until all ingredients are well blended.

Pour into Bundt pan and bake 1 hour at 325° or until cake tests done. Invert on a cake plate and prick all over before spooning on glaze.

**GLAZE:**

4 tablespoons butter
¾ cup sugar
¼ cup water
⅓ cup apricot brandy

Heat butter, sugar, and water in small saucepan until butter is melted and sugar is dissolved. Remove from heat; add apricot brandy, mixing well. Prick cake on top and sides with fork. Spoon glaze slowly over cake, letting cake absorb liquid before adding additional glaze. If freezing, wrap in heavy aluminum foil; leave out overnight. Wrap additionally in freezer wrap; tape all open edges closed and freeze.

To serve: Place on a cake plate, surround with fresh holly; place sprigs of fresh holly on top of cake, and tuck either red maraschino or candied cherries in and among the holly leaves. Serves 18-20.

*It's Christmas!*

# Whole Wheat Angel Food Cake

This cake is a great variation on the basic Angel Food Cake. It has added texture and a wonderful taste. It is excellent for people watching their cholesterol and consumption of fat.

¾ cup whole wheat flour
¼ cup cornstarch
1½ cups sugar
12 large egg whites
½ teaspoon salt

1½ teaspoons cream of
   tartar
1 teaspoon vanilla
1 teaspoon almond extract

Heat oven to 375°. Combine flour, cornstarch and ¾ cup sugar in a small bowl. Stir until thoroughly mixed; set aside. Separate eggs, being sure there is no yolk mixed with the whites. Add salt and cream of tartar. Whip until whites will stand in peaks. Gradually add remaining ¾ cup sugar and flavorings. Sprinkle ⅓ of the flour mixture over the beaten whites; fold in carefully. Repeat twice with the remaining flour mixture, folding the last ⅓ only until it is thoroughly mixed. Pour into 10-inch angel food cake pan. Bake 35-40 minutes. Invert pan to cool. Serve slices of cake with Strawberry Glaze.

**STRAWBERRY GLAZE:**
¾ cup sugar
3 tablespoons cornstarch
¾ cup lemon-lime
   carbonated beverage

Red food coloring
1 pint strawberries

Combine sugar and cornstarch in a medium saucepan. Gradually stir in carbonated beverage. Cook over low heat, stirring constantly, until smooth and thickened. Stir in a few drops of red food coloring. Wash strawberries and remove stems. Spoon glaze over berries.

*From the Ozarks' Oven...*

# Pumpkin Cheesecake

**CRUST:**

1½ cups graham cracker
  crumbs
½ cup almonds, ground

½ teaspoon ginger
½ teaspoon cinnamon
⅓ cup butter, melted

Preheat oven to 425°. Combine ingredients and press in an even layer on the bottom of a 10-inch springform pan. Bake for 10 minutes or until the crust is lightly browned. Reduce the oven temperature to 325°.

**FILLING:**

32 ounces cream
  cheese, softened
1¼ cups sugar
3 tablespoons maple syrup
3 tablespoons cognac
1 teaspoon ginger

1 teaspoon cinnamon
½ teaspoon nutmeg
4 large eggs, room
  temperature
¼ cup heavy cream
1 cup cooked pumpkin

Beat the cream cheese until smooth. Gradually add the sugar, beating it until fluffy and light. Add the maple syrup, cognac, ginger, cinnamon, and nutmeg, blending well. Add the eggs, one at a time, beating thoroughly after each addition. Add the cream and the pumpkin and mix well. Pour the filling mixture into the cooled crust and bake for 45 minutes.

Turn off the oven. Do not open the oven door during baking time or for 1 hour after the oven is turned off. Then remove the cake.

**TOPPING:**

2 cups sour cream
¼ cup sugar
1 tablespoon maple syrup

1 tablespoon cognac
¼ cup almonds
1 tablespoon butter

Preheat oven to 425°. Blend the sour cream, sugar, maple syrup, and cognac. Spread over the cake and bake for 10 minutes. Allow the cheesecake to cool at room temperature for 1 hour. Sauté the almonds in the butter. Arrange in a ring around the perimeter of the cake. Chill for at least 3 hours before removing the sides of the pan. Serves 12.

*Note:* This cake freezes well.

*Bouquet Garni*

# Chocolate Turtle Cheesecake

2 cups vanilla wafer crumbs
6 tablespoons margarine, melted
1 (14-ounce) bag caramels
1 (5-ounce) can evaporated milk
1 cup chopped pecans, toasted

2 (8-ounce) packages cream cheese, softened
½ cup sugar
1 teaspoon vanilla extract
2 eggs
½ cup semi-sweet chocolate chips, melted

Combine crumbs and margarine. Press into bottom of 9-inch springform pan. Bake at 350° for 10 minutes. Melt caramels with milk in 1 ½-quart heavy saucepan over low heat, stirring frequently, until smooth. Pour over crust. Top with pecans.

Combine cream cheese, sugar and vanilla, mixing at medium speed until well blended. Add eggs, 1 at a time, mixing well after each addition. Blend in chocolate. Mix well. Pour over pecans. Bake at 350° for 40 minutes. Loosen cake from rim of pan. Cool before removing rim completely. Chill. Makes 10-12 servings.

*Delicious Reading*

# Surprise Cupcakes

**FILLING:**

1 (8-ounce) package cream
  cheese, softened
1 egg
⅓ cup sugar

½ teaspoon salt
6 ounces semi-sweet
  chocolate chips

**BATTER:**

3 cups flour
2 cups sugar
½ cup cocoa
1 teaspoon salt
2 teaspoons soda

⅓ cup vegetable oil
2 cups water
2 tablespoons vinegar
2 teaspoons vanilla

Combine filling ingredients except chocolate chips; beat until smooth and add chocolate chips. Set aside. Sift together all dry ingredients. Add all liquids to sifted ingredients and blend until smooth. Fill cupcake tins ⅔ full and drop in a heaping teaspoon of filling. Bake at 350° for 25 minutes. Makes 26 cupcakes.

*Company's Coming*

# Surprise Lemon Pudding
# Under Golden Cake Topping

1 cup sugar
¼ cup sifted enriched
  flour
Dash salt
2 tablespoons melted butter
  or margarine

5 tablespoons lemon juice
2 teaspoons grated lemon
  peel
3 well beaten egg yolks
1½ cups milk, scalded
3 stiff-beaten egg whites

Preheat oven to 325°. Combine sugar, flour, salt, and butter; add lemon juice and peel. Combine the beaten egg yolks and milk; add to first mixture. Fold in egg whites and pour into 8 greased 5-ounce custard cups (Pyrex).

Bake in pan of hot water in slow oven (325°) 45 minutes. When baked, each dessert will have custard on the bottom and sponge cake on top. Makes 8 servings.

*Covered Bridge Neighbors Cookbook*

# Cookies and Candies

*Mark Twain's Statue appropriately looks out over the*
*Mississippi River that he wrote about and loved. Hannibal.*

# Brown Edge Cookies

You can't make enough!

| | |
|---|---|
| 1 cup butter | 1 teaspoon vanilla |
| ²/₃ cup sugar | 1½ cups flour (sifted) |
| 2 eggs | ¼ teaspoon salt |

Cream butter and sugar. Add eggs, beating well. Add vanilla. Mix in flour and salt. Drop by teaspoon on greased cookie sheet. Bake in preheated 350° oven for 10 minutes. Makes about 60 cookies.

*Note:* Allow space between dropped dough because cookies spread.

*The Cook Book*

# Lazy Sugar Cookies

| | |
|---|---|
| ½ cup butter or oleo | 1 egg |
| ½ cup vegetable shortening | ½ teaspoon cream of tartar |
| ½ cup sugar | ½ teaspoon baking soda |
| ½ cup powdered sugar | ½ teaspoon salt |
| 1½ teaspoons vanilla extract | 2¼ cups flour |

Cream butter, shortening, and sugars. Add vanilla extract, egg, cream of tartar, baking soda, and salt; blend. Add flour and mix well. Roll dough into walnut-size balls, roll in sugar and place on a cookie sheet about 2 inches apart. Flatten with glass dipped in sugar. Bake in 350° oven for 10-12 minutes. Makes about 3-4 dozen cookies.

*Steamboat Adventures*

# Irish Lace Sandwich Cookies

½ cup (1 stick) butter
1 cup sugar
1 egg
1 teaspoon almond extract

2 tablespoons flour
⅓ teaspoon salt
1 cup quick-cooking oats

Cream softened butter and sugar in a mixing bowl. Add egg and almond extract, mixing well. Add flour, salt, and oats. Line a baking sheet with aluminum foil. Use a melon baller (for more uniform shapes) or drop by ½ teaspoonfuls onto foil. (Use only this small amount; dough will spread to give a lacy effect in the finished cookie.) Place only 6 cookies at a time on an average-size baking sheet.

Bake in a 350° oven 5-8 minutes, or until light brown. Slide foil off sheet and completely cool cookies before removing from foil. (If they resist at all, they are not completely cool.)

**FILLING:**

4 ounces bittersweet or
   semisweet chocolate
1 tablespoon butter

2 tablespoons grated orange
   zest
1 tablespoon Grand Marnier

Melt chocolate and butter in top of a double boiler or in a microwave at MEDIUM POWER. Stir in orange zest and Grand Marnier. Cool slightly. Spread mixture on flat side of 1 cookie and sandwich with a second. Let cool and serve. Makes 18 sandwich cookies.

**Note:** Serve these light treats with a scoop of vanilla ice cream or orange sherbert, and a cup of cinnamon-flavored coffee.

*Above & Beyond Parsley*

---

Twelve exhibits in the Hallmark Visitors Center in Kansas City tell visitors the story of this world famous greeting-card company.

# Sour Cream Cashew Drops

The best cookie we've tasted for your Christmas goodies tray.

| | |
|---|---|
| 2 cups sifted flour | ½ cup soft butter |
| 1 teaspoon baking powder | 1 cup brown sugar |
| ¾ teaspoon soda | 1 teaspoon vanilla |
| ¼ teaspoon salt | ½ cup sour cream |
| 1 egg | 1½ cups cashew nuts |

Sift flour, baking powder, soda, and salt together into mixing bowl. Put egg, butter, brown sugar, vanilla, and sour cream in blender container. Cover and run on medium speed until smooth. Stop blender and add nuts. Cover and run on medium speed until nuts are coarsely chopped. Pour into flour mixture and stir to mix. Drop by teaspoonfuls onto lightly greased cookie sheets. Bake at 375° for 10 minutes or until golden brown. Cool and frost with a white butter frosting.

**FROSTING:**

| | |
|---|---|
| 2 cups powdered sugar | 2 tablespoons cream |
| 4 tablespoons butter | 1 teaspoon vanilla |

Cream butter and vanilla. Add remaining ingredients and beat until smooth.

    Can be frozen—frost before freezing. Makes 5 dozen.

*Finely Tuned Foods*

# Big Fat Cookies

| | |
|---|---|
| 1 (18.5-ounce) package yellow or devils food cake mix with pudding | 2 eggs |
| | 1 cup semi-sweet chocolate chips |
| ½ cup water | |

Prepare the cake mix as directed on package except use ½ cup water and 2 eggs—omit salad oil. Drop by tablespoons onto greased cookie sheet. Sprinkle with 1 cup chocolate chips. Bake 8-10 minutes at 375° or until almost no impression remains when a cookie is touched lightly. Yield: 3 dozen.

*Chockful O' Chips*

# Monster Cookies

12 eggs
2 pounds brown sugar
4 cups sugar
1 tablespoon vanilla
1 tablespoon syrup or honey
1 pound butter (no substitutions), softened

3 pounds peanut butter
18 cups oats
1 pound chocolate chips
1 pound M&M's candy

Needed: One strong-armed man to mix in large dishpan all ingredients in order given. Drop by tablespoonfuls and flatten on ungreased cookie sheets. Bake at 350° for 10-12 minutes. Do not overbake. Let cool on cookie sheet. Bake cookies until you are tired. Freeze remaining dough in Ziploc bags. Makes 200 cookies.

*Note:* There really is no flour in this recipe.
*Variation:* Add 8 teaspoons baking soda.

*Delicious Reading*

# Chocolate Chip Cookies
### (Sugar Free)

1 cup flour
½ teaspoon soda
¼ teaspoon salt
½ cup butter
4 teaspoons liquid sugar substitute

½ teaspoon vanilla
1 egg, beaten
½ cup semi-sweet chocolate chips

Sift together dry ingredients. Cream butter. Add sugar substitute, vanilla and egg, blending well. Add flour mixture and beat well. Stir in chocolate chips. Drop by teaspoons onto a greased baking sheet. Bake for 10 minutes at 375°.
Yield: 3 dozen.

*Chockful O' Chips*

# Coconut Cookies

2 cups sifted flour
½ teaspoon salt
2 teaspoon baking powder
½ cup shortening

1 cup sugar
2 eggs
½ teaspoon vanilla
1½ cups coconut

Sift together flour, salt, and baking powder. Mix until creamy the shortening, sugar, eggs, and vanilla. Mix in flour mixture, then add coconut. Mix well. Refrigerate for 1 hour or more.

Form dough into 1-inch balls. Place on cookie sheet; flatten with bottom of a glass covered with cheesecloth or dipped in sugar. Bake in a 350° oven, about 12 minutes or until done.

*Recipes Old and New*

# Biscotti Italian Cookies

1 cup shortening or
   margarine
3 eggs
5 cups flour
½ teaspoon salt (optional)
1 cup sugar

⅓ cup milk
1 teaspoon vanilla extract
4 teaspoons baking powder
1 package mini chocolate
   chips

Mix all ingredients. Knead a little. Make cookies into 2-inch finger shape size and place on ungreased baking sheet. Bake at 350° for 10-12 minutes or until light brown. When cool sprinkle with powdered sugar. This recipe is an old Milanese recipe.

*St. Ambrose "On the Hill" Cookbook*

# Melt In Your Mouth
# Chocolate Cocoanut Macaroons

Everybody's favorite.

1 cup sweetened condensed
  milk
4 cups cocoanut
⅔ cup mini semi-sweet
  chocolate bits

1 teaspoon vanilla extract
½ teaspoon almond extract

Preheat oven to 325°. Combine sweetened condensed milk and cocoanut. Mix well by hand—mixture will be gooey. Add chocolate bits, vanilla, and almond extract. Stir until all ingredients are well blended.

Lightly spray a "non stick" (Teflon coated) cookie sheet with a "no stick" cooking spray. Drop by teaspoonfuls onto cookie sheet, one inch apart. Cook 12 minutes or until lightly brown on top.

Remove from pan with a Teflon coated spatula and let cool. Store in an airtight container or in Ziploc freezer bags. Freezes well. Yields 50-55 cookies.

*It's Christmas!*

# Chocolate Chip Cream Squares

2 (16-ounce) rolls chocolate
  chip cookie dough
1 (16-ounce) package cream
  cheese, softened

2 eggs
½ cup sugar
½ teaspoon vanilla

Pat one roll of dough in bottom of greased 9x13-inch pan. Cream together cream cheese, eggs, sugar, and vanilla. Spread mixture on top of dough in pan. Crumble the second roll of dough on top of cream mixture. Bake about 30 minutes at 350°. Dough will be soft in center. Yield: 2 dozen.

*Chockful O' Chips*

# Marguerites

No one around 1900 would have thought of giving a reception, tea, or such entertainment without making the then popular "Marguerites" which were made on the expensive and select Saratoga crackers. Have on hand the crackers, any quantity of egg whites sufficient for the crackers, chopped black walnut meats and shredded coconut.

Crackers
2 egg whites
½ cup sugar
⅛ teaspoon salt

½ teaspoon vanilla
1 cup chopped black walnuts
Shredded coconut

Beat the egg whites to a very stiff foam, then add sugar in the proportion of ½ cup to each 2 egg whites and ⅛ teaspoon salt, adding the sugar by the teaspoonful and whipping with a flat wire whip. When very stiff, add ½ teaspoon vanilla and about 1 cup chopped nut meats. Spread this on the crackers. Sprinkle with coconut if you so desire. Place on cookie tins and pop into the oven to brown lightly and beautifully.

(*Editor's Note:* Bake at 250° about 20 minutes until dried but not browned, then turn off heat and leave in oven till cool, about an hour.)

*The Shaw House Cook Book*

# Soda Cracker Bars

Soda crackers may sound like an unlikely ingredient, but once these cookies are baked, no one knows what the crust is. These bars are quick and easy—and unbelievably delicious. I use unsalted crackers.

Saltine crackers
1 cup dark brown sugar
1 cup (2 sticks) butter or margarine, melted

1 (12-ounce) package semi-sweet chocolate morsels

Line a jelly roll pan (or cookie sheet with sides) with foil. Cover foil with 1 layer of crackers (breaking them as necessary to have sides touching). Mix brown sugar and melted butter in saucepan. Bring to a boil and continue boiling for 3 minutes. Remove from heat and spread mixture over crackers.

Bake 5 minutes in a 400° oven. While cookies are hot, sprinkle chocolate morsels over them. As chips melt, spread chocolate evenly with a spatula. Store in the refrigerator or a cool place. Makes 30 bars. Best to cut while still warm.

*USO's Salute to the Troops Cookbook*

# Old-Fashioned Oatmeal Apple Cookies

¾ cup butter Crisco
1¼ cups packed brown sugar
1 egg
¼ cup milk
1½ teaspoons vanilla
3 cups quick cooking oats
1 cup flour

1¼ teaspoons cinnamon
¼ teaspoon nutmeg
½ teaspoon soda
½ teaspoon salt
1 cup peeled and diced apples
¾ cup raisins
¾ cup walnuts

Cream Crisco, brown sugar, egg, milk, and vanilla. Combine all dry ingredients and add to creamed mixture. Mix well. add nuts and apples. Stir in oats. Drop by tablespoons on greased cookie sheet. Bake at 375° for 13 minutes.

*Home Cookin'*

# Scrumptious Chocolate Surprises

Make ahead and freeze.

1¼ cups (1½ sticks)
butter or butter substitute,
room temperature
2 cups sugar
2 eggs
2 teaspoons vanilla extract

¾ cup unsweetened cocoa
powder
2 cups all-purpose flour
1 teaspoon soda
1 teaspoon salt

Preheat oven to 350°. In a large bowl, cream butter, sugar, eggs, and vanilla. Add cocoa and mix until well blended. Add flour, soda, and salt. This mixture will seem very thick. Mix until well blended. Drop by one-half teaspoonfuls on a greased cookie sheet—or use a Teflon, no stick cookie sheet. Bake 8 minutes at 350°.

TOPPING:
1 (10-ounce) bag large
marshmallows

1 (6-ounce) bag semi-sweet
chocolate chips

While cookies are baking, quarter marshmallows and set aside. (Dip scissors into cold water if they become sticky.) Remove cookies from oven at 8 minutes, top each cookie with one quarter of a marshmallow and return to oven. Cook 4 minutes. Remove from oven and place one semi-sweet chocolate chip in center of each marshmallow. Gently press chocolate chip into marshmallow. Heat from cookie will slightly melt bottom of chip and allow chocolate chip to adhere to marshmallow. Let cool completely and store in an airtight container, or freeze up to 2 months. Yields 6 dozen.

*It's Christmas!*

Laura Ingalls Wilder won international fame as the author of *Little House on the Prairie* and seven other "Little House" books for children. She came to live at Mansfield in the Missouri Ozarks in 1894. She was 65 when in 1932 she wrote her first book, and retired after her eighth in 1943.

# Strawberry Squares

| | |
|---|---|
| 1 cup sifted all-purpose flour | 2 egg whites |
| ¼ cup brown sugar | 1 cup sugar, granulated |
| ½ cup black walnuts, chopped | 2 cups strawberries, sliced |
| | 2 tablespoons lemon juice |
| ½ cup butter, melted | 1 cup whipping cream, whipped |

Mix first 4 ingredients; bake in shallow pan at 350° for 20 minutes. Stir occasionally. Sprinkle ⅔ crumbs in 13x9x2-inch pan. Combine egg whites, granulated sugar, berries, and lemon juice. Beat at high speed about 10 minutes. Fold in whipped cream. Top with remaining crumbs. Freeze 6 hours. Serves 12.

*The Never Ending Season*

# Key Lime Squares

A new twist to an old favorite.

**CRUST:**

| | |
|---|---|
| 1 cup margarine | 2 cups flour |
| ½ cup powdered sugar | Pinch of salt |

Combine margarine, powdered sugar, flour, and salt with pastry blender or mixer. Pat into a well-greased 9x12x2-inch pan. Bake at 350° for 15-20 minutes.

**FILLING:**

| | |
|---|---|
| 4 eggs | 6 tablespoons flour |
| 2 cups sugar | Rind of one lime, grated |
| 6 tablespoons lime juice | |

Beat eggs and add sugar, lime juice, flour, and lime rind. Put on top of baked pastry and bake for 25 minutes. Sprinkle with powdered sugar while warm. Cut into squares.

*Finely Tuned Foods*

# Apricot Butter Bars

½ cup finely snipped
  apricots, cooked
¾ cup cold butter
1½ cups sifted flour
1 egg

½ cup brown sugar, firmly
  packed
½ teaspoon vanilla extract
½ cup pecans, chopped
Lemon Glaze

Put snipped apricots into a heavy saucepan with a small amount of water, 5-6 tablespoons. Cover and cook over low heat until water is absorbed. If they are still in firm pieces, mash them with a fork or give them a buzz in the food processor. Cool.

Cut butter into flour until particles are the size of a rice kernel. Press evenly into a 9x13-inch baking pan. Bake at 350° for 15 minutes. Beat egg, brown sugar and vanilla until thick. Stir into mixture of apricots and pecans. Spread evenly over partially baked layer in pan. Return to oven and bake about 20 minutes, or until light brown around the edge. Remove from oven and immediately spread Lemon Glaze over top. Cut when cool.

**LEMON GLAZE:**

¾ cup confectioners' sugar     ¼ teaspoon lemon extract
2 tablespoons lemon juice

Blend and spread on top of apricot mixture.

*Eat Pie First...Life is Uncertain!*

# Yum Yum Bars
### *(Dates)*

1 egg
1 cup sugar
1 cup flour
2 tablespoons baking powder
½ teaspoon salt

½ cup milk
1 cup chopped dates
1 cup chopped nuts
Powdered sugar

Beat egg well, add sugar, mixing well.  Combine flour and baking powder, and salt.  Add milk and dry ingredients to sugar mixture.  Fold in dates and nuts.  Bake at 350° for 30-35 minutes.

While hot, cut into squares and roll in powdered sugar. Store in tight container so they will not dry out.  Use a 9x9-inch baking pan.

This comes from a cookbook of the 1920s that my mother had.  She prepared these for Christmas when I was a child. It was a treat at Christmas time.

*Recipes & Stories of Early-Day Settlers*

# Coconut Bars

10 slices white bread
(sandwich)
⅓ cup plus 1 tablespoon
white corn syrup

⅛ teaspoon vanilla
1 small can evaporated milk
1 (12-ounce) package
shredded coconut

Use 2 or 3-day old bread.  Trim crust and cut each slice into halves.

Put corn syrup in measuring cup, add vanilla, fill to 1 cup with evaporated milk, stir to blend.  Pour in shallow bowl. Grind or chop 1 cup of the coconut to consistency of coarse cornmeal; put in second bowl.

Lightly grease a cookie sheet and preheat oven to 375°.

Dip bread into milk, roll in coconut and place on cookie sheet. Sprinkle tops with some of the regular shredded coconut and bake for 15-17 minutes or until golden brown.  Remove with spatula and allow to cool on waxed paper.

*The Sportsman's Dish*

# Toffee Nut Bars

½ cup butter
½ cup brown sugar
1 cup flour, sifted
2 eggs, well-beaten
1 cup brown sugar
1 teaspoon vanilla

2 tablespoons flour
1 teaspoon baking powder
½ teaspoon salt
1 cup coconut, shredded
1 cup almonds, sliced,
   or pecans, chopped

Cream butter and ½ cup brown sugar. Mix in flour and press into ungreased 9x13-inch baking pan. Bake at 350° for 10 minutes. Cool.

Combine eggs, 1 cup brown sugar, and vanilla. Add flour, baking powder, and salt. Add coconut and almonds, and spread mixture over first layer. Return to 350° oven for 20-25 minutes or until topping is golden brown. Cool and cut into 24 bars.

*Company's Coming*

# Chewy Noels

These are good and easy to make.

2 tablespoons margarine
2 eggs
1 cup brown sugar (packed)
5 tablespoons flour

⅛ teaspoon soda
1 cup chopped nuts
1 teaspoon vanilla
Powdered sugar

Heat oven to 350°. Melt margarine in a 9-inch square pan over low heat, then remove from heat. Beat eggs slightly. Combine sugar, flour, soda, and nuts and stir into beaten eggs. Add vanilla. Pour over melted margarine; don't stir, but spread evenly. Bake 20 minutes. Turn out onto rack, sprinkle bottom with powdered sugar, then cut in oblongs. Serves 18.

*Treasured Recipes Book I*

# Swedish Raspberry Shortbread

1 (18½-ounce) box butter
  cake mix
½ cup finely chopped
  pecans
¼ cup butter, softened
1 egg

1 (10-ounce) jar raspberry
  preserves
½ cup powdered sugar
2½ teaspoons water
½ teaspoon almond extract

Preheat oven to 350°. Grease and flour a 9x13-inch pan. In a large bowl combine cake mix, nuts, butter, and egg. Mix at low speed until crumbly. Press mixture on bottom of prepared pan. Spread with preserves. Bake 25 minutes or until edges are light brown. Combine sugar, water and almond extract and mix until smooth. Drizzle over warm shortbread. Cool completely and cut into bars. Makes 3 dozen.

*Sassafras!*

# Cherry Bar Squares

1 cup oleo, softened
1¾ cups sugar
4 eggs
3 cups flour
1½ teaspoons baking
  powder

¼ teaspoon salt
1 teaspoon vanilla
1 can cherry pie filling
Powdered sugar and milk
  to make glaze

Cream together oleo and sugar. Add eggs, 1 at a time, beating well after each addition. Add flour, baking powder, and salt. Mix well. Add vanilla and stir again. Batter will be thick. Spread ¾ of the batter in a greased jelly roll pan. Then put 1 cup of cherry pie filling on top, spreading the cherries as evenly as possible Put remaining batter in dollops over all. It will spread as it bakes. Bake at 350° for 40-45 minutes. Remove from oven and while still warm, ice with powdered sugar icing by drizzling over baked bars—won't take much, mostly to make it look pretty!

*Remembering the Past—Planning for the Future*

# Yum Yums

50 light caramels
²/₃ cup evaporated milk
1 (17½-ounce) package
  German chocolate cake mix
²/₃ cup butter or margarine,
  melted

1 cup nuts, chopped
1 cup semi-sweet chocolate
  morsels

Combine caramels and ⅓ cup evaporated milk in top of a double boiler. Cook and stir over boiling water until caramels are melted; set aside.

Combine dry cake mix, butter, remaining ⅓ cup milk and nuts in a large mixing bowl. Stir until dough holds together. Press half the dough into a greased and floured 13x9-inch pan, reserving remaining dough for topping. Bake at 350° for 6 minutes. Sprinkle chocolate pieces over baked crust. Spread caramel mixture over chocolate pieces; crumble remaining dough over caramel mixture. Return to oven and bake 15-18 minutes longer. Cool slightly, then chill for 30 minutes. Cut into bars. Makes 36 bars.

*Gourmet Garden*

# Cheesecake Brownies

**CHEESE MIX:**

1 (8-ounce) package cream
  cheese, softened
½ teaspoon vanilla

⅓ cup sugar
1 egg

In a bowl, combine cheese mixture ingredients and set aside. Preheat oven to 350°.

**BROWNIE MIX:**

1¼ cups sugar
2 eggs
½ cup butter or margarine,
  melted

¾ cup flour
¼ cup cocoa
1 teaspoon vanilla

Grease and flour a 8 or 9-inch pan. In a bowl combine sugar and eggs. Add the melted butter; mix in flour, cocoa and vanilla. Pour ¾ of the brownie mixture in the pan. Cover with cheese mixture and top with remaining brownie mixture. Swirl mixtures, but do not mix together. Bake 45 minutes. Set aside to cool.

**FROSTING:**

3 tablespoons butter
2 cups powdered sugar
½ teaspoon vanilla

2 tablespoons cocoa
2-4 tablespoons milk or
  cream

Combine butter, sugar, vanilla and cocoa. Add milk or cream as needed for spreading. Frost brownies. Easy. Can freeze. Yields 16-24 pieces.

*Variation:* For a larger yield, double brownie and cheese mixture ingredients using a 9x13-inch pan. (Follow recipe instructions, bake 45-55 minutes). To frost use 4 tablespoons butter, 3 cups powdered sugar, 1 teaspoon vanilla, 3-5 tablespoons milk or cream and 3 tablespoons cocoa.

*Cooking in Clover II*

# Killer Brownies

4 beaten eggs
2 cups sugar
1 cup melted margarine
1½ cups flour

1 teaspoon baking powder
6 tablespoons cocoa
1 teaspoon vanilla

Combine and cream eggs and sugar. Add melted margarine alternately with combined, sifted dry ingredients. Add vanilla. Bake in a 9x13-inch cake pan in a 350° oven for 27 minutes  Frost with Cocoa Satin Frosting.

COCOA SATIN ICING:
½ cup margarine
½ cup cocoa
1 pound confectioners'
   sugar, sifted
7 tablespoons milk

1 teaspoon vanilla
1 cup nuts (if you're making
   brownies it has to be black
   walnuts)

Melt the shortening in a saucepan, add the cocoa and heat for a minute until they are smooth, stirring constantly. Remove from heat and alternately add sugar and milk, beating to spreading consistency. Blend in vanilla and nuts.

*Eat Pie First...Life is Uncertain!*

# Triple Chocolate Coffee Brownies

1 beaten egg
1 (21½-ounces) package
   fudge brownie mix
¼ cup oil
¼ cup coffee liqueur or
   strong coffee
¼ cup strong coffee or water

¾ cup white baking pieces
   with cocoa butter (optional)
¾ cup milk chocolate pieces
½ cup semi-sweet chocolate
   pieces
½ cup chopped walnuts or
   pecans

In a large mixing bowl combine egg, brownie mix, oil and liquids. Stir in white baking pieces, chocolate pieces and nuts. Spread in a greased 9x13x2-inch baking pan. Bake in a 350° oven for 30 minutes. Cool completely, cut into bars. Makes 36 bars.

*Lavender and Lace*

# Spiced Candy Cake Roll

½ pound whole shelled
   Brazil nuts (1 cup)
½ pound pitted dates,
   uncut (1 cup)
1 (⅛-ounce) jar red maraschino cherries, drained
   (cut)
½ pound fine crushed
   graham crackers

½ pound marshmallows
1 tablespoon orange rind,
   grated
⅓ cup orange juice
⅛ teaspoon cinnamon
⅛ teaspoon nutmeg
⅛ teaspoon cloves
⅛ teaspoon allspice
⅛ teaspoon ginger

Mix nuts, dates, cherries and graham crackers well. Melt marshmallows with orange rind, orange juice, cinnamon, nutmeg, cloves, allspice and ginger in top of double boiler until melted. Stir into fruit and nut mixture. Divide and shape into 2 rolls. Wrap in aluminum foil. Chill 6-8 hours.

Unwrap and cover each roll in ¼ cup finely chopped nuts. Rewrap and freeze until ready to use. Cut ¼-inch thick. (I never freeze—we eat it throughout the holidays and eat it promptly.)

*Cooking on the Road*

# Truffles

| | |
|---|---|
| 8 ounces German sweet chocolate, broken into pieces | 2 tablespoons unsalted butter, room temperature |
| ⅔ cup heavy cream, scalded | ¼ cup unsweetened cocoa, mixed with a little |
| 1½ tablespoons Grand Marnier or favorite liqueur | cinnamon, or coarsely chopped toasted nuts |

Melt chocolate in a double boiler, stirring until smooth. Add cream, whisking vigorously until mixture is smooth. Stir in liqueur. Refrigerate at least 4 hours or overnight.

Beat chilled chocolate mixture and butter until smooth. Form into 1-inch balls and roll in cocoa and cinnamon mixture or nuts. (Chill if mixture gets too soft.) They will look rough and uneven like real truffles. Cover and refrigerate. Truffles may be kept in refrigerator up to one month, or frozen for several months. Approximately 70 truffles. Nestle truffles in a little silver basket.

***Beyond Parsley***

# Peanut Clusters

| | |
|---|---|
| 2 pounds white almond bark | 1 (12-ounce) package chocolate chips |
| 1 square unsweetened chocolate | 2 pounds dry-roasted peanuts |

Melt first 3 ingredients in crock pot or double boiler. Add dry roasted peanuts. Stir until coated.

Drop by spoonful on waxed paper. Cool. Makes 100-120.

***Covered Bridge Neighbors Cookbook***

Diamond is the birthplace of George Washington Carver, the first black scientist to achieve nationwide prominence. Carver's best-known work was his discovery of over 300 by-products of the peanut, which would become one of the South's most important crops.

# Almond Brittle

| 1 cup blanched whole | ½ cup sugar |
| almonds | 1 teaspoon vanilla |
| 2 tablespoons plus 1 | Salt |
| teaspoon butter | |

In a heavy skillet combine almonds, butter, and sugar. Cook over medium heat, stirring constantly with a wooden spoon until mixture caramelizes (turns golden caramel brown). This process takes approximately 20 minutes. Immediately add vanilla and mix through quickly. Pour onto sheet of heavy duty aluminum foil and spread as thin as possible quickly. Sprinkle lightly with salt. Cool thoroughly. Break into clusters. Store in airtight containers up to 4 months.

If recipe is doubled, the caramelizing process will take approximately 10 minutes longer. Easy. Can do ahead.

*Cooking in Clover*

# Microwave Almond Butter Toffee

| ¼ pound butter (do not use | 1 (4-ounce) package sliced |
| margarine) | or slivered almonds |
| 1 cup sugar | 4 ounces semisweet or milk |
| ½ teaspoon salt | chocolate |
| ¼ cup water | Additional butter for |
| | greasing |

Butter a 2- to 3-quart bowl appropriate for microwave cooking along the top edge. Place ¼ pound butter in the bowl. Pour sugar directly on butter and avoid getting sugar on the sides of the bowl. Add salt and water. Place in microwave and cook on HIGH for 7 minutes. Add time in 30-second intervals until mixture is the color of light brown sugar. Meanwhile place almonds on a greased cookie sheet.

When candy is ready, pour over almonds. Do not scrape bowl; let cool. Melt chocolate in microwave on HIGH for about 1½ minutes. Spread chocolate over candy and let cool. (If doing in warm weather, refrigerate.) Break candy into pieces. Easy. Can freeze. Serves 10.

*Cooking in Clover II*

# Persimmon Candy

5 cups sugar
½ cup light corn syrup
1 teaspoon salt
¾ cup persimmon pulp
1½ cups canned milk
  (evaporated)

1 teaspoon vanilla
4 tablespoons butter
½ cup chopped hickory nuts

Combine all ingredients except vanilla, butter, and nuts, in a heavy pan. Cook to a hard ball stage (approximately 32 minutes) over medium heat. Stir continually. Blend in vanilla and butter and vanilla. Set aside until cool. Beat mixture until it becomes dull. Add nuts. Pour into greased 9x12-inch dish and let stand until firm (at least 12 hours). Cut into 1-inch squares. Yield: 70 pieces.

*Steamboat Adventurés*

# Molasses Pull Taffy

"Taffy Pulls" were a popular form of entertainment around the turn of the century.

Combine one cup of molasses, two cups of sugar, one tablespoon of vinegar, and a little butter and vanilla. Boil for 10 minutes, then cool slightly. While still warm, pull the taffy again and again until it is white and thoroughly cooled. Cut into bite-size pieces. The taffy will keep for quite a long time.

*á la Rose*

# Carmel Corn

1 cup popcorn
2 cups brown sugar
1 cup margarine (2 sticks)

Pinch salt
1 teaspoon vanilla
½ teaspoon baking soda

Pop the popcorn. Boil sugar, margarine, and salt 5 minutes. Remove from heat. Add baking soda and vanilla and stir until white. Pour over popped corn. Put in large flat pan in 250° oven for 1 hour. Stir twice. Let cool. Break up and store in covered container.

*Treasured Recipes Book II*

## Pies and Desserts

Missouri's State Capitol sits atop a beautiful bluff overlooking
the Missouri River. Jefferson City.

# Caramel Apple Pecan Pie

³/₄ cup sugar
¹/₄ cup flour
1 teaspoon cinnamon
Dash of salt
¹/₈ teaspoon nutmeg

6 cups of peeled and sliced
   Jonathan or Granny Smith
   apples
Pastry for a double crust pie
1 tablespoon butter

Combine sugar, flour, cinnamon, salt, and nutmeg. Toss apples and sugar-flour-cinnamon mixture. Turn into a 9-inch pastry shell. Dot with butter. Cover with top crust. Moisten, seal, and flute edges with fingers or fork. Prick or slit top crust to allow steam to escape. Bake at 450° for 10-15 minutes, then reduce heat to 350° for 40-45 minutes. Remove from oven, and cool pie. Top with caramel topping.

**CARAMEL-PECAN TOPPING:**

8 ounces Kraft caramels
2 tablespoons evaporated
  milk

¹/₂ cup chopped pecans

Place caramels and milk in double boiler and heat, or melt in a microwave until smooth. Add ¹/₂ cup chopped pecans and spread over top of pie.

*Baked With Love*

# Green Apple Pie

1 pastry for double crust
Approximately 8 green apples
  (Lodi), pared, thinly sliced
¼ stick butter

½ cup sugar
½ cup brown sugar
3 tablespoons flour
¼ cup water

Make a bottom crust and fit it into a 9-inch pan, then fill with the sliced apples. Make a lattice top and place over the apples. Next, melt butter and add combined sugars, flour, and water; cook this until it starts to boil. Pour this mixture over the apples through the lattice top. Bake at 450° for 15 minutes, then reduce heat and finish baking at 350° for 45 minutes.

Wherever you take it, someone wants the recipe!

*Home Cookin'*

# Sugarless Apple Pie

6 medium Red Delicious
  apples, peeled and sliced
1 (6-ounce) can frozen apple
  juice (without sugar),
  thawed
1½ tablespoons cornstarch
⅓ cup water

1 teaspoon cinnamon
3 tablespoons margarine
2 (9-inch) unbaked pie
  crusts
Margarine, melted for
  basting

Place apples and undiluted apple juice into a large pan. Bring to a boil; reduce heat and simmer, covered, for about 5 minutes. Dissolve cornstarch in the water. Gently stir cornstarch into apple mixture. Bring to a boil, reduce heat and simmer, covered, for 10 minutes, or until apples begin to soften. Stir in cinnamon. Fill 1 (9-inch) pastry shell with apples, dot with 3 tablespoons margarine, and cover with top crust. Bake at 350° for 45 minutes. Baste with margarine after baking.

*Remembering the Past—Planning for the Future*

# Grated Apple Pie

| | |
|---|---|
| 1½ cups apples, grated | 1 teaspoon vanilla |
| 1 cup sugar | ½ teaspoon cinnamon |
| 1 tablespoon flour | ½ teaspoon cloves |
| 1 stick margarine, melted | ½ teaspoon ginger |
| 2 eggs, beaten | 1 (9-inch) unbaked pie crust |

Mix all ingredients together and put in unbaked pie crust. Bake for 20 minutes at 350°, then add the Coconut Topping:

| | |
|---|---|
| 1⅓ cups coconut, flaked | ¼ cup milk |
| ½ cup sugar | ½ teaspoon vanilla |
| 1 egg, well beaten | |

Mix topping ingredients and put on top of grated apple pie that has already cooked 20 minutes. Bake for another 25-30 minutes at 350°.

*Apples, Apples, Apples*

# Applescotch Crisp

| | |
|---|---|
| 4 cups peeled and sliced apples (4 medium) | ½ cup firmly packed brown sugar |
| 1 tablespoon flour | ¼ cup milk |
| ½ cup water | |

Combine in large bowl; mix well. Pour into ungreased 9-inch square baking pan.

| | |
|---|---|
| ⅔ cup flour | ½ cup butter or margarine, melted |
| ½ cup quick oatmeal | 1 (4-serving-size) package dry butterscotch or vanilla pudding mix (not instant) |
| ½ cup chopped nuts | |
| ¼ cup sugar | |
| ½ teaspoon salt | |
| 1 teaspoon cinnamon | |

Combine in medium bowl; mix until crumbly. Sprinkle over apples. Bake at 350° for 45-50 minutes, until apples are tender and topping is golden brown.

*Home Cookin'*

# Favorite Apple Betty

4 cups cooking apples,
   peeled and sliced
⅓ cup sugar

1 teaspoon cinnamon
¾ cup hot water

Combine apples, sugar, cinnamon, and water. Simmer 10 minutes or until tender. Pour into ungreased 9-inch pie pan. Sprinkle the following crumb topping over the apples:

**TOPPING:**

½ cup brown sugar
¼ cup shortening
2 tablespoons butter or
   margarine

1 cup flour
1 teaspoon baking powder
¼ teaspoon salt

Blend brown sugar, shortening, and butter. Add remaining ingredients and mix well. Mixture will be crumbly. Sprinkle over apples.

   Bake at 350° for 25-30 minutes. Serve warm or cold. Yield: 6 servings.

   Call it Apple Betty, Brown Betty or Blue Betty, it is absolutely the best Betty!

*From the Apple Orchard*

# Juicy Apple Dessert

2 eggs, beaten
1 cup sugar
4 cups apples, peeled and
  finely chopped
¼ cup vegetable oil

2 cups flour
1 teaspoon baking powder
1 teaspoon salt
1 teaspoon cinnamon
⅓ cup walnuts

Stir sugar into beaten eggs. Add chopped or grated apples and oil. Stir in sifted dry ingredients. Spread in greased 9x13-inch pan and bake at 350° for 35-40 minutes. When done, poke holes in cake with fork and pour hot topping over cake. Cover pan with aluminum foil and let cool.

**TOPPING:**

½ cup granulated sugar
½ cup brown sugar
2 tablespoons flour
¼ teaspoon salt

2 cups water
½ cup (1 stick) butter or
  margarine
1 teaspoon vanilla

Mix the sugars, flour, and salt in 1-quart saucepan. Add water and cook for 3 minutes. Add butter and vanilla.
  Yield: 16-20 servings.

*From the Apple Orchard*

# Ozark Pudding

This is well remembered as Mrs. Harry S. Truman's simple Missouri pudding during World War II.

1 egg
¾ cup sugar
2 tablespoon flour
1¼ teaspoons baking
  powder

⅛ teaspoon salt
½ cup chopped nuts
½ cup chopped apples
1 teaspoon vanilla
Whipped cream or ice cream

Beat egg and sugar until creamy. Add dry ingredients to eggs and sugar. Mix well. Add nuts, apples and vanilla. Bake in greased 9-inch square Pyrex baking dish at 350° for 35 minutes. Serve warm with whipped cream or ice cream.

*Cooking on the Road*

# Apple Roll

| | |
|---|---|
| 1½ cups sugar | 6 tablespoons shortening, |
| 2 cups water | cut in flour mixture |
| Handful of red hots | ⅔ - ¾ cup milk |
| 2 cups flour | 3 cups cut up apples |
| 3 teaspoons baking powder | 1 tablespoon butter |
| 2 tablespoons sugar | Sprinkle of cinnamon |
| 1 teaspoon salt | Whipped cream |

Place sugar, water, and red hots in 13x9-inch pan. Put in oven for sugar and red hots to melt and make syrup. In meantime, sift together flour, baking powder, sugar, and salt. Cut in shortening. Stir in ⅔ - ¾ cup milk to make soft dough.

Roll ⅓-inch thick into 6x12-inch oblong. Spread with 3 cups cut up apples, 1 tablespoon butter, and a sprinkle of cinnamon. Roll into a long roll. Pinch edges into roll to seal. Slice 1½ inches thick and quickly place slices into pan of hot syrup. Bake at 450° for 20-25 minutes, and serve warm with whipped cream. Makes 8 servings.

*Home Cookin'*

# Red Cinnamon Apple Rings

| | |
|---|---|
| 5 cooking apples | 2 or 3 sticks cinnamon, |
| 2 cups water | 2½ inches long |
| 2 cups sugar | |
| ½ teaspoon red food coloring | |

Peel and core apples. Slice in ¾-inch rings. Combine water, sugar, food coloring, and cinnamon in large skillet. Stir over low heat until sugar is dissolved. Bring mixture to boil, stirring often. Reduce heat; simmer 10 minutes. Arrange apple rings in syrup. Cook over low heat, basting often until rings are tender. Makes about 15 rings.

*Home Cookin'*

# Raspberry Bavarian Pie

2 egg whites
10 ounces raspberries (if frozen, thaw and drain)
1 cup sugar
1 tablespoon lemon juice
¼ teaspoon vanilla
¼ teaspoon almond extract
⅛ teaspoon salt
1 cup whipping cream
1 graham cracker crust

Beat egg whites. Add all ingredients, except whipping cream and crust. Beat for approximately 15 minutes. Whip cream and fold into raspberry mixture. Pile into graham cracker crumb crust and freeze for at least 8 hours.

This can also be used as a pudding without the crust.

*Heavenly Delights*

# Raspberry Dessert

2 (10-ounce) packages frozen red raspberries
1 cup water
½ cup sugar
2 teaspoons lemon juice
4 tablespoons cornstarch
¼ cup cold water
50 large marshmallows
1 cup milk
2 packages Dream Whip
1½ cups graham cracker crumbs
¼ cup chopped nuts
¼ cup margarine, melted

Heat raspberries with water, sugar, and lemon juice. Dissolve cornstarch in cold water, stir into raspberries, and cook until thick and clear. Cool. Melt marshmallows in milk. Cool thoroughly. Whip Dream Whip and fold into marshmallow mixture. Mix crumbs, nuts, and margarine, and spread over bottom of a 9x13-inch pan. Spread marshmallow mixture over crumbs. Spread raspberry mixture over top. Refrigerate until firm. Serves 15-18.

*Treasured Recipes Book II*

# Banana Split Pie

Mary's favorite!

3 egg yolks
½ cup granulated sugar
3½ tablespoons cornstarch
¼ teaspoon salt
2½ cups milk

½ cup crushed pineapple,
  well drained
1 teaspoon vanilla
1 large banana
8-10 maraschino cherries
1 prebaked pie crust

TOPPING:
Whipped cream
Maraschino cherries
Pecan pieces

¼ cup semi-sweet chocolate
  pieces, melted

Beat yolks and set aside. Combine sugar, cornstarch, and salt in saucepan. Add milk. Cook over medium heat until pudding begins to thicken. Add pineapple. Add egg yolks (to which some of hot filling has been added.) Cook until pudding has thickened. Add vanilla. Remove from heat. Cool to room temperature.

Add banana, sliced or chopped, and chopped maraschino cherries. Pour into prebaked pie crust. Top with whipped cream. Garnish with maraschino cherries, chopped pecans, and drizzle melted semi-sweet chocolate over pie. Serves 6.

*Luncheon Favorites*

Union Station in St. Louis was the largest and busiest rail terminal in the world in the '40s. Having undergone a massive historic preservation project, it is now a marketplace with more than 100 specialty shops and restaurants. It features a beautiful stained glass window under the famous Whispering Arch, where a word whispered on one side can be clearly heard on the other.

# Peaches and Cream Pie

¾ cup sugar
¼ cup quick cooking
  Tapioca
¼ teaspoon salt
¼ teaspoon nutmeg

1 cup whipping cream
  (½ pint)
1 (9-inch) pie shell, baked
1 quart peaches or
  nectarines, sliced and
  peeled (4 cups)

Combine sugar, Tapioca, salt and nutmeg, pour in cream; stir until blended. Let stand 30 minutes. Prepare pie shell. Fill shell with sliced peaches or nectarines, and pour in cream mixture. Bake at 400° for 40 minutes.

*Gourmet Garden*

# Rhubarb Goody

4 cups rhubarb (cut in
  ¼ - ½-inch pieces)
1 cup sugar

4 tablespoons flour
½ teaspoon cinnamon

Put rhubarb in a bowl; add sugar, flour, and cinnamon; stir to mix. Place mixture in an 8x8x2-inch greased pan.
  Preheat oven to 375°.

TOPPING:
1 cup flour
½ cup quick oats

1 cup light brown sugar
1 stick margarine

Mix flour, oats, and brown sugar together. Cut in margarine with a fork and stir until mixture is crumbly. Sprinkle topping over rhubarb. Bake for 35 minutes or until rhubarb is tender and top is golden brown.

*The Sportsman's Dish*

# Banbury Tarts

| | |
|---|---|
| 1 lemon | 1 egg, beaten |
| 1 cup raisins | 1 cup sugar |
| 2 soda crackers | Pie crust dough |

Grind lemon, raisins, and crackers, then mix with egg and sugar. Roll pie crust dough thin, cut in 4-inch squares or in rounds with a cookie cutter. Put a spoonful of the mixture on half of the square, fold over the dough and press edges together. Do the same with the rounds, except use 2 whole rounds, then press together. Puncture a few holes in the top with a fork to let steam escape. Place on a greased pan and bake until golden brown.

*Treasured Recipes Book I*

# Orange Chiffon Pie

| | |
|---|---|
| 1 envelope unflavored gelatin | 2 tablespoons fresh orange peel, grated |
| 1 cup sugar | ¼ cup lemon juice |
| ¼ teaspoon salt | ½ teaspoon fresh lemon peel, grated |
| ¾ cup milk | |
| 3 egg yolks, slightly-beaten | 10-inch pastry shell, baked |
| ⅓ cup orange juice concentrate, undiluted | 1 cup heavy cream, whipped |
| | Grated orange peel for garnish |

Combine gelatin, sugar, and salt in saucepan. Add milk and egg yolks. Cook and stir over medium heat until thickened slightly. Remove from heat and add juices and grated peels. Chill until partially set, at least 2 hours. Fold in all except ¼ cup whipped cream. Chill until mixture mounds. Pile into pastry shell and chill. Garnish with remaining whipped cream and grated orange peel. Serves 8.

*Company's Coming*

# Good Good Pie

¾ stick margarine, melted
3 eggs
3 tablespoons flour
1½ cups sugar

1 cup crushed pineapple, drained
1 cup coconut flakes
1 (9-inch) unbaked pie shell

Mix first 6 ingredients, pour into pie shell. Bake 1 hour at 350° or until set and brown.

*Kitchen Prescriptions*

# Hawaiian Coconut Cream Pie

½ cup sugar
3½ tablespoons cornstarch
¼ teaspoon salt
½ cup flaked coconut
2½ cups milk
3 egg yolks
½ cup crushed pineapple, drained

1 teaspoon vanilla
1 banana
1 (9-inch) pie shell, prebaked
1 cup whipping cream, whipped

In heavy saucepan or top of double boiler, combine sugar, cornstarch, salt, and coconut together. Add milk and stir constantly with wire whisk until mixture thickens. Add some cream mixture into egg yolks and then return to cream mixture, continually stirring over heat until mixture is thick. Add crushed pineapple and mix well. Add vanilla and remove from heat.

Let filling cool at room temperature. Slice banana into filling. Pour into pre-baked pie shell, and top with whipped cream. Garnish with toasted coconut and 6 whole Macadamia nuts, if desired.

*Baked With Love*

# Lime Pie

**CRUST:**

1½ cups graham cracker crumbs

¼ cup sugar

⅓ cup melted, unsalted butter

Preheat oven to 375°. In a mixing bowl combine crumbs, sugar and butter. Press into a 9-inch pie pan, bottom and sides, and bake 8 minutes. Let cool. Reduce oven temperature to 300°. (If using store-bought crust, preheat oven to 300°).

**FILLING:**

3 eggs, room temperature and separated

½ cup lime juice

1 (14-ounce) can sweetened condensed milk

Pinch of salt

1 tablespoon sugar

In a large mixing bowl beat egg yolks until pale yellow, then gradually add lime juice and condensed milk. In another bowl beat egg whites, salt and sugar until stiff peaks form. Fold one-third of the whites into yolk mixture, then adding remaining whites, folding gently. Pour into pie shell. Bake 15 minutes. Cool on a rack to room temperature. Refrigerate for 6 hours or overnight.

**TOPPING:**

1 cup whipping cream

3 tablespoons powdered sugar

4 lime slices, cut in ½ for garnish (optional)

Beat whipping cream, gradually adding the sugar until stiff. Spread on top of pie. Can be kept in refrigerator for 1 hour with the whipped cream topping. Decorate with lime slices if desired. Must do ahead. Serves 8.

*Cooking in Clover II*

# Chocolate Meringue Pie

2½ cups milk
¾ cup sugar
4 tablespoons cornstarch
½ teaspoon salt
4 tablespoons cocoa
(slightly heaped)
3 eggs separated

1 teaspoon vanilla
Gob of butter (about 2
tablespoons)
8 or 9-inch pie shell
(baked)
6 tablespoons sugar

Heat 2 cups milk over medium heat until scalding, in the meantime blend ½ cup milk, the sugar, cornstarch, salt, cocoa and egg yolks. Add to warm milk, cook until thick, remove from heat, add vanilla and butter, pour in pie shell. Make meringue with 3 egg whites and 6 tablespoons sugar. Beat egg whites on high speed with mixer. When they begin to foam up good, start adding sugar 1 tablespoon at a time. When it stands in a peak, place on top of pie and bake in 350° oven until brown.

### *Variation:*

Coconut Cream Pie: Leave out the cocoa and add coconut when you add the vanilla and butter. Top meringue with coconut.

Banana Cream: Leave out the cocoa, place bananas in bottom of crust, fill with about half of the filling, more bananas, and finish filling with filling.

Plain Cream: Leave out the cocoa. Sometimes, I want one cream pie and one chocolate pie, so I double the recipe, leaving out the cocoa, fill the crust for the cream pie, and add either semi-sweet chocolate chips or unsweetened chocolate to the remainder to make the chocolate pie.

Peanut Butter: Cream pie filling plus 1 or 2 tablespoons peanut butter until it looks and tastes right.

*A Collection of Recipes from the Best Cooks*
*in the Midwest*

# Lemon Angel Pie

4 egg yolks
½ cup sugar
¼ cup fresh lemon juice
1 tablespoon grated lemon
  peel

1 (9-inch) meringue crust
  (see below)
Whipped Cream Topping (see
  below)

Beat egg yolks until thick and lemon-colored. Gradually beat in sugar. Stir in lemon juice and grated peel. Cook in double boiler over simmering water, stirring constantly, until mixture is thick, about 5-8 minutes. Mixture should mound slightly when dropped from spoon. Cool. Spread into meringue crust. Top with Whipped Cream Topping. Chill 12 hours or overnight.

**MERINGUE PIE SHELL:**
3 egg whites (room
  temperature)
¼ teaspoon cream of tartar

⅛ teaspoon salt
½ teaspoon vanilla
½ cup sugar

Combine egg whites, cream of tartar, salt and vanilla. Beat until frothy. Gradually add sugar and beat until stiff and glossy peaks form.

Spread on bottom and sides of a well greased 9-inch pie pan. Build up the sides. Bake in a 275° oven for 1 hour. It will be light brown and crisp. Let cool in pan away from drafts. Spoon in the filling and chill. These crusts often collapse in the center and it doesn't make any difference at all.

**WHIPPED CREAM TOPPING:**
1 cup whipping cream
¼ cup sifted con-
  fectioners' sugar

½ teaspoon vanilla
¼ cup sour cream

Whip the cream and fold in vanilla and sugar. Stir in sour cream. Spread over the pie leaving about a 2-inch circle open in the middle. Garnish with a little lemon zest.

*Eat Pie First...Life is Uncertain!*

# Cherry Cobbler

1 cup flour
1 cup sugar
3 teaspoons baking powder
　(Clabber Girl)
½ cup milk
1 tablespoon margarine
1 (No. 303) can sour
　cherries

Combine flour, ½ cup sugar and baking powder. Mix well.
Blend milk and margarine. Stir into flour mixture until moistened. Pour batter into a 9-inch baking pan. Combine cherries, juice and remaining sugar in a saucepan. Bring to a boil. Pour hot sweetened cherries over batter. Bake at 350° for 30 minutes or until golden. Serves 9.

*Heavenly Delights*

# Plum or Peach Buckle

1 stick butter or margarine
½ cup sugar
1 cup flour
1½ teaspoons baking powder
¾ cup milk
¼ teaspoon cinnamon
½ cup sugar
1 dozen prune plums, pitted,
　halved or 2 cups sliced
　peaches
Grated orange or
　lemon rind

Melt butter in 8-inch baking pan round or square. In bowl, mix sugar, flour, baking powder, and milk. Pour over butter slowly and evenly and do *not* stir. Arrange plums or peaches on top of mixture. Sprinkle fruit with rind and mixed sugar and cinnamon. Bake in 350° oven for 40-50 minutes. Batter will rise to top and form a broken but firm crust. Serve with whipped cream or Cool Whip if desired.

*Tasty Palette*

# Fruit Crumble
## *(Microwave)*

3 cups fruit (raspberries,     ½ cup flour
    blueberries, apples,     ⅔ cup quick-cooking oats
    peaches, cherries, etc.)     ½ cup margarine, softened
2 tablespoons lemon juice     ¾ teaspoon cinnamon
⅔ cup brown sugar, packed     ¼ teaspoon salt

Spread fruit in 8x8x2-inch baking dish. Sprinkle with lemon juice to prevent discoloring. Mix brown sugar, flour, oats, margarine, cinnamon, and salt, and sprinkle on top.

Microwave, uncovered, on HIGH (100%) until hot and bubbly, 7-10 minutes. Let stand 10 minutes. Serve with warm cream or ice cream.

*Tasty Palette*

# Apricot Almond Tart

**TART SHELL:**

½ cup butter, cut in
    pieces
⅓ cup almonds, finely
    ground

¾ cup flour
2 tablespoons powdered
    sugar

Combine all ingredients for shell in a food processor until mixture resembles coarse meal. Press into greased and floured 11-inch fluted flan or tart pan. Bake at 425° for 8-10 minutes. Cool and loosen slightly.

**MARZIPAN FILLING:**

½ cup almond paste
¼ cup powdered sugar
1 egg yolk

2 tablespoons butter (room
    temperature)

Beat all filling ingredients together in small bowl. Spread marzipan over cooked shell.

**APRICOT GLAZE:**

1 cup dried apricots,
    chopped
1 cup water

2 tablespoons brown sugar
1 tablespoon Grand Marnier

Combine chopped apricots, water, brown sugar, and Grand Marnier in medium size pan. Heat over medium heat for 10-15 minutes; drain. Cool. Spread on tart.

**GARNISH:**

1 cup dried apricots
1 cup water
½ cup almonds, sliced

1 cup heavy cream, whipped
1 teaspoon sugar
1 teaspoon Grand Marnier

Simmer apricots in water for 15 minutes; drain and cool. Place apricots in concentric circles on top of apricot glaze. Place almonds in between apricots. Whip cream and fold in sugar and Grand Marnier. Put whipped cream in pastry bag and decorate around fruit and almonds. Refrigerate. Cut in wedges to serve. Can do ahead. Serves 8.

*With Hands & Heart Cookbook*

# Citrus Blossoms

8 ounces phyllo dough
½ cup (1 stick) unsalted
butter, melted

1 cup fresh or frozen
blueberries, raspberries, or
blackberries
24 mint leaves

Brush 1 sheet of phyllo with melted butter. Top with another sheet and brush with melted butter. Cut into 4-inch squares. Carefully place each square into a muffin tin. Add 2 more squares to each tin, rotating each slightly to make "petals." Repeat to make cups.

Bake phyllo cups at 375° for 8-12 minutes or until golden brown. Remove from pans. Spoon in 1 rounded teaspoon of Lime Curd. Top each with berries and a mint leaf. Makes 24.

LIME CURD:
4 egg yolks
6 eggs
2 cups sugar
1 cup fresh lime juice

2 tablespoons grated lime
zest
1 cup (2 sticks) unsalted
butter

In a heavy saucepan, combine egg yolks, eggs, sugar, lime juice, and lime zest. Cook over low heat, stirring constantly with a whisk until thickened (curd will coat the back of a spoon). Do not allow curd to boil. Remove from heat and gradually whisk in butter. Cool in a glass or plastic container. Refrigerate until ready to serve.

**Note:** A striking centerpiece on a buffet table. Both the phyllo cups and the Lime Curd may be prepared ahead and then assembled just before serving.

*Above & Beyond Parsley*

Kansas City and St. Louis are host cities to professional sports teams offering fans major league enjoyment year round. Baseball: KC Royals and SL Cardinals; Football: KC Chiefs; Hockey: KC Blades and SL Blues; Soccer: KC Attack and SL Storm.

# Cream Puffs

**CREAM PUFFS:**

| | |
|---|---|
| 1 cup water | 1 cup flour |
| ½ cup butter or margarine | 4 eggs |

Heat oven to 400°. Heat water and butter to rolling boil. Stir in flour. Stir vigorously over low heat for about 1 minute or until mixture forms a ball. Remove from heat. Beat in eggs, all at one time; continue beating until smooth. Drop dough by scant ¼ cupfuls 3 inches apart onto ungreased baking sheet. Bake for 35-40 minutes or until puffed and golden. Cool away from draft. Fill with pudding filling. Dust with powdered sugar.

**FILLING:**

| | |
|---|---|
| 1½ cups scalded milk | 3 eggs, separated |
| ¼ cup flour | 2 tablespoons butter |
| ½ cup sugar | ½ teaspoon vanilla |
| ¼ teaspoon salt | 6 tablespoons sugar |

Scald milk; mix flour, sugar and salt. Add milk and cook until thick and smooth. Beat egg yolks; stir in a little of the hot mixture and pour back into pan. Cook for 2 minutes, stirring constantly. Remove from heat and add butter and vanilla. Beat egg whites until stiff and gradually beat in 6 tablespoons sugar. Fold in about one-third of the egg whites into the cooled pudding. Use remainder of whites for another purpose.

*Kohler Family Kookbook*

---

At the turn of the century, it was almost a fifty mile drive from Springfield to Bonniebrook, which took two days by wagon. It was necessary to cross Bear Creek 32 times, and you ended up on the same side! Bonniebrook in Taney County near Branson is the home of Rose O'Neill, the founder of the Kewpie Doll.

---

# Strawberry Pizza

**CRUST:**

1 stick oleo
1 cup flour

¼ cup powdered sugar

Melt oleo in pan; add flour and sugar. Mix; pat out on pizza pan. Bake at 350° for 10 minutes or until golden brown.

**FILLING:**

1 (8-ounce) package cream
  cheese
1 can Eagle Brand sweetened,
  condensed milk

⅓ cup lemon juice
1 teaspoon vanilla

Mix until smooth; spread on cooled crust.

**TOPPING:**

2 pints sweetened
  strawberries

4 tablespoons cornstarch

Mix well and heat over low heat until thick. Spread on pizza and chill. Top with Cool Whip.

*Cooking on the Road*

# Never Fail Meringue

1 tablespoon cornstarch
1½ tablespoons cold water
½ cup boiling water

3 egg whites
6 tablespoons sugar
2 tablespoons vanilla

Dissolve cornstarch in cold water in a small saucepan. Add the boiling water and cook over medium heat. Stir constantly till thick and clear. Set aside to cool.

Meanwhile, beat the egg whites in a large bowl to soft peaks. Beat in the cooled paste. Continue to beat till very firm peaks are formed. Gradually add the sugar, then beat in vanilla. Pile onto pie. Bake at 375° for 6-10 minutes, till peaks are golden.

*From Granny, With Love*

# Woodford Pudding

½ cup butter
¾ cup sugar
3 egg yolks
1 cup strawberry jam
1 cup bread flour
½ teaspoon baking soda

1 teaspoon cinnamon
¼ teaspoon allspice
⅓ cup sour cream or thick
   buttermilk
3 egg whites, stiffly beaten

Cream the butter and sugar together. Add the egg yolks and strawberry jam. Sift the flour with the baking soda and spices, then add the dry ingredients alternately with the sour cream to the creamed mixture. Fold in the beaten egg whites. Grease a loaf pan with salad oil and dust lightly with flour. Bake at 375° for an hour, or until the pudding tests done. This keeps well, and mellows a day after baking. Serve with:

**EGG-NOG SAUCE:**
4 egg yolks
⅓ cup sugar
1 cup light cream

2 tablespoons rum
Dash of nutmeg

Beat the egg yolks with sugar until thick. Add cream and cook in a double boiler until thick, stirring frequently. Remove from the heat, cool slightly, add the rum and nutmeg. Refrigerate or serve warm, as desired.

*The Shaw House Cook Book*

The Katy Trail State Park stretches for more than 200 miles across the state, from St. Charles to Sedalia and beyond. The former route of the Missouri-Kansas-Texas Railroad, better known as "the Katy", the new compacted limestone surface is ideal for hiking and bicycling along the scenic route that follows the Missouri River.

# Cottage Pudding

This recipe has an unusual name, but the origin is unknown. It was one of my mother's favorite recipes, and was a favorite when I was a child 60 years ago. It's especially good served warm, with the Lemon Sauce.

| | |
|---|---|
| ⅓ cup butter | ¼ teaspoon soda |
| 1 egg | ¼ teaspoon salt |
| ⅔ cup sugar | 1 cup sour milk |
| 1¾ cups flour | 1 teaspoon vanilla |
| 2 teaspoons baking powder | |

Cream butter, egg, and sugar together. Sift flour, baking powder, soda, and salt together, add to cream mixture alternately with the sour milk. Add vanilla and beat hard. Bake in greased pan at 350° for 25-30 minutes.

LEMON SAUCE:

| | |
|---|---|
| 1 cup sugar | 2 tablespoons lemon juice or |
| 2 tablespoons flour | extract |
| Dash of salt | 2 tablespoons butter |
| 1 cup boiling water | |

Mix sugar, flour, and salt together. Add boiling water and lemon juice. Add the butter. Cook in double boiler pan until done. Serve hot over the Cottage Pudding.

*Recipes & Stories of Early-Day Settlers*

# Lemon Mousse with Strawberry-Raspberry Sauce

Ambrosial!

**MOUSSE:**

4 eggs
3 eggs, separated
9 tablespoons sugar, divided
2 envelopes unflavored
  gelatin
3 tablespoons lemon juice

3 tablespoons water
Grated rind of 1 lemon
¼ cup frozen lemonade
  concentrate, defrosted
2 cups heavy cream,
  whipped

Beat eggs, the 3 egg yolks and 6 tablespoons of sugar until thick and smooth. In a heatproof measuring cup, soften gelatin in lemon juice and water for 5 minutes. Place cup in simmering water and stir until gelatin dissolves, add to egg mixture with lemon rind and lemonade. Fold in whipped cream. Beat the 3 egg whites and remaining sugar until stiff peaks form, fold into mousse.

Pour into a straight-sided crystal bowl or an 8-inch soufflé dish which has had a lightly-oiled collar of waxed paper tied or taped around the outside, extending 2 to 3 inches above the rim. Smooth top with a spatula, chill 6 hours or until firm. Remove collar and serve with Strawberry-Raspberry Sauce.

**STRAWBERRY-RASPBERRY SAUCE:**

1 (10-ounce) package
  sweetened frozen
  strawberries, defrosted
1 (10-ounce) package
  sweetened frozen
  raspberries, defrosted

2 teaspoons cornstarch
1 teaspoon water
1 teaspoon lemon juice
⅓ cup currant jelly
1 tablespoon kirsch
1 teaspoon Frambois

Place strawberries and raspberries in a food processor or blender, purée. Strain through a sieve lined with cheesecloth. Dissolve cornstarch in water. Combine purée and cornstarch in a saucepan, cook over low heat until mixture begins to thicken. Add lemon juice and jelly, stir until jelly dissolves. Remove from heat, cool. Blend in kirsch and Frambois, chill. Serves 8.

*PAST & REPAST*

# White Chocolate Mousse with Raspberry Sauce

2 pounds white chocolate
10 eggs
1 cup simple syrup (1 cup water to ½ cup sugar)

3 cups heavy whipping cream
Semi-sweet chocolate shavings for garnish

Melt chocolate and set aside to cool. Separate eggs and set whites aside. Slowly whip simple syrup into yolks. Put mixture in double boiler over boiling water and whisk until mixture is warm to the touch. Remove and continue whipping by hand for another 2 minutes until mixture forms a "ribbon" of yolks and sugar. Slowly add melted chocolate to yolk and syrup mixture, and blend well. Continue to whip until smooth. Whip cream until it forms soft peaks, then set aside. Whip egg whites until they form soft peaks and set aside. Fold whipped cream into the chocolate mixture first, then the whipped egg whites. Be careful not to overblend (you don't want to collapse the cream or egg whites by adding too much too fast). Chill mixture at 35° for 8 hours.

Spread a pool of Raspberry Sauce onto dessert plates, followed by a serving of mousse. Garnish each with chocolate shavings. Serves 8-10.

**RASPBERRY SAUCE:**

10 ounces frozen raspberries, thawed and drained
2 tablespoons water

3 tablespoons sugar
3 tablespoons fresh lemon juice
2 teaspoons light rum

In a saucepan combine raspberries with water and bring to a boil over moderate heat, stirring occasionally. In a food processor fitted with the steel blade or in a blender, purée the raspberry mixture with the sugar, lemon juice, and rum. Force the purée through a fine sieve into a small bowl and cover. Let chill overnight. Makes about 1½ cups.

*Kansas City Cuisine (Cafe Allegro)*

# Death by Chocolate

1 (19.8-ounce) family size
  fudge brownie mix
¼ - ½ cup kahlua or
  coffee liqueur*

3 (3.5-ounce) boxes
  chocolate mousse
8 Skor or Heath bars
1 (12-ounce) carton Cool
  Whip

Bake brownies according to directions on package. Cool. Punch holes in brownies with fork and pour kahlua over brownies.

Whip up chocolate mousse according to package directions. Break Heath bars into small pieces with hammer (in the wrapper). Break up half the brownies and place in the bottom of a glass trifle dish. Cover with half the mousse, half the candy and half the Cool Whip. Repeat layers.

*Instead of liqueur, you may substitute a mixture of 1 teaspoon sugar and 4 tablespoons leftover black coffee.

*Covered Bridge Neighbors Cookbook*

# Sweet Noodle Kugel

2 (12-ounce) packages
  medium noodles
6 eggs, beaten
1 cup margarine, melted
4 large apples, peeled and
  grated

1⅔ cups sugar
2 teaspoons cinnamon
15 ounces golden raisins

Cook noodles in boiling salted water until tender. Drain and rinse. Mix eggs, margarine, grated apples, sugar, raisins and cinnamon with noodles in a large bowl. Pour into a greased 13x9x2-inch glass baking dish. Bake at 350° for 45 minutes. Serves 12-14.

*From Generation to Generation*

# Chocolate Layered Dessert

**FIRST LAYER:**

1 cup flour ½ cup oleo
¼ cup powdered sugar

Mix flour, sugar and oleo like a pie crust. Press into a 9x13-inch pan. Bake at 350° for 15 minutes.

**SECOND LAYER:**

1 (8-ounce) package cream 1 cup powdered sugar
  cheese 8 or 9 ounces Cool Whip

Mix softened cream cheese, powdered sugar, and Cool Whip. Spread onto cooled crust. Let set in refrigerator for 30 minutes.

**THIRD LAYER:**

2 (3-ounce) packages 3 cups cold milk
  instant chocolate pudding

Mix chocolate pudding and milk. When very thick, spread onto cream cheese mixture.

**FOURTH LAYER:**

Whipping cream Chopped nuts, optional

Top with whipped cream and sprinkle with nuts (optional). Cut into 2-inch square pieces.

*Heavenly Delights*

# Frozen Lemon Dessert

**CRUST:**

1 cup flour
¼ cup brown sugar
½ cup chopped pecans or
   walnuts

½ cup melted margarine or
   butter

Stir together the flour, brown sugar, nuts and margarine, and spread evenly in a shallow baking pan. Bake at 350° for 20 minutes, stirring often to make crumbs. Watch carefully so they don't burn. Sprinkle ⅔ of these crumbs in an ungreased 9x13-inch pan.

**FILLING:**

4 egg whites
1 cup sugar
4 egg yolks
1 teaspoon grated lemon peel

½ cup lemon juice
8 ounces pareve (non-dairy)
   whipped topping

Beat egg whites until soft peaks form. Gradually add sugar, beating into stiff peaks. Set aside. Beat egg yolks until thick. Fold yolks, peel and juice into whites. Fold in whipped topping and pour into pan over crumb crust. Sprinkle remaining ⅓ of crumbs over lemon filling. Cover pan and freeze. Will keep several weeks in freezer if well covered. Serves 12.

*From Generation to Generation*

# Frozen Lemon Crunch

2 tablespoons butter
½ cup crushed cornflakes
3 tablespoons brown sugar
½ cup pecans, chopped
3 egg yolks
½ cup sugar

3 tablespoons lemon juice
2 tablespoons lemon rind, grated
3 egg whites
¼ teaspoon salt
1 cup heavy cream, whipped

Melt butter in skillet; add cornflakes, brown sugar, and pecans. Cook and stir until sugar melts and caramelizes slightly. Set aside.

In small saucepan beat egg yolks and sugar until light and foamy. Cook over low heat until thick. Add lemon juice and rind. Cool.

In large bowl, beat egg whites with salt until stiff. Fold in cooled egg yolk mixture and whipped cream. Place half of cornflakes mixture on bottom of springform pan. Pour in lemon mixture and top with remaining cornflakes mixture. Freeze a minimum of 4 hours. Serves 10.

*Company's Coming*

# Fruit Sherbet

Juice from 4 oranges
Juice from 2 lemons
½ cup crushed pineapple

1½ cups sugar
1 cup crushed banana
3 cups whole milk

Mix first 5 ingredients and cool overnight. Mix in whole milk. Freeze in shallow dish. When almost set, beat, and then refreeze till firm.

*Kitchen Prescriptions*

Because of the abundant walnut trees in the area, Warsaw produces almost 90% of the world's gunstocks.

# Oreo Ice Cream Pie

24 Oreo cookies, crushed
½ stick oleo, melted
½ gallon vanilla ice cream
1 can Eagle Brand condensed
  milk

1 stick oleo or butter
1 (8-ounce) can Hershey
  chocolate syrup
1 (9-ounce) carton Cool Whip

Crush 24 cookies; place them in a 9x13-inch pan. Pour melted oleo over crumbs; freeze. Soften ice cream; place 1 layer over crumbs. Freeze.

To make sauce, combine Eagle Brand milk, 1 stick butter, and chocolate syrup; place in a saucepan. Bring to a slow boil; simmer for 5 minutes. Pour sauce over hardened ice cream; freeze. Top with Cool Whip. Cover with foil.

*Note:* After each step, freeze for a least 30 minutes.

*Recipes Old and New*

# My Favorite Ice Cream

2 cups sugar
2 heaping tablespoons flour
6 eggs, separated
1 quart milk

½ pint whipping cream
½ pint half-and-half
1 large can evaporated milk
2 tablespoons vanilla

Cook sugar, flour, egg yolks (beaten), and milk until thick. Strain and pour in freezer. Beat egg whites, add cream, whites and vanilla into gallon freezer.

You may substitute 1½ cartons coffee rich for the whipping cream and half-and-half; also increase the sugar ½ cup. For chocolate, increase flour 1 heaping tablespoon and add 1 can (1 pound) chocolate syrup. Add chocolate last. Freeze according to freezer directions.

*A Collection of Recipes from the Best Cooks*
*in the Midwest*

# Coffee-Toffee
# Ice Cream Pie

1 (9-inch) graham cracker
crust, baked
1 jumbo size chocolate
almond bar (½ pound)

¼ cup coffee
1 quart coffee ice cream,
slightly softened
3 Heath candy bars

Melt chocolate almond bar with coffee in double boiler. Spread over crust and cool. Fill chocolate lined pie crust with coffee ice cream. Top with crushed Heath bars (crush better when frozen). Freeze. Remove 10-15 minutes before serving. Serves 6-8.

*Note:* The size of Heath candy bars makes no difference. The more the better!

*The Cook Book*

---

 Maintained by the Missouri State Park Board, the Sandy Creek Covered Bridge in Jefferson County was originally built in 1872. It is still open to vehicular traffic.

---

# Watermelon Popsicles

½ Missouri watermelon
2 teaspoons fresh lemon
  juice

½ cup sugar
½ cup distilled water

Cut watermelon into cubes and rub through a strainer to remove seeds, making 3 cups watermelon juice.

In small saucepan mix together sugar and water, simmer 3 minutes. Remove from heat, stir in watermelon juice and lemon juice. Turn into 2 ice trays. Freeze until very mushy and insert a popsicle stick in each cube. Freeze. Makes about 36 small popsicles.

*The Never Ending Season*

The Gateway Arch in St. Louis is our country's tallest monument (630 feet). Visitors (over 2 million each year) board a unique 5-passenger capsule-transporter that runs on special tracks up the hollow, curving legs of the Arch. The panoramic view from the observation room at the top is nothing short of spectacular.

# Index

*Excursion boats reflect in the Mississippi River along with the St. Louis skyline and the impressive Gateway Arch.*

# Index

# INDEX

**271**

# INDEX

**273**

# INDEX

# INDEX

# Catalog of
# Contributing
# Cookbooks

*The Liberty Memorial pierces the night skyline of Kansas City.
At the base of the memorial is the only US World War I Museum.*

# Catalog of Contributing Cookbooks

All recipes in this book have been submitted from the cookbooks shown on the following pages. Individuals who wish to obtain a copy of a particular book can do so by sending a check or money order to the address listed. Prices are subject to change. Please note the postage and handling charges that may be required. State residents add tax only when requested. Retailers are invited to call or write to same address for wholesale information. Some of these contributing cookbooks have gone out of print since the original publication of this book. See page 285 for a listing of these out-of-print cookbooks.

### ADVENTURES IN GREEK COOKING

St. Nicholas Philoptochos Society        314-361-6924
4967 Forest Park Boulevard
St. Louis, MO 63108

A compilation of favorite recipes from members of our organization and community. 255 pages; approximately 400 recipes.

$20.00 Retail price
$4.00 Postage and handling

Make check payable to St. Nicholas Philoptochos Society

### À LA ROSE

Kay Cameron        www.camerons-crag.com
P. O. Box 526        kay@camerons-crag.com
Point Lookout, MO 65726        417-335-8134

A collection of Ozark recipes that were favorites during Rose O'Neill's era from the late 1800s to the early 1940s. Rose O'Neill, mother of the Kewpies, was at-home in the Ozarks at Bonniebrook, north of Branson. "O'Neilliana," Ozark colloquialisms and traditions, and O'Neill-style Kewpie illustrations also featured. 100 pages, spiral-bound.

$4.95 Retail price        ISBN 1-879945-02
$.30 Tax for Missouri residents
$1.50 Postage and handling

Make check payable to Katydid Publications

### THE ART OF HELLENIC CUISINE

Assumption Greek Orthodox Church        314-966-2255
1755 Des Peres Road        314-966-2416
Town & Country, MO 63131

Within 151 pages you will travel all over Greece through your taste buds. Ladies of Philoptochos (Friend of the Poor) created this book to raise funds for charity. Over 200 recipes are original, centuries old, never written, passed from grandmother to mother to daughter. They are simple to prepare; easy diagrams to follow.

$15.00 Retail price (Allow 4-6 weeks for delivery)
$3.00 Postage and handling

Make check payable to Assumption Greek Orthodox Church

## BAKED WITH LOVE

The Blue Owl Restaurant & Bakery     www.theblueowl.com
P. O. Box 98                              636-464-3128
Kimmswick, MO  63053

*Baked With Love,* our first cookbook, celebrated the fourth anniversary of our restaurant. It features many favorite recipes which bring our customers back time after time. Includes fresh, flaky pies, old-fashioned cobblers, rich, irresistible cheesecakes, and buttery pastries. Custom artwork in shades of blue and peach.

$14.95  Retail price (includes tax and postage)
Make check payable to The Blue Owl

## BLUE RIDGE CHRISTIAN CHURCH COOKBOOK

Christian Women's Fellowship          816-353-1632
3625 Blue Ridge Boulevard
Independence, MO  64052

Our cookbook consists of 119 pages and 325 recipes. There is a picture of our church at the front, when the church and CWF started. It has three pages of kitchen hints, four pages of calorie counters, and seven categories in the table of contents. Book has laminated cover with a country look, and a spiral ring to lay flat.

$2.00  Retail price
$2.00  Postage and handling
Make check payable to Christian Women's Fellowship

## BREAKFASTS OZARK STYLE

Kay Cameron          www.camerons-crag.com
P. O. Box 526         kay@camerons-crag.com
Point Lookout, MO  65726     417-335-8134

A lively 155-page collection featuring treats suitable for breakfast, brunch, lunch, a late-night snack, or any time! Includes "Nearly Gourmet" recipes, an "On-The-Run" section, tips to make cooking easier, and "painless" nutrition suggestions.  155 pages, 8½ x 7, spiral-bound.

$7.95  Retail price         ISBN 1-879945-00
$.48  Tax for Missouri residents
$1.50  Postage and handling
Make check payable to Katydid Publications

## A COLLECTION OF RECIPES FROM THE BEST COOKS IN THE MIDWEST

Nellie Ogan              660-584-4235
1201 W. 19th Street, Apt 115C
Higginsville, MO  64037

As the name implies, this is a thirty-year collection containing original, old family, and those great "pass-around" recipes. A cookbook you will use. The book is 8½x11 inches, spiral-bound, 312 recipes on 101 pages.

$10.00  Retail price
$.66  Tax for Missouri residents
$1.50  Postage and handling
Make check payable to Nellie Ogan

## FROM GENERATION TO GENERATION COOKBOOK II

B'nai Amoona Women's League                     314-576-9990
324 S. Mason Road
St. Louis, MO  63141

Over 600 kosher recipes in 400 pages.  Includes dietary laws, holiday obser-
vances, kid's section, quantity food preparation, low-calorie and special diet
recipes, beverage buying guidelines, and substitution and equivalent tables
for rice, heart-healthy foods, dairy, chocolate, baking, apples, and strawberries.

$14.95  Retail price (discount for 10 or more)
  $4.00  Postage and handling

Make check payable to B'Nai Amoona Women's League

## FROM THE APPLE ORCHARD

Lee Jackson                          www.imagesunlimitedpub.com
P. O. Box 305                                   660-582-4279
Maryville, MO  64468

A collection of treasured apple country recipes!  From thirst-quenching
Apple Tangy Fizz, apple fritters, streusel-filled apple muffins, to microwave
apple pancakes, plus pies, cakes, cookies, and more.  The answer to "What
will I do with all these apples?!"  A real treat for apple lovers everywhere!

$12.95  Retail price                      ISBN 0-930643-00-3
  $.57  Tax for Missouri residents
 $1.50  Postage and handling

Make check payable to Images Unlimited

## FROM THE OZARKS' OVEN...

College of the Ozarks                   417-334-6411 ext. 3395
Attn:  Fruitcake Dept.
Point Lookout, MO  65726

The cookbook was written as a convenient source of recipes emphasizing
the use of whole-grain meal and flour milled at the Edwards Mill, located
on the campus of the College of the Ozarks.  It has 173 pages containing
191 recipes.

$6.50  Retail price
  $.18  Tax for Missouri residents
 $1.50  Postage and handling

Make check payable to College of the Ozarks

## GRANDMA'S OZARK LEGACY

Kay Cameron                          www.camerons-crag.com
P. O. Box 526                          kay@camerons-crag.com
Point Lookout, MO  65726                        417-335-8134

A unique collection of "old-timey" Ozark recipes and methods, most of
which were in use at the "turn-of-the-century."  Recipes are written in
prose form, like "handed-down receipts" in old books.  Colloquialisms
indicative of that era in the Ozarks are included.  100 pages, spiral-bound.

$5.95  Retail price                       ISBN 1-879945-0-1
  $.36  Tax for Missouri residents
 $1.50  Postage and handling

Make check payable to Katydid Publications

## HOOKED ON FISH ON THE GRILL

Pig Out Publications, Inc.                    913-789-9594
6005 Martway #107                        Fax 913-789-3119
Mission, KS 66202

This grill book will have you dining on the back deck with fast, easy, and healthy fare like Stir-Grilled Catfish, Lemon-Lime Monkfish, and Pepper Tuna. Compiled by Karen Adler, Rich Welch, and Carolyn Wells. 96 pages, softcover.

$9.95  Retail price                          ISBN 0-925175-16-1
$.71  Tax for Missouri residents
$3.85  Postage and handling
Make check payable to Pig Out Publications

## LUNCHEON FAVORITES

The Blue Owl Restaurant & Bakery          www.theblueowl.com
P. O. Box 98                                636-464-3128
Kimmswick, MO 63053

*Luncheon Favorites* is an accumulation of requested recipes from our customers, and a celebration of the fifth anniversary of our restaurant. Recipes include soups, salads, quiches, casseroles, and additional desserts that were not included in *Baked With Love,* our first cookbook. Delightful country artwork in shades of pink and blue.

$14.95  Retail price (includes tax and postage)
Make check payable to The Blue Owl

## REMEMBERING THE PAST: PLANNING FOR THE FUTURE

Lawson United Methodist Church             816-296-7793
P. O. Box 127
Lawson, MO 64062

A unique easel 3-ring binder allows the 286-page indexed cookbook to stand while working with any of the 700 recipes. Clever angel cartoons, cooking tips, and hints adorn multi-colored tabbed dividers for 15 sections. Quantity recipes are included. *Remembering the Past* is a reprint of nostalgic 1950 recipes and advertisements of that era.

$10.00  Retail price
$2.00  Postage and handling
Make check payable to Lawson United Methodist Church

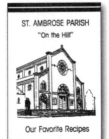

## ST. AMBROSE PARISH "ON THE HILL" COOKBOOK

St. Ambrose Church                          314-771-1228
5130 Wilson Avenue
St. Louis, MO 63110

This beautiful cookbook contains over 450 recipes in 178 pages. It is a tribute to the Italian heritage of St. Ambrose Parish. This book explains the authentic art of Italian cooking. It is spiral-bound and indexed.

$10.00  Retail price
$2.00  Postage and handling
Make check payable to St. Ambrose Church

## STEAMBOAT ADVENTURES:
### Recipes & Stories of Early-Day Settlers
by Kenneth C. Weyand
Discovery Publications                    816-474-1516
104 E. 5th Street • Kansas City, MO  64103
A unique mix of old-time recipes and tall-but-true tales from our past. The book chronicles the earliest trips down the Mississippi, and battles with the Mighty Missouri. There is also a wonderful array of home remedies and even a recipe for "leanness." 152 pages, more than 250 recipes.

$7.95  Retail price                    ISBN 1-878496-02-6
$.51  Tax for Missouri residents
$3.00  Postage and handling

Make check payable to Discovery Publications

## THE TASTY PALETTE COOK BOOK
South County Art Association
c/o June Sadler                        314-647-2754
5115 Annette Avenue
St. Louis, MO  63119

St. Louis is a melting pot of many cultures in the heartland of the country. The many ethnic groups living here each contributed their own delicious specialties. There are 600 tried-and-true recipes and helpful hints to choose from. Proceeds help toward scholarships for needy art students.

$7.95  Retail price
$.56  Tax for Missouri residents
$1.95  Postage and handling

Make check payable to South County Art Association

## WITH HANDS & HEART COOKBOOK
Bethesda Hospital                        314-727-4291
9751 Old Warson Road
St. Louis, MO  63124

*With Hands & Heart Cookbook* is a 243-page cookbook with over 400 tested recipes. Published in 1990 by the Bethesda Hospital Women's Board, the book includes fabulous recipes from Barbara Bush, Corinne Quayle, and many well-known St. Louis restaurants and clubs. *With Hands & Heart* has also been featured on national television.

$8.95  Retail price
$2.00  Postage and handling

Make check payable to Bethesda Hospital

# Out-of-Print Cookbooks

The cookbooks listed below are out of print and may no longer be available for purchase. Quail Ridge Press is pleased to offer a selection of the most popular recipes from these cookbooks in fulfillment of our mission of *Preserving America's Food Heritage*.

**ABOVE & BEYOND PARSLEY**
Junior League of Kansas City, Missouri, Inc.

**APPLES, APPLES, APPLES**
by Ann Clark • Marionville, MO

**BEYOND PARSLEY**
Junior League of Kansas City, Missouri, Inc.

**BOUQUET GARNI**
Independence Regional Health Center Auxiliary • Independence, MO

**CHOCKFUL O' CHIPS**
by Peggy Seemann

**COMPANY S COMING**
Junior League of Kansas City, Missouri, Inc.

**THE COOK BOOK**
Nation Council of Jewish Women, Greater Kansas City Section • Shawnee Mission, KS

**COOKING FOR APPLAUSE**
Repertory Theatre of St. Louis Backers Board • St. Louis, MO

**COOKING IN CLOVER**
Jewish Hospital Auxiliary • St. Louis, MO

**COOKING IN CLOVER II**
Jewish Hospital Auxiliary • St. Louis, MO

**COOKING ON THE ROAD (AND AT HOME TOO)**
by Montana Whitfield • Steele, MO

**COVERED BRIDGE NEIGHBORS COOKBOOK**
Covered Bridge Neighbors • St. Peters, MO

**DELICIOUS READING**
Friends of the St. Charles City/County Library District • St. Peters, MO

**EAT PIE FIRST . . . LIFE IS UNCERTAIN**
by Joan Jefferson • Freeman, MO

**FINELY TUNED FOODS**
Symphony League of Kansas City Leawood,KS

**FROM GRANNY, WITH LOVE: Recipes from My Heart**
by Pat Neaves • Kansas City, MO

**FROM SEED TO SERVE**
by Leanna K. Potts • Joplin, MO

**GATEWAYS**
Auxiliary—Twigs—Friends of St. Louis Children's Hospital • St. Louis, MO

**GOURMET GARDEN**
Menorah Medical Center Auxiliary Kansas City, MO

**HEAVENLY DELIGHTS**
Mothers and Daughters of Zion Independence, MO

**HOME COOKIN': Apple Recipes from Missouri Apple Growers**
Missouri Apple Growers • Wellington, MO

**IT'S CHRISTMAS!**
by Dianne Stafford Mayes and Dorothy Davenport Stafford • Carthage, MO

## KANSAS CITY BBQ
Pig Out Publications, Inc. • Mission, KS

## KANSAS CITY CUISINE
Pig Out Publications, Inc. • Mission, KS

## KITCHEN PRESCRIPTIONS
American Academy of Family Physicians
Kansas City, MO

## KOHLER FAMILY KOOKBOOK
by the descendants of John and Margaret
Watkins Kohler • Harrisonville, MO

## LAVENDER & LACE
Arlingon United Methodist Women
Bridgeton, MO

## THE NEVER ENDING SEASON
Missouri 4-H Foundation • Columbia, MO

## THE PASSION OF BARBECUE
The Kansas City Barbeque Society
New York, NY

## PAST & REPAST:
## The History and Hospitality of the
## Missouri Governor's Mansion
Missouri Mansion Preservation, Inc.
Jefferson City, MO

## RECIPES & STORIES OF EARLY-DAY SETTLERS
by Kenneth C. Weyand • Kansas City, MO

## RECIPES FROM MISSOURI . . . WITH LOVE
by Sandy Buege • Prior Lake, MN

## RECIPES OLD AND NEW
St. Catherine of Alexandria Ladies' Society
St. Louis, MO

## RUSH HOUR SUPERCHEF!
by Dianne Stafford Mayes and Dorothy
Davenport Stafford • Carthage, MO

## SASSAFRAS!
Junior League of Springfield, Missouri
Springfield, MO

## THE SHAW HOUSE COOKBOOK
Missouri Botanical Garden
St. Louis, MO

## SILVER DOLLAR CITY'S RECIPES FROM AMERICA'S HEARTLAND
by Judy Miller • Branson, MO

## SING FOR YOUR SUPPER
The River Blenders • O'Fallon, MO

## THE SPORTSMAN'S DISH
by Jack Caraway • Hamilton, MO

## TALK ABOUT GOOD III
Forsyth Library Friends • Forsyth, MO

## THYME FOR KIDS
by Leanna K. and Evangela Potts
Joplin, MO

## TREASURED RECIPES I
Taneyhills Library Club • Branson, MO

## TREASURED RECIPES II
Taneyhills Library Club • Branson, MO

## TURN OF THE CENTURY COOKBOOK
Alberta L. Hensley • Grain Valley, MO

## USO'S SALUTE TO THE TROOPS COOKBOOK
by James S. McDonnell USO
St. Louis, MO

## THE VEGETARIAN LUNCHBASKET
by Linda Haynes/Nucleus Publications
Willow Springs, MO

## WANDA'S FAVORITE RECIPES
by Wanda Brown/Cass Medical Center
Foundation • Harrisonville, MO

# Best of the Best State Cookbook Series

Best of the Best from
## ALABAMA
288 pages, $16.95

Best of the Best from
## ALASKA
288 pages, $16.95

Best of the Best from
## ARIZONA
288 pages, $16.95

Best of the Best from
## ARKANSAS
288 pages, $16.95

Best of the Best from
## BIG SKY
Montana and Wyoming
288 pages, $16.95

Best of the Best from
## CALIFORNIA
384 pages, $16.95

Best of the Best from
## COLORADO
288 pages, $16.95

Best of the Best from
## FLORIDA
288 pages, $16.95

Best of the Best from
## GEORGIA
336 pages, $16.95

Best of the Best from the
## GREAT PLAINS
North and South Dakota,
Nebraska, and Kansas
288 pages, $16.95

Best of the Best from
## HAWAI'I
288 pages, $16.95

Best of the Best from
## IDAHO
288 pages, $16.95

Best of the Best from
## ILLINOIS
288 pages, $16.95

Best of the Best from
## INDIANA
288 pages, $16.95

Best of the Best from
## IOWA
288 pages, $16.95

Best of the Best from
## KENTUCKY
288 pages, $16.95

Best of the Best from
## LOUISIANA
288 pages, $16.95

Best of the Best from
## LOUISIANA II
288 pages, $16.95

Best of the Best from
## MICHIGAN
288 pages, $16.95

Best of the Best from the
## MID-ATLANTIC
Maryland, Delaware, New
Jersey, and Washington, D.C.
288 pages, $16.95

Best of the Best from
## MINNESOTA
288 pages, $16.95

Best of the Best from
## MISSISSIPPI
288 pages, $16.95

Best of the Best from
## MISSOURI
304 pages, $16.95

Best of the Best from
## NEVADA
288 pages, $16.95

Best of the Best from
## NEW ENGLAND
Rhode Island, Connecticut,
Massachusetts, Vermont,
New Hampshire, and Maine
368 pages, $16.95

Best of the Best from
## NEW MEXICO
288 pages, $16.95

Best of the Best from
## NEW YORK
288 pages, $16.95

Best of the Best from
## NO. CAROLINA
288 pages, $16.95

Best of the Best from
## OHIO
352 pages, $16.95

Best of the Best from
## OKLAHOMA
288 pages, $16.95

Best of the Best from
## OREGON
288 pages, $16.95

Best of the Best from
## PENNSYLVANIA
320 pages, $16.95

Best of the Best from
## SO. CAROLINA
288 pages, $16.95

Best of the Best from
## TENNESSEE
288 pages, $16.95

Best of the Best from
## TEXAS
352 pages, $16.95

Best of the Best from
## TEXAS II
352 pages, $16.95

Best of the Best from
## UTAH
288 pages, $16.95

Best of the Best from
## VIRGINIA
320 pages, $16.95

Best of the Best from
## WASHINGTON
288 pages, $16.95

Best of the Best from
## WEST VIRGINIA
288 pages, $16.95

Best of the Best from
## WISCONSIN
288 pages, $16.95

*All cookbooks are 6x9 inches, ringbound, contain photographs, illustrations and index.*

## Special discount offers available! *(See previous page for details.)*

To order by credit card, call toll-free **1-800-343-1583** or visit our website at **www.quailridge.com.**
Use the form below to send check or money order.

*Call 1-800-343-1583 or email* **info@quailridge.com** *to request a free catalog of all of our publications.*

# Order form

Use this form for sending check or money order to:
**QUAIL RIDGE PRESS • P. O. Box 123 • Brandon, MS 39043**

❑ Check enclosed

Charge to: ❑ Visa ❑ MC ❑ AmEx ❑ Disc

Card # _____

Expiration Date _____

Signature _____

Name _____

Address _____

City/State/Zip _____

Phone # _____

Email Address _____

| Qty. | Title of Book (State) or Set | Total |
|------|------------------------------|-------|
|      |                              |       |
|      |                              |       |
|      |                              |       |
|      |                              |       |

Subtotal _____

7% Tax for MS residents _____

Postage ($4.00 any number of books) **+    4.00**

Total _____